THE ROMANCE OF THE INDIAN FRONTIERS

THE ROMANCE OF THE INDIAN FRONTIERS

LT-GEN. SIR GEORGE MACMUNN

GYAN

Published by

GYAN

Gyan Publishing House
5, Ansari Road
Daryaganj, New Delhi-110002
Phone 011-47034999, 9811692060
E-mail: books@gyanbooks.com

Distribution Network
gyanbooks.com
India, USA, Canada, UK, Australia

ISBN: 978-93-6433-389-4 (PB)
First Published, 1931

2rd Impression 2024

Printed at: Gyan Press, Delhi.

THE ROMANCE OF THE INDIAN FRONTIERS
Author: Lt-Gen. SIR GEORGE MACMUNN

THE ROMANCE OF THE INDIAN FRONTIERS

A WAZIRI 'MALIKH' OR HEAD-MAN COMES TO DRAW HIS ALLOWANCE

Frontispiece

THE ROMANCE OF THE INDIAN FRONTIERS

BY

LT.-GEN. SIR GEORGE MACMUNN
K.C.B., K.C.S.I., D.S.O.
Colonel-Commandant the Royal Artillery

JONATHAN CAPE
THIRTY BEDFORD SQUARE
LONDON & AT TORONTO

CONTENTS

CONTENTS

CONTENTS

CONTENTS

LIST OF ILLUSTRATIONS

LIST OF ILLUSTRATIONS

MAPS

THE ROMANCE OF THE INDIAN FRONTIERS

CHAPTER ONE

THE FRINGES AND FRONTIERS OF INDIA

§ I

THE WIDE-FLUNG FRONTIERS

IT is instinctive in our minds when the frontier of India is mentioned, to think of the 'North-west Frontier' as the only frontier worthy of the name. That is more than unreasonable as a glance or even a thought of the map of India will show. The North-west Frontier is more west than north, but then we have no northern frontier, since the two faces are north-west and north-east, the former over 1000 miles in length and the latter 1700, exclusive of the frontier of Burma, which is close on 2000 miles more. The latter 1700 miles brings us into touch with Russia and China and the states of Nepal and Tibet, while the former, for the most part, marches with Afghanistan and Persia. The frontier of Burma marches with France as well as with China and Siam, so that the foreign relations of India are complicated by actual land frontiers bringing almost daily problems of trade, intercourse, and disagreement with Russia, China, France, Persia, Afghanistan, Tibet and Nepal. Such a sweep and range of varied neighbours must mean unlimited occasion for incident and romance of all kinds, and so the British have found it.

As we study the subject we shall see that while the North-eastern Frontiers have lain much as they lie now from far back in the ages, the present North-west Frontier is a thing of yesterday and that India once marched on the Oxus, and that in very modern times it extended as far as the Hindu Kush. And the story thereof includes the epic of Alexander of Macedon, the scourgings of Mahmud of Ghazni, and the glorious coming of Baber the Turk, King of Kabul, to found that great splendour, the Mogul Empire, which crumbled to pieces for the British to rebuild.

Between the march of the phallanxes and the day when the British horse under Sir John Gilbert chased the last of the Afghan horse 'like dogs' as the Sikhs said, through the Khaiber, there is such colour and romance, such love and lust, such tragedy and glory as would fill ten thousand volumes. Since then with our own people, it has been one story of derring do, and stirring endeavour to help and tame a wild people, amid

> 'The flying bullet down the pass
> That whistles shrill all flesh is grass.'

This North-west Frontier, the land which was long the home of earlier Hindus and Buddhists, now the hunting-ground of the Sons of the Prophet, is full of strange relics of the past that can hardly yet be peaceably explored. . . .

> 'Some arms deep rusted, an old-world rhyme,
> A broken idol, a ruined fane,

May linger as waif of the wild fore-time
When the Gods were cruel and men were slain.'

It is proposed in this book to try to strike old broken strings, to see the frontiers through the ages with all their romance, and visions of the armed hordes threading the mountains of Roh to the Eldorado of the Ganges plains, the gentle Buddhist pilgrims on their way from China, the Ghilzais in their mountains and the horses of the Turkomans harnessed to the guns of the Russian Tsar. Of Baber among his Kabul gardens, his Tartar maidens and the narcissi on the hill-side, and of Tommy Moore who sang so gloriously of what he had never seen.

Mingled at every turn are nature's sweet, familiar things – the Prophet's Flower on the hill-side, the silvery reeds by the flowing water, the narcissi in the rills that Baber loved, and through it all

'Dead women of the bygone years who swayed
The passionate songs of lips that love you well,
Dead cities where the princes, shade with shade,
In phantom honours dwell.'

§ 2

THE GREATER GEOGRAPHY

The geography of India as it stands to the rest of Asia that fringes its frontiers, is an amazing thing, only to be fully realized before a relief map. Such a map alone can make the mind's eye take in the world plateau of Tibet, the drop from the Himalayas, down to the Gangetic plain, the whorl of hills that divide the Oxus from the Indus, and the incredible maze of parallel gorges of the rivers of China, east of the Burman frontier. Eleven hundred miles from the northernmost point above Kashmir to Robat on the frontier of Persia in the south-west, runs the North-west Frontier. For 1700 miles from the same point, to the south-east, and later to the east as it curves, runs the frontier on the Himalayan side to the point beyond Tibet where it strikes the water divide of the Salween River. Thence, lest anyone should think that Burma is a small province, let it be said that the Eastern Frontier drops due south for close on 2000 more indented miles, till it slithers into the Bay of Bengal and touches the Malay Peninsula. Lest that should not be enough, let us remember, as already stated, that here we march for several hundred miles with French Indo-China and Siam. The scenery, the climate, the flora and the fauna vary through every possible extreme, as do the races with whom our officers come in contact. From the Persian border round, we may begin with Arab and Semite and countless varieties of the Moslem Aryan, and then through the refugee pockets of ancient Dravidian races escaping from invaders, to every variety of Tartar and Mongol. From every possible blend of these with Aryan and early Indian races we come to such different people as Muhammadan Chinese, and varieties of the ancient Shan kingdoms and races. Out of China and Tibet flow the great rivers of India and Burma, the Indus itself, the Chenab, which but means the river of China, the Ganges, the Brahmaputra, the Irrawaddi and the Salween.

If the reader would get some faint conception of it into his mind's eye, let him pass through the mountains of Kashmir in imagination and look down from the Pamirs, 'The Roof of the World,' and see how 'the Hills in order stood' before the Aryans' waves set the world a-growing. He must realize how the great heaving mass of the world, like the breaking crown of a cake risen by mighty baking powder, runs from the top in a thousand whorls and fissures. To the south-east the Himalayas themselves, 'The abode of snow,' roll away for hundreds of miles, ridge on ridge and crest on crest, amid the thunder of the avalanches that feed the rivers. To the south-west the great world-tops quickly descend to the lesser mountains of Afghanistan through the dark ravines of Kafiristan, throwing, however, one mighty spur – the Hindu Kush – across to Herat, which men have called the 'Key of India.' The British officers of the administration on their frontiers in the last century and a half, and the scientists and missionaries who work under their protection, have added countless chapters to the whole world's knowledge of these enormous areas.

§ 3

THE NORTH-WEST FRONTIER HILLS

The thousands of miles of the Eastern and North-eastern Frontiers, however, are largely closed to the come and go of the world's races, by very reason of their tumbled masses and inaccessible gorges. On the North-west Frontier, however, the migrations of great hungry races in evolution on the Central Asian steppes have come down to warm and hospitable India since time was. Here is movement, battle, might and dominion, and it is here that our own history makes stirring reading. Through these hills came the long procession of mighty conquerors whose names have crimsoned the histories of the world, and it is here that our minds and hearts can stir more readily than amid the snows of the sparsely trod Himalayan passes.

The great whorls from the Pamirs on this side throw off the great range referred to – the Parapomisus of the ancients – the Hindu Kush, then the hills of Kabul Kohistan and the Ghazni uplands, cribbing the rivers in narrow gorges for a while, and taking the Indus out to the northern plains of India, hedged by the Mountains of Solomon on the west, but free on the east to widen its own *kăchch* or unbaked mud-bed at will. In these mountains we find the tribes of the Afghan and Pathan races, Moslems all, whose origin will be described later.

Our relief map will show us on the right bank, halfway on its course to the sea, a big peak towering far above the Suleimans. It is no less a place than the *Tahkt-i-Suleiman*, the Throne of mighty Solomon himself where tradition says he sat, as he sat on Mount Tabor, to counsel the world. Below, the sheen of the Derajat when the wheat grows green lies, like Issachar, a fat ass, rolling and sprawling, a prey to the men of the mountain. Legend also has it that here on the *Takht*, the great king rested a while, when flying back to Jerusalem on a magic carpet -- rested, because in his rôle as the world's greatest lover, he had an India princess beside him, who would fain stop and gaze farewell on her native land. The which is an allegory.

Indeed, as you look on your map, or better still, come with the writer to the Throne of Solomon, or to the great mountains behind Kashmir, you will say with the Psalmist, 'Why hop ye so, ye high hills?' These lower frontier hills of India are so torn and storm-swept, that you will agree that only the pen and brush of Gustave Doré could draw them and gain inspiration for his illustrations of the *Inferno* therefrom.

Then let us stand at Attock on the Indus, or at Darya Khan some hundred miles lower down by the land of those who dwell in tents, and we will see the same sight, the great swelling circle of snowy hills round the Peshawar Valley, or the bigger lines in the Derajat of ridge piled on ridge, and snow upon snow.

Then let us carry our line of sight in our imagination further over the Afghan hills and we shall see another green streak of corn land, and that is the bed of the Oxus that men now call the Amu Darya on its way to the inland sea of Aral. Then we shall notice as from the bird's eye, the tumbled mass of mountains between, through which we can see the passes threading their way from Balkh and Kabul and from Herat and Kandahar to India.

'When Spring-time flushes the desert grass,
Our *kafilas* wind through the Khyber Pass,
Lean are the camels but heavy the frails,
Light are the purses but heavy the bales,
When the snowbound trade of the north comes
down,
To the market square of Peshawar town.'

'The Ballad of the King's Jest.' – R. K.

Then you will realize that what men now call Afghanistan but which once was India, lies for the most part between the Oxus and the Indus. Later on we will look at the people therein, those who still call themselves the Children of Israel and have the names of Scripture, and those of the almond-eye whom Genghis Khan planted in his passage.

South of Solomon's Throne lies British Baluchistan, the famous passes leading to Multan, the inner Key of India, as Herat is the outer, whence came all or almost all the main invasions of India. These hills contain two differing races, some the Pathan tribes who count kin with the Children of Israel, as will be described later on, and others the Baluch, whom older custom wrote Belooch, a different race, descended probably from those Arabs who came in the days of Kasim of Basra, in the eighth century. Among them, not of them, are a race called the Brahui, who are not Pathan and are not Baluch, and who speak a Dravidian tongue, so that they well may be descendants of the older Dravidian inhabitants of India, another of those pushed-aside pockets which we shall find in the deep glens as we probe the border round. South of British Baluchistan so called – the part in which we come and go freely as necessary to our plans for the defence of India – lies the great area of tribal Baluchistan under the control, for the most part, of the Khan of Kelat, British so far as the outer world is concerned, but otherwise severely enjoying itself in its own way. The Baluch, with his Arab extraction, is even more Semitic of appearance than the Afghan proper, and with his long locks parted in the middle, might sit any day as a model for a picture of the Last Supper. Baluch and Pathan then are the peoples of the North and West Frontier hills until we reach the small states farther north beyond the main paths of the invading and migratory ways to Hindustan, and some of the refugee pockets to which allusion has been made.

§ 4

THE FRONTIER STATES OF THE NORTH

The most northerly road to India from Central Asia is that from Kabul to Peshawur, either by the Khaiber, or the adjacent ways north of the Kabul River which avoid that ill-omened opening. North of this outside Afghanistan are a series of small states, and I will ask you to follow me among them for a brief glimpse before the reel takes us farther east round the frontiers. We shall see states under the shadow of the Roof of the World whose princes still claim descent from Alexander of Macedon, and where raw gold and turquoise bind maidens' hair.

We have already looked from the walls of Attock Fort westward, and seen the sweep of snow-clad hills. West we have seen the portals of the Khaiber and the great White Mountain, to our right, among the mountains across the Indus after the tribal hills, we come to certain states. First is the Pathan state of Dir, and then beyond Chitral, whose story will be outlined later. It is a state close under the Dorah Pass on to the Pamirs, which holds a British garrison lest the Cossack once again come to destroy peace of mind among small chieflets. The people of Dir are Pathans, but in Chitral we come to one of the ancient Dard pockets, with a people who had managed to resist the Aryan influx in ancient days, and the pressure of those who turned Moslem in the years to follow, and now call themselves Pathan. Beyond Chitral the small states run who own sway of the Kashmir Government, Yasin and Hunza-Nagar, the Kanjuti states, in a country where the three passes on to the Pamirs admitted, in the 'eighties and 'nineties of last century, filibustering parties of Cossacks in the endeavour to reap where they had not sown. Then the determination of the British Government to slam the doors in the Bear's face, to close the Killik, the Baroghil and the Dorah Passes, sent joint garrisons of British and Kashmir troops into the Gilgit Agency. There followed the Hunza-Nagar campaign of most romantic interest, and the affairs which led to the Defence of Chitral and the dramatic incidents involved therein, the former of which was so famously told in Mr. Knight's *Where Three Empires Meet.* The 'Thum' of Hunza is one of those who claim descent from large-

MEN AND BOYS IN A TRANS-FRONTIER VILLAGE

To face page 26

hearted Alexander of Macedon. Not long after, there followed the tripartite boundary commission on the Pamirs which settled which of the Pamirs, Alichur, Tagumdash, or what not was to belong to each of the three, Britain, Russia and China, and the enterprising Cossack retired to the Pamirski Post and then began to bother his Afghan neighbours in Shignan and Roshan, which but meant a fresh crop of anxieties for the British to settle amicably.

On the hither bank of the Indus are found some Pathan clans of the Yuzafzai fraternity, who inhabit the Black Mountain. Here British and Kashmir troops have carried out joint expeditions on several occasions, in which the 'Burning of Alai' – '*Jab Alai Phunka*' – was long a remembrance in the army of Jammu and Kashmir. One road to Gilgit runs up from the British frontier district of Hazara to Chilas on the Indus, far up its gorges, via the Khagan valley and a country where the chiefs known as the Sayads of Khagan claim to be and are recognized as descendants of the Prophet, the other, by Astor and Bunji, starts on the Woolar Lake in Kashmir.

§ 5

KASHMIR

And this brings us by a long and difficult route to consideration of the state of Jammu and Kashmir, the only one of the Indian feudatories that is on the outer frontiers of India, and that shares as a matter of routine the duties of the frontier watch and ward, since its confines march with both Russia and China. This valley of Kashmir all the world knows, because of its fabled beauty, its great mountains and its sport, and its position as the playground of the British in India and, as Indians grow wiser, for Indians too. The winding valley of the Jhelum, some 5000 feet above sea-level, is the basis of the country, from which long valleys emanate and small khans own principalities which long ago were brought under the control of the Kashmir throne.

A thousand years ago, Kashmir was a prosperous Hindu kingdom, a seat of great culture and learning, with a strong Brahmin oligarchy in control. Then came the fierce proselytizing forces of Islam, which made a waste, destroying the beautiful stone temples which stand to this day as picturesque ruins, and forcing all except the Brahmins to accept the Faith or perish. So to this day the people, save the Brahmins, are Moslems. Magnificent of thew are they, tall and handsome but with the heart of a louse, so completely has long generations of cruel oppression at the hand of Mogul and Afghan trampled any manly spark from their bosoms.

Till 1820, Kashmir was a province of Afghanistan, wrested a generation or so earlier from the Mogul. For twenty-five years it remained an appenage of the Sikh ruler of Lahore who had evicted the Afghans. After the first Sikh War, to weaken the power of the Sikhs lest they again invade British India unprovoked, Rajah Gulab Singh of Jammu, a Rajput chief, was offered the chieftainship of Kashmir as a vassal of the British Crown, on his offering to pay the Sikh War indemnity. When the Sikhs made their mad invasion of British India in the winter of 1845, Gulab Singh, who had a large army in subordination to the Sikhs, held aloof. Since then he and his descendants have served the British loyally, sending a contingent to the Siege of Delhi in 1857, and taking a part in several frontier expeditions. In the World War the Kashmir forces went far afield. Thus, as Lord Harding planned in 1846, so have things remained. Kashmir, as well as having the unique position of being a frontier state, is also one specially formed by the British, under their own conditions. The Kashmir army is furnished by the Dogra Rajputs of Jammu, the big burly Kashmiri being worthless as a soldier, though a few Afghans settled in the valley retain some of their martial proclivities.

The beautiful valley of Kashmir is separated from British India by a subsidiary range of snowy mountains, the Pir Panjal, which presents a magnificent panorama from the cantonments of Siakot and Jhelum and to those who travel in winter-time down the main line from Peshawar southwards. In the summer-time the pea-soup haze of dust and heat, that so adds to the season's horrors, blots out effectively all hint even of the Abode of Snow.

South-east of Kashmir comes a long fringe of little Rajput states subject to the British, that nestle under the mighty massif of Tibet, the people Aryan in the outer hills and often passing to Mongoloids and refugee Dravidian pockets nearer the snow wall. Deep are the gorges, well tilled the buckwheat-terraced fields of the hill folk, and you look down on flat-topped homesteads on which the crimson amaranth and love-lies-bleeding blaze colour to the green.

As we pass down the eastern plains we shall see the twin peaks, where rise Jamna and Ganga, great snowy breasts like towers, that men call Jamnotri and Gamnotri, kissed of the clouds, since man cannot venture. Towards these go the crowds of Hindu pilgrims seeking the Infinite and peace on a road untold, men by themselves, men with families – *un qui marche, un qui tette, un qui vient* – crowding out, stumbling as they go. . . .

'March, brothers, march! for the hills are far,' and above them the eternal snows.

And then, after a while, you come again to a frontier state which alone of those under the Tibetan wall is not part of British India. For five hundred miles along the plains lies Nepal, running up the valleys towards the never-never country for about a hundred miles. Nepal also is a Rajput state, aboriginals and Mongoloids conquered by Rajput invaders from the plains. The latter are the ruling race and some of their followers remain still largely Aryan, who are known to the Army as the *Khas* Gurkhas, those near and special to the throne. But the mass of men who enlist are the aboriginal and Mongoloid tribes, such as Magar and Gurung, Hinduised to some extent, and granted special status, who enter the Indian army in large numbers with the cordial approval of the Nepal Durbar or Government.

Nepal, friendly and peaceful enough towards British India and Britain, is the one potential danger to India on the North-east Frontier. Early in the nineteenth century Nepal was encroaching on India for a distance of many miles right up to the Simla hills and even on to the Punjab. The Rajput district of Kumaon and Garhwal was occupied, and harsh and heavy and ruthless was the rule of the invader. Though it is over a hundred years since their outrageous incursions compelled the British Government at the time of Waterloo to take action, yet to this day if any Government subordinate or any officer looking for transport in a hurry, behave in an overbearing manner, at once do the people of Kumaon say, '*Oho, phir Gurkha Raj agya.*' – 'So the Gurkha rule is back again!'

The war with Nepal was fought for two years, and the British for a while took several repulses as they endeavoured to storm the Gurkhas' forts. The famous Rollo Gillespie of Comber, the hero of the Vellore Mutiny and then a major-general, lost his life at the assault on Kalunga. It was not till wise Sir David Ochterlony, the 'Lony Ochter Sahib,' of the Eastern diction, was given command of all the columns, that victory to British arms was assured, and the scornful invaders driven back into their own hills. After the manner of the English, the Gurkha prisoners of war were then and there enlisted into the levies which soon became the Gurkha corps that are now so famous.

§ 6

TIBET, SIKKIM AND BHUTAN

We are now coming to the part of the frontier that has a very definite and peculiar romance of its own, far different from that of the fierce Jewish Pathans, Afghans and what not among the Graeco-Bactrian ruins of Swat and the Khaiber. Some hint of China comes in at every stage, even the Hindu temples in the Simla hills are curling at the eaves with a suggestion of Pekin and the Tartar city. Behind Kashmir and Nepal and all the other states on our North-eastern Frontier lies the vast upland of Tibet, the abode of lamas, prayer-wheels, turquoises and everything that is different from Aryan life. In the distance too looms China herself with her tradition of authority long since lost, but boldly asserted on every possible and impossible occasion, so that till quite lately states actually within the Indian range sent annual tribute and missions. Far away in the mountains too lay Lhasa, the capital of Tibet which, with Kafiristan, was one of unsolved mysteries of the East. Now since Macdonald and Younghusband's Mission in 1904 that veil has been lifted, and yet was not a myth as was the Macedonian pocket in Kafiristan.

British relations with this great territory have always been friendly, even during the hostilities that occurred in this mission. Her policy has been to let Tibet remain as a great contented *inconnue* on India's border, free of Chinese domination, and defended from Russian aggression. Imperial Russia after some considerable pressure did formally and openly declare, somewhat to the chagrin of her frontier-mongers, that Tibet was entirely outside her ambitions, but with the Soviet Government and its desire to disturb and upset any civilization and to fish in any troubled waters, the matter is otherwise. By 1930 the relations between Britain and Tibet have grown more and more cordial and enlightened, as will be described hereafter. Apart from politics lies all the simple romance that is implied in prayer-wheel and lama, the delightful lama of *Kim* – by no means a creature of imagination – the *chela*, the Way and the Arrow, the queer bronze utensils and objects of art, raw lumps of turquoise, and the like.

This vast upland plateau has, since time was, acted as a great buffer between India and the teeming hordes of the yellow races, the races of the 'Mongol fold,' *i.e.* the almond-eye. There have been, contrary to popular impression, many inroads into India even through the Himalayas and over the Tibetan plateaus, but never in the swamping proportions which but for its existence would surely have occurred. The plateaus of Tibet, over 1200 miles from east to west, and 7500 miles from north to south, have never less than an altitude of 11,000 feet, and often, apart from the actual mountains, which are far higher, a level of 16,000 feet. Races and peoples, to say nothing of flora and fauna, who live at this height must develop a very different mentality and psychology to races or peoples of the same race who live near the sea-level, and this alone is enough to account for the strange and picturesque appearance of its people and country, and its domination by an intense form of the amiable philosophic atheism which men call Buddhism.

The real Tibet is only touched by our actual Indian border for about a hundred miles north of Garhwal, behind the popular hill resort of Naini Tal. Here alone does British India administer the border districts directly, in the hill tracts inhabited by the semi-Rajput Garhwalis of military fame, until the hills ascend into the uninhabited peaks and gorges where somewhere lies the undefined Indo-Tibetan boundary. Along its other borders lie the buffer states of Kashmir, the Simla statelets, independent Nepal, dependent Sikkim and Bhutan, and then east of Bhutan the mass of wild tribal country which will be outlined. But all along this frontier the actual points of joining, save for a few routes of penetration, lie high up in the uninhabited mountain tops and eternal glaciers, so that frontier questions rarely arise.

Sikkim is a small Tibet-like principality with which at times we have had some words and over which we have had to exercise a benevolent compulsion. Occasionally from Sikkim, as from Tibet, treatment so arrogant and contemptuous – the vice of China – has been experienced that only some show of force could bring courtesy and wisdom into the relationship. Eastward of Sikkim comes the large, somewhat indefinite state of Bhutan, also of semi-Tibetan folk with whom British relations are cordial enough. Soon after the Mutiny an expedition against the Bhutanese was necessary, and a clasp, *Bhootan*,[1] is carried on the India Medal of 1854.

§ 7

THE ASSAM BORDERS

We now come on this screen of the North-east Frontier, which, it may be remarked incidentally, now faces due north for many hundreds of miles, to the most fascinating and interesting province of Assam. To follow this we must be enterprising enough to look at the map. If we turn to Bhutan, after noticing with surprise the very long stretch of the frontier spanned by Nepal, we shall note how the Brahmaputra, having joined the Ganges, runs into the Bay of Bengal in a direction that is practically south.

But close up to the hills its course turns due east, and we find this mighty stream running to us from the east for 350 miles. We are, of course, talking backwards, so we will now re-trace our steps to Lhassa, and there we see that the Brahmaputra runs at levels far above that of the Assam plains due west for 300 miles. Then it starts on its astounding task of cutting its way through the Himalayas. How this was done was for long a mystery. In fact so great was the drop to be accomplished, that geographers for many years imagined that somewhere was a mighty waterfall that could alone get the river down the required thousands of feet; before this, it was said, Niagara and the Victoria Falls would be a bagatelle.

[1] The earlier spelling of Bhutan.

Alas for such excitements! The Abor Expedition, which took place in 1911-12, added to one or two subsequent botanical explorations, has dispelled the hope of a fall. A series of great rapids, stupendous in their force and length, during the 150 miles down which the river, turning due south, cuts its way through the Himalayas, succeeds in bringing the river down to the required level. Having turned a right angle on the high plateau, the river, now at Kobo, turns again through 90 degrees and flows slightly south of west for 350 miles as related, and at Dubri makes the third right-angled turn to the sea. The long arm that flows westward comprises a large part of fertile tea-planting Assam, but the lower spurs of the Himalayas on the north side and a long range of hills on the south, both in some sense have constituted frontiers in that they hold a mass of hill tribes whom we do not administer directly, and who during a long series of years have presented, though in a minor degree, the same problems as the Mountains of Roh on the North-west Frontier. North of the river are such Mongoloid and perhaps aboriginal tribes as Miris, Abors and Mishmis. The southern range of hills, civilized enough in its western end of the Garao Hills and the Kasi and Jaintia Hills, spreads eastwards into the wild uncivilized frontier tracts that lie between the Brahmaputra and the valleys of the Chindwin and Irrawaddi Rivers in Burma. These hills consist of inaccessible forest areas containing such people as Nagas, Hkamtis, Lushais, Singhos, Daphlas, Akkas, etc. The tribes are all Mongoloid Tibetan, except the

Akkas and Nagas, who are of some Indian origin and the Hkamptis, who are Shans. The Nagas have long been inveterate head-hunters whose propensities have been very slowly overcome. All these tribes have for countless generations raided into India for slaves, and their racial make-up has been to some extent altered thereby. It will be remembered how, in the last few years, by the exertions of the Governments of Burma and Assam, all slave-holding has been abolished, and how Sir Harcourt Butler, as Governor of Burma, extended this arrangement, a matter of great difficulty, to the Kachins of 'The Triangle' and to the more distant Chin tracts. Assam, thus bordered on three sides by wild tribes, has a long military record of the kind where activity, endurance, and self-reliance were the important factors. Three regular Gurkha battalions were stationed for many years on this frontier, and there has long been an efficient military police force which now can maintain peace on these borders unaided.

Within the boundaries of Assam and among her frontier problems has been the Indian state of Manipur which lies between Assam and the Chin Hills of Burma. This state, which within the Indian Empire has carried on a contented life for many years, was in 1891 in some disorder owing to the pretensions of the Senapatti, or Commander of the State troops. An attempt by the British to remove him by force resulted in the massacre in open durbar of Mr. Quenton, the Commissioner, and Colonel Grimwood, the military commander. The escort of some four hundred Gurkhas was heavily attacked and was unable to give a good account of itself. Several individual military acts of fame took place, and eventually a British force restored the situation.

The occurrence led to prodigious rumours in Calcutta and Bengal, and gossip persisted in the quite unfounded tale that the Tangal-General who was involved in the trouble and murders, and who was an old man, was none other than the long-lost Nana, the Dundoo Punt of Cawnpore horror, whose fate was wrapt in mystery.

The seat of government of this interesting and prosperous province is on the beautiful down-like upland of Shillong in the Jaintia Hills. The Brahmaputra being a navigable river carries a large steamer flotilla which has not, like that on the Ganges, withered as railways progress. Some more detailed account of the military expeditions on the North-east Frontier in the last hundred years will be given further on.

It will be realized that interesting and important as the whole of this frontier is, the passes therethrough lead to no great world routes and invaders' roads. The work of development and civilization therefrom goes on more for its own sake than as part of a world trade policy or a strategical plan.

The two exceptions to this are Tibet, where the former world policy of China in regard thereto may be revived, and the attitude hereafter of the hitherto friendly and helpful Nepal towards India or Tibet. Save for these two factors the North-east Frontier is a stable one.

NAGAS IN THE HILLS BETWEEN BURMA AND INDIA, WHO SACRIFICE HUMAN BEINGS AND HUNT HEADS

THE KOHAT PASS

To face page 39

§ 8

THE EASTERN FRONTIER

Proceeding east from Assam we come to the tumbled series of mountains and forests with Chin and Kachin inhabitants, whose affairs are the affairs of the Burma Province. If you take a bee-line across the map to the east from Dibrugarh on the Brahmaputra, you find that you come after some miles of confused hills to the River Nmali-kha, the more westerly of the two branches of the Irrawaddi, and you will see that to the north, till you reach the Chinese border, there is no frontier line. The British border just fades away into an unexplored unknown tangle of gorges. You will also notice a curious feature, viz. the existence of numerous rivers whose mouths are far distant from each other, but which here seem to be gathered in a bundle, their course running parallel and close together in deep gorges, which are separated by stupendous steep ranges of mountains. These are the Nmali-kha already just referred to, the Nmai-kha, the eastern branch of the Irrawaddi, the Salween, the Mekong, and the Yang-tse, flowing into such widely separated oceans as the Bay of Bengal, the Gulf of Cambodia, the China Sea and the Pacific, while at the latitude of Dibrugarh a hundred miles would cover the whole five. This frontier without a border is largely inhabited by tribes of the Kachin race, quite the most interesting and intelligent of all the Mongoloid tribes of the Eastern Frontier, who for generations have been pressing down on Burma and the Shan country from the north, and who must have had their origin in the Desert of Gobi, that matrix of lost races.

The frontier districts include such interesting localities as the Hukawng Valley, the Khamti Plain, Putao, and 'The Triangle,' as the space between the two branches of the Irrawaddi is called. The Kachins, against whom in the last forty years considerable operations have been necessary, before they would accept the *Pax Britannica*, are now for the most part quiet and content and are furnishing admirable soldiers to the Burman battalions of the Indian Army. A battalion almost entirely Kachin distinguished itself in operations against the Kurds far north of Bagdad in 1919, and also in the recent operations against the rebels in Burma.

By the time the Chinese border is reached on the high range above the Salween, the frontier has been clearly delimited and our officers are in touch with the Chinese frontier officers.

For many miles down the frontier the tribes, chiefly Kachin, are very lightly administered, and so long as they do not molest the caravans on the trade routes that connect with China, all is well. This Eastern Frontier, as already mentioned, is approaching 2000 miles in extent, marching for long distances with French Indo-China, and with Siam. Half-way down the border it will be noticed that there is a great bulge of country, which is the Shan States, curling outward into French territory, and in the past disputes as to the boundary line have been serious, now, however, happily settled. At one point the frontier meets a curve of the Mekong itself. This long frontier is far more in touch with the territories across the border than on the North-east Frontier. Well-frequented trade routes exist at many points, through which in the past Chinese influence and also Chinese armies have come. The wide-flung pretension of China to hold jurisdiction over distant states, including the suzerainty of Burma, has not been without its diplomatic difficulties in the past. At Bhamo on the Irrawaddi in the Kachin country there is a large Chinese settlement in close touch with Yunnan. The mules of the Muhammadan Chinese, known as Panthays, carry all sorts of merchandise from China and conduct the jade trade from the famous jade mines in the Burman district of Mogaung. These Panthay mule-owners used constantly to hire themselves to the British military columns operating in the frontier hills, though of late years the Chinese Government, for no adequate reason, has endeavoured to stop the practice. But the existence of the Chinese trade routes and traders lent romance and attraction to this border, while a special interest lies in the origins of the tribes themselves, who are in a primitive state of religious conceptions which should throw considerable light on the development of religion among earlier man. The languages of the frontier folk all belong to the monosyllabic agglutinative type, which distinguishes races of Tartar origin throughout the world. The Kachin language, which is the most generally spoken, and kindred tongues were unwritten till civil officers and missionaries reduced them to the English alphabet.

Reference has already been made to the slave releases along this frontier. This feat, largely achieved by prestige in the years just past, marks a very definite advance. The prevalence of the slave-raiding habits may account for the strangely different features that are to be seen among the Mongoloids. I have seen a Kachin with the face and mien of a Jesuit priest, amid a crowd of snub-nosed, almond-eyed Mongols, only explicable by some incident of Aryan concubinage.

CHAPTER TWO

THE NORTH-WEST FRONTIER THROUGH THE AGES

§ 1

THE COMING OF THE ARYAN

So far as the North-west Frontier is concerned imagination must roam far back in the mists of time before it can grasp the present, for the story of to-day is intimately connected with the story of many thousands of years ago.

The Hindu Kush, the 'point where the Hindu perishes,' runs at great altitude for many miles north of Kabul. The passes over it are not negotiable for several months in the year, and even then present great difficulties to forces marching from the Oxus. For this reason all invasions of India from that direction must bear off towards the low portion of the range, the Parapomisus of history, and make for Herat, a fertile valley amid arid tracts and bare hills. So Herat has come to be spoken of as the 'Key of India,' since all must come that way.

The second principal offshoot of the high whorl is the range of mountains close to the Afghan side of the Indus, generally known as the Mountains of Solomon. Speaking roughly, the country which we now call

Afghanistan lies between the Oxus and the Indus, and those who would enter Afghanistan from Central Asia must do so over the Hindu Kush or via Herat to Kandahar, Ghazni or Kabul, and thence through the deep gorges and passes of the mountains. Since the word *Kush*, the root of the Persian *kushidan*, 'to kill,' resembles the word *khush*, meaning 'happy,' there has arisen the old strategical and psychological *mot* that the way to hold India was to 'Keep the Hindu khush.'

The migrant waves coming to India with caravans and flocks having reached the oasis of Herat and of Seistan, will then have wound up the valleys of Ghazni and Kabul, or on to Kandahar, and from thence reached India by one of the many roads through the Mountains of Solomon. These to this day are famous thoroughfares – the Khaiber in the North, the Kurram and the Tochi leading to the Indus ferries of Dhankot and the like, the group of passes from Ghazni, of which the Gomal is the most known, or from Kandahar by a group which converges through the Solomon Mountains or Suleimans, and lead by various most historic roads to Mooltan and India.

There was a time when India was inhabited by a group of people usually termed Dravidian, themselves foreigners of earlier date and distinct from the surviving aboriginal folk who still remain. The Dravidians must have lived as far north as the Suleiman Mountains, for we find the Brahuis (p. 24) who live among the Baluch speaking a Dravidian tongue, and tucked away in the more inaccessible whorls of the ranges south of the Pamirs we find people who to this day are called

Dards – already mentioned – and people of other non-Aryan and non-Semitic types, such as the Kafirs of that mysterious Kafiristan which we so long imagined contained a Macedonian pocket.

Somewhere, far back in the ages, some world trouble set the Aryan tribes moving from their pastures and fields in Central Asia. They are strange things these movements of ancient peoples, and our knowledge of what set them moving hard to follow. Probably the rotting sand-hills began to smother somebody's fields, and set the owners pressing into others, thus starting a great shuffle, and then the news came of new and better lands. Whatever it was, the great white race that we call Aryan, set itself a-moving, and its trek followed three lines – to Europe via the Caucasus, to Persia, and to India.

Across the Oxus over the Hindu Kush, settling for generations in the Afghan valleys, then passing on, or passing their kinsmen through, the flow swirled round the bases of the mountains and watered valleys, and then came through the Suleimans to the Indus Valley and down the great rivers of the Punjab, which is but Persian for 'Five Rivers.' On and on pressed the white stream, across the Punjab, and then it came to the country now called Sirhind, the top of India, and thence ran downhill as it were to the fertile plains of the Jamna and holy Ganges herself. There was the centre of civilized and powerful Aryana, and the great king to whom Greek Megasthenes was accredited. But the Hindu, that is to say the Aryan, kingdoms stretched from the Oxus downwards to the Ganges mouth, and for many a century the old fortified city of Balkh, not far from the Oxus, whose old walls still show a few miles from the modern Balkh of the caravans, stood as a bulwark against another great wave of race movement.

The great wall of gorge and jungle which the Aravalli Mountains of Central India presented, and the jungles farther south, called a halt. The Aryan kept to the open plains and the line of least resistance. The Dravidians he drove before him or absorbed with the aboriginal tribes he came across, into a system of slavery and concubinage whence derive India's untouchables. The interesting point to remember is that in this great stretch of Aryana reaching from the Oxus almost to the Bay of Bengal, the ruling race and principal occupiers of land were the Aryans of the three twice-born classes and clans – Brahmin, Rajput and Vaisya, and the frontier of India was the Oxus.

§ 2

ALEXANDER OF MACEDON

The great figure who had stretched forth the hand of might and conquest across half the civilized world was not destined to let India escape him. Anatolia, Syria, Egypt, Mesopotamia and Persia had felt his might and become part of his empire, and from Persia came to him the story of India. Nearly two centuries before him, Darius the Persian had invaded northern India, swung down through those same passes whose names are emblazoned on the devices of British regiments, and exercised for a while dominion over the northern province that borders the Indus and the Kabul provinces of India. But the Persian power had passed, the Indian kings ruled again over their countrymen of the Kabul Kohistan, in Kabulistan and Zabulistan, in Ghazni, and in the valleys that trend towards the Oxus.

The march of Alexander through Persia and Afghanistan to the Indus is often spoken of with bated breath as the last word in enterprise and wonder, but if we reflect on the conditions of the time, we may realize that it was not so wonderful. For some generations Mesopotamia and Persia, far more civilized than ever since, had been honeycombed with Greek influence. Xenophon's march from Babylonia to the sea was before the days of Alexander. Greek mercenaries served the Persian rulers in Babylon and the territories of Mesopotamia, Greek traders followed the 'Silk road' and Greek clerks were probably in request. The Persian Empire was a mighty empire from which Rome did not disdain to learn. The imperial roads were roads as we understand the term, and Alexander's march, so far as his main routes were concerned, was well staged with transport animals and wheeled vehicles, with food contractors and shops, and the handy ubiquitous Greek was trading and clerking then as now. Alexander's young men were as good at training local legions as are the British to-day, and both the Turkish tribes he encountered in North Persia and the Aryans of the Cis Oxus took to their leading. Entering the Herat Valley by the great road, he turned down towards Kandahar, which some say conceals his name, and then must have gone via Ghazni or the adjacent parallel valleys over the great pass between the latter place and Kabul, as did Donald Stewart and Roberts, and Keane and Nott before them, down into Kabul. Before he made for India, the conqueror turned across the Hindu Kush to capture Balkh and overrun the valleys and plains on the Afghan side of the Oxus, even establishing an Alexandria far off over that river. Re-crossing the stupendous passes of the Hindu Kush he was ready at Nyssa in the vicinity of modern Kabul for his march into India. From there the Khaiber Pass, held then as now by the lawless *Aparoetae*, was not the safest road into India, so he crossed the Kabul River in the vicinity of Jalalabad and came down into the Euzafzai Plain by way of the Kunar Valley, Swat, and what we now call the Malakand. The long Macedonian columns, followed by their convoys of elephants and camels, slowly wound along the valleys and over the passes, making apparently for the Indus ford at Amb.

It is very easy to see in the mind's eye this arrival of the Macedonian forces in the Indus Valley. If you stand on the bastions of the historic fort at Attock by the Indus shore and look round from north to west you will see the great tumbled ranges of the Indus Kohistan range upon range, peak upon peak, snow piled on snow. Then as you gaze round that great gallery of hills your eye strikes the black masses that mean the portals of the Khaiber, and behind them the solid white wall of the Safaid Koh, the 'White Mountain.' The serrated ridges behind the Malakand, show you where the Macedonian filed down to the plains, and you can almost hear the Macedonian staff swear as the column turns in again through one of the passes to the lower Siwaliks of Buner . . . swear at the hostile slingers on the crag tops who have just brought down a camel, and whose stones are rattling round a brigadier and his entourage. Swiftly are orders given to some of the light spearsmen to go up the crag and picket the gorge while the convoy follows through, and 'Look slippy and be damned to you, or Basileus will know why.'

There are elephants in the convoy, too, packed with engineer stores for crossing the Indus and artillery stores for battering great walls.

Alexander, good soldier that he was, is turning aside to carry the stronghold of Aornos, rather than leave it a thorn in his side to worry him later. A sad difficulty has this same Rock of Aornos been to the historian and the geographer, these eighty years and more, when the coming of the British to the Indus turned full light on to Macedonian history. The story of this great Rock, this mountain place of assembly, had been read and re-read in the search for its identification. Almost every likely hill-top in that chain has had its turn in the fashion, and yet none would fit the story or the actual description. At last scientific people were fain to say that Arrian had invented it and that it was a boastful fairy tale. Standing out above Buner and close to the Indus is a great mountain known as Mahaban. Here folk said the site must be, if Aornos ever had foundation in fact. Dr. Aurel Stein, some years before the War was, by the good offices of Sir Harold Deane, the Chief Commissioner of the frontier, and certain chiefs of Euzafzai, taken up to the mountain-top. But search as he would he could not fit it to what was required. Here and there a ruin, the trace of a wall of no great antiquity, but nothing that would be described as a vast place of refuge and stronghold. The matter was given up as hopeless, and a travellers' tale! But the persistent Aurel Stein, now a knight, would not let the matter rest. The *Pax Britannica* was spreading, the deadly hatred and unreliability of the tribesmen was mellowing. It was possible to get a safe and friendly escort to hills farther up the Indus on the tribal side, and far from the actual British border-line in the Peshawar Valley, and Sir Aurel went, after the lapse of a dozen years.

This time he found beyond all doubt what it was he was looking for.

It is pretty well accepted that Alexander found political conditions that suited his aim. Along the line of the Indus were apparently various chiefs and kinglets, who were at variance with King Porus the overlord. Among these was the chief of Taxila who was waiting the Macedonian's arrival across the Indus. Together they marched on to the Jhelum, and on the hitherside of that river fought the famous battle with Porus, on or close to Lord Gough's battlefield of Chillianwallah. By the camp fires ninety years ago this is the chorus that the British Army roared:

'Fight where fought Alexander –
Oh, Paddy Gough's a cross betwixt
Hero and Salamander.'

Porus the noble, beaten but not crushed, accepts subsidiary alliance with the Macedonian conqueror, and on the phallanxes march to conquer the great Hindu Empire of Magadha. But the battle is not always to the swift, and Alexander's Europeans were, in modern phraseology, fed up. They were not going to cross the River Sutlej or Hyphasis, and the Basileus had to give way. Then it was that, leaving what we should call his C.3 men in garrison, he marched and sailed away down the rivers of the Punjab to the Indus, and battling and marching, took his way by the devil coast of Baluchistan to Babylon, the great Greek Babylon that had been grafted on to the Neo-Babylon of Nebuchadnezzar and Darius, arriving in 325 B.C. There, as all the world knows, he died as his troops filed past his bed. What the world does not know is the resting-place of his ashes.[1]

The rule that he had founded in India was not to endure. While his empire broke off into pieces, the garrisons in India were destroyed or perhaps were absorbed as mercenaries and settlers, no new thing to Greeks. But in cooler Bactria the rule remained for several generations, till the coming of the Yue-Chi, another Tartar horde, and the forced transference of the Greek rule to the Indus, of which more anon.

[1] In 1931 said to have been discovered near Alexandria.

§ 3

THE COMING OF THE TARTAR

Mention has already been made of the old stronghold of Bactria, which was practically Balkh, and how it and its colonists were for long a buttress against another world movement. It is part of the great struggle between Iran and Turan which still obtains in some form to this day. In Mogul politics in India the tug between the Lords of Iran and the Lords of Turan was a never-ending feature of disruption, and it was a contest between races whose whole biological and physical make-up are so widely different, that it has been felt that whatever the manner of the evolution of the human race, the origin of Iran and Turan must be widely different. It is the story of the Aryan race against that strange and numerous people who have the almond-eye – the Mongol fold as it is called – and it is all so fascinating, that not only for its connection with the Indian frontiers, but for the sheer evolutionary romance of it all, it is worthy of being dwelt on.

Somewhere in Central Asia, where the Desert of Gobi and the sand-buried cities of Khotan now stand, was apparently the home of the ramifications of the Tartar race, be they known as Manchus, Tartars, Turks, Mongols, Urghurs, the 'ogres' of nurserydom, and the like.

Set moving by hordes, pressed it is thought by the smothering of pastures and cornfields by the wind- and water-borne sand from rotting sandstone mountains, as well as by their birth-rate, a *trek* outwards began which grew and grew with the centuries. We see it flowing periodically into Europe in great waves with Attila, Genghis Khan, Timur, all marking the epochs. We see large parts of Europe colonized with Tartar offshoots and whole provinces of South Russia. We see the Mongol fold and the high cheek-bone, to this day, where the waves lapped round Russia to follow the Baltic shores even to East Prussia. We know that in St. Albans herrings in the season of 1237 were selling at fifty a penny because, owing to the Huns threatening the German coasts, no one came to buy the British catch. Wherever this hand of the Tartar has fallen and remained, we find a people whose inherent respect for human life and whose conception of ruth is far lower than that of the rest of mankind.

So widespread has this domination been, that we see four great Tartar dynasties ruling the whole of Asia from the Pacific to the Bosphorus, and for the most part till after or just before the World War. These were the Manchu dynasty of China, pure Tartar, the Mogul dynasty of Delhi, the Khajiar in Teheran, and the Ottoman in Constantinople. The Mogul was the first to go, and that lasted in some sort till 1857, the Manchus till a year or so before the War, the Ottoman and the Khajiar since, all of them mighty empires and now 'none so poor as do them reverence.' People who ponder over these things, and are perplexed that in Russia the Jews should take so prominent a part in the horrible cruelties which the Soviets accept as part of their routine, have remembered that the great part of the Jews of Russia are not racially Jews, and have nothing akin to the Semite. When the mass of the Tartars, many centuries ago, accepted Islam, the Tartars of South Russia adopted Judaism as their religion, and hence the Russian Jew – the flat-nosed Jew men call him.

Those there be who, believing that there is nothing in Genesis that is not founded on some early fact in the history of man, however obscurely recorded and inaccurately interpreted, think that the Mongol fold, *i.e.* the almond-eye, is the 'brand' put on Cain, and further that the almond-eyed races are the descendants of Cain, the murderer. There is some interesting collateral argument that is relevant. Up till the sixth chapter of Genesis, Cain and his descendants and their cities are freely referred to. Then there descends a silence, a *tabu* – neither Cain *nor* any of the Tartar races are ever mentioned in the whole of Holy Writ. In none of the genealogies, in none of the tables of races in which Misr and Javan figure is there any mention of Tartary or China.

The silence is so complete as almost to be intentional. Possibly the Horses of Togomar may refer to Turkish hordes, but no more. It is a romantic and attractive suggestion that tinges with interest the whole story of the Tartar races. There is one more curious point that is germane to the problem: apparently the different races of the world have a peculiar liaison with the ways of the great apes. The Aryan, in a state of *dementia praecox* sits as the ourang, sits with his hands on his knees as do the great gods at Abu Simnel, while the

Mongol or Tartar sit as do the chimpanzi, feet crossed and hands on lap, as also sit the statues of the Buddha. There is some yet unfathomed secret here, something on which the researches in southern Mongolia of Dr. Roy Chapman Andrews may throw light. Further intimately connected with this problem is the strange incidence of 'Mongolism' among mentally deficient children, which when traced to its real cause may have some strange light to throw on human origins.

Whatever the causes or mainsprings that affect human life and have produced this portion of the human race, certain it is that the movements of these races from Gobi brought them surging against the Aryan settlements on the Oxus, and it would appear that ancient Balkh was the great buttress of Iran against Turan. Trans-Oxus the Tartar tribes were circling round against Persia by way of the Silk Road and Rhagae, and the destruction of the Iranian barons in North-east Persia by the Macedonians did a great deal to weaken that part of the Aryan line and admit the invaders into Persia itself in the years to follow.

§ 4

THE SPREAD OF BUDDHISM

No study of the history of the Indian frontiers would be complete without some reference to the share and the signs of Buddhism, and the great philosophy that Prince Gautama brought into the world. In 557 B.C. was born to the wife of Suddhodana, King of the

Sakyas, a boy who was called Siddartha – but more commonly known by the family name of Gautama – who was brought up as a young prince and trained to war and hunting. Legend says that the slaying of a hind suddenly awoke his sympathy with all that were poor and oppressed, and from his reflections and actions arose Buddhism, the faith – or rather the philosophy – that he, Buddha, the wise old sage who lived, preaching, until he was eighty, taught. It spread among the simpler Aryans, weary of the complicated religion that the Brahmins had evolved from their earlier beliefs. We need not follow the spread of the Way. It took many generations to come north and in the days of Alexander, in 327, had not yet come to the Punjab. Hindu dynasties flourished in Magadha, and in 267 B.C. Asoka succeeded to his father Chandra Gupta, the founder of the Mauriya dynasty of that realm. His father was a professing Hindu, but Asoka eagerly adopted the Buddhist rule, and having carried the confines of his kingdom to the borders of Bactria in the north and the banks of the Kishna River in the south, he spread Buddhism with it. Far up the valleys from the Indus to the Hindu Kush are to be found the remains of Buddhist stupa and monasteries. The whole of the inhabitable valleys of the Swat and Kunar Rivers are full of Buddhist remains to this day, mingled with the Greek carvings and temples of the Graeco-Bactrian kingdoms on the Indus already referred to. The short period of King Amanullah's activities in Kabul helped French and German archaeologists to explore still further the remains in Afghanistan and bring more Buddhist work to light, showing how far the faith had spread under a cultured Government that encouraged and protected builders.

Here the Tartar invasions that were beginning to break through the Aryan fence also adopted the Way, and it is interesting to note that while Brahminism after a while re-asserted itself and drove out Buddhism among the Aryan races, that faith seems to have remained among the Tartar and Mongoloid folk, and to be more suited to their mentality than to Aryan and Semite races. Many of the Tartar folk in closer touch with Islam did, it is true, become Moslems, but it is to be noted that they rarely have been affected by the enthusiasms for the creed of the Prophet in the same way as the Semitic races. The indifference of modern Turkey to the creed is a case in point. We know a good deal of the Buddhists of northern India and in the region of the Indus, from the itineraries of the Chinese Buddhist pilgrims who came into India by way of Kashmir to visit the great monasteries on the Indus, and to pay homage to the shrine of the ashes of Buddha, in the Kanishka Stupa outside modern Peshawar. This shrine, lost for many hundred years, complete with casket and ashes, was found by the enterprising Dr. Spooner of the Indian Archaeological Department, through the careful and imaginative study of these said itineraries, of Fa Hian in the fifth century, and of Houen Hsang a couple of centuries later. Of late, Sir Aurel Stein in the same journey that showed him Aornos, came on more of the monasteries of the Pilgrim Route.

Therefore in thinking of the North-west Frontier of India we must think of it as a country full of remains of the ancient Way, presenting countless unexplored sites, and an immense wealth of Buddhist as well as Greek remains, and not merely as the bare snowswept or sunscorched hills, inhabited by uncouth fanatical Moslem tribes. We must picture to ourselves cross-legged ascetics and kindly philosophers sitting in the monasteries and shrines on the hill-side, telling their beads and teaching fat, round-eyed children, where in our time Chikai the free-booter would swagger and shoot.

§ 5

THE JĂTS OR GETAE; THE SIKHS AND KENT

When Alexander led his men over the Indus, he was in alliance with the Chief of Taxila, the fascinating site at the opening of the Hazara Valley not many miles from Rawalpindi, once the village or Pind on the Rawal stream, now the Aldershot of northern India. Apparently his successes were, as already mentioned, much aided by the fact that several chiefs of lesser states in the upper Punjab were in semi-rebellion to King Porus, the ruler of the northern Hindu state. These kinglets were, it is believed, some of the earlier settlers of another great colonizing stream from Central Asia which, coming down by Herat and through what we now call southern Afghanistan and the passes in Zhob, had worked up the Indus. This race we know as the Jăts, the Getae of history, who drove the purer Aryan folk into the mountains, or farther down into India or else agreed to mingle. We find them to this day as far south as Delhi and the neighbouring country, where they call themselves Jāt, and all over the Punjab, Jăt. Round Delhi they are Hindu, and as such serve in certain class regiments in the Indian Army, and one of their corps was so distinguished in the World War, as to be, with one or two others, the first among the units of the Indian Army to be called 'Royal.' The Sikh fraternity is very largely composed of the Jăt tribes in the eastern Punjab, who were and are famous as cultivators and farmers – in fact the word 'Jăt' is almost synonymous with cultivator. A considerable portion of this race adopted Islam in the Punjab, but not in Hindustan, and a few have remained Hindu. Ethnologically they must have been closely allied to the original Aryan colonists, were admitted to recognized Hinduism, and wear the sacred thread. They would like to be recognized as Rajputs, literally the 'Sons of Princes' as the descendants of the ancient Tshatrayas or warriors of the Aryan waves called themselves. Hindu opinion, lay or priestly, has never conceded this, but that Brahmin nest of anti-British intrigue and venom against which we have always had to guard, would be prepared to consider their claims to Rajput origin would they turn sour against the British, so strange and involved are the under-currents we have to deal with.

Let us for the moment jump two thousand years or

so, before we go back to Alexander – for in this astounding land years are but as days – to the time of Ranjhit Singh, the great Maharajah of the Punjab, who in the first thirty years of the nineteenth century picked up the ends of the Sikh folk – Sikh being a religion of all those folk who had become the *sikh* or 'learner' from the saintly Baba Nanak and his warlike successors – and who was a Jăt Sikh, viz. born of that portion of the Jăt race who had turned 'learners' or disciples. Anyone of any race or faith might join the religion evolved by Baba Nanak in the days when Martin Luther was setting a torch to Europe, a simple, kindly faith that was more readily accepted by Hindus than by others. It was generations of oppression at the hands of the Mogul and Moslem rulers of Delhi that produced the martial people we now know. Guru Govind was the leader who taught the simple, austere warrior faith, and gave his followers the Rajput cognomen of *Singh* or 'lion.'

It will be remembered how, when old Ranjhit Singh died in 1839, worn out by the debauchery of his later years, there arose in Lahore such a reign of murder and counter-murder as destroyed the thirty-year-old state. The great army raised by Ranjhit Singh, trained by French and American officers, was egged on to fling itself against the British bayonets, rather than eat up its own ineffective regency. After the First Sikh War, the British, it will again be remembered, endeavoured to restore a Sikh kingdom with the putative small son of the aged Ranjhit Singh on the throne. Again the Sikh army and chiefs combined to destroy the British, and the Punjab after a sanguinary campaign was annexed. The Sikh Wars are not very germane to this frontier story, save for the interesting story that I am about to tell. The boy ex-king, little Dhulip Singh, was first of all placed under tutelage in India, but eventually it was decided to bring him to England, where he eventually became a country gentleman. A house for his residence was obtained in Kent, and here is the point of the story. His friend, the famous Colonel Sleeman, one of that early band of most sympathetic Indian administrators and political officers, wrote to the lad when leaving for Kent, 'You are Jăt, and in Kent you will be among your own people, for they are all Jăts from Jutland.' And so they were, for one wave of semi-Aryan Jăts had followed the earlier Aryan waves to Europe.

§ 6

THE SAKAS AND THE GRAECO-BACTRIAN KINGDOMS ON THE INDUS

It has already been related that Alexander's successes in India were assisted by the support that he received from northern chiefs and princes who were probably Jăts. It was therefore among and over a mixed Jăt and Aryan population that the Macedonian province of Bactria controlled. On the death of Alexander and the subsequent absorption or destruction of his Indian garrisons, the Bactrian kingdom at Balkh remained for many years, and continued to function as the buttress of Aryan civilization against Tartar influences and inroads. But again and again these hordes in some form or other swelled on the Oxus, and a fresh wave, generally spoken of as Scythian or in the East the Sakas, became too strong for the Macedonian control. After a series of Greek kings who bewilder us by the multitude of their mintings, they seem to have been driven eastward to the Indus, and being Graeco-Bactrian, that is to say a mingling of Greek with Bactrians, viz. Jăts and Aryans, set up without difficulty a series of Graecoid (if one may coin a word) states on both sides of the Indus which endured for several generations. Their mintings, too, are numerous, and it is these same settlements which are responsible for Greek civilizations one hundred and fifty years after the coming of Alexander, rather than the conquerors' own Greek remains, that are so frequently met with in the Indus vicinity. Along our frontiers, as has been mentioned, are the remains of the Graeco-Bactrian frontier posts set to keep, as now, the hill tribes off their herds and fields. Remains of their cities abound. All over the country-side aged countrymen to this day will untie their shirt-tails and offer to sell you Greek coins wrapt therein. Near Kabul, and within our own borders at Akra near Bannu, coins are found in great quantities among the ruins. In the valley of Swat across our borders north of Peshawar the Graeco-Buddhist remains are innumerable, with carvings on stone of great beauty, friezes of Greek singers and dancers and the like. These have unfortunately been much injured by the Moslem thirst to destroy all representations of the human figure as impious, and by the desire of the British in the past to purchase figures broken off the ancient temples which the traders would bring in. Not far from the frontier station of Mardan stands a hill covered with ruins, known as Takht-a-bhai, and there was the amusing story of an Irish medical officer who had climbed up to see them, who reported, that 'Ye could tell they were Graeco-Bactrian by the Roman t*o*gas depicted.' You must get the broad sound on the 'o,' the 'o' *majul*, as the Arabs would call it, to feel the joy of the remark.

These kingdoms must have held sway for a century and more, for they greatly influenced the growing Buddhism and probably merely melted into the indigenous rulers, or perhaps were, as powers, destroyed by Tartar hordes who were soon to establish a northern dynasty.

But among the good-looking village lads in the North-west Punjab and in the frontier hills many a pure Greek profile is to be seen to this day, clearer and purer as the years roll on, the ancient blood seemingly resisting, as the stronger strain, Dravidian or Tartar defilements. Perhaps the reason is but the common Aryan strain in Greek and Rajput, but whatever the cause, the observer will be struck with the result. There is a drifting story of a recruit, a Brahmin from the Punjab, a splendid lad, who now and again would go awry, with the epileptic hunch from which the great Macedonian suffered, to the anger and horror of the drill havildar. It was not till one of his officers visited Florence and saw the portrait of Alexander with his head on one side that he exclaimed, 'Why, there is Duni Chand the recruit who gave us so much trouble and could not stand straight.' For the Alexandrine strain seems to have found its way into several families, as already related, and Brahmins keep their blood so pure, including an imperial defilement, that the tale might easily be more than coincidence.

The museum at Lahore, that at which Rudyard Kipling's father was curator, has a very fine gallery of Graeco-Buddhist and Graeco-Bactrian carvings as they gradually merge into the Indian forms, and the controversy sometimes launched, as to how much Indian Art owes to Greece seems to be eloquently answered here. Close to the frontier where the Hazara Valley opens out is Taxilla, the capital of the king who welcomed Alexander, now laid bare to wondering generations, much as is Pompeii, by the energies and scientific research of Sir John Marshall and the Indian Archaeological Department, which owed the greater part of its origin to Lord Curzon's wise thought. The Buddhist monasteries discovered in the gorges close to the city are themselves astounding works of intricate and fantastic carvings. Especially does one note the conception that mounts the great figures of the Buddha on pedestals supported by men and beasts writhing under the strain.

A new chapter on the Bactrian kingdoms was half-opened during the days of Amanullah, and no doubt as Nadir Shah restores the amenities of that Afghanistan the scientists and archaeologists will be able to work

GREYBEARDS IN THE KHAIBER

THE BUDDHIST STUPRA OF SHPOLA IN THE KHAIBER, BUILT IN THE DAYS OF THE KUSHANS AT THE COMMENCEMENT OF THE CHRISTIAN ERA. ON TOP IS A WATCHMAN'S TOWER BUILT IN QUEEN ANNE'S REIGN OF THE MOGUL EMPEROR AURUNGZEB

To face page 64

in safety. The Moslem himself has no great interest in the past; especially where it is to him an idolatrous past, and genuine archaeologists are hard to find among Easterns, though Sir John Marshall's enthusiasms have produced them in India.

CHAPTER THREE

TURK, AFGHAN AND MOGUL

§ 1

THE COMING OF ISLAM

UP to the seventh century we may think of Afghanistan and the frontier generally as either Hindu or Buddhist, sometimes subject to Tartar conquerors, sometimes ruled by their own Aryan Buddhist or Hindu kings. Then occurred that astounding happening, which affected the world in a manner only second to the coming of Christ and the rise of the Christian faith, the birth of Islam, which means 'The Submission,' *i.e.* 'The submission to the Will of God.' The spread of Islam, however, appearing as it did among tribes and races too fierce and wild to absorb the Christianity which for some centuries had been impinging on them, followed a very different course to Christianity. Not for Moslems was the persecution by the great pagan civilizations, not for them the martyr's death. The fierce Arabs turned on their neighbours, demanding acceptance of their faith at the point of the sword, added to their harems countless women of conquered races, from whom they bred tens of thousands of children to bring up in the fierce proselytizing faith. In an incredibly short time the Arab faith and the

Arab rule spread over the Eastern and North-African world. It swept across over Persia and towards China; it ran along North Africa, completed the destruction of the kingdoms that the Vandals had humbled, and even surged across into Spain. Swelling up through Persia and into Central Asia, the waves lapped round the Parapomisus and up from holy Meshed into the mountains of Ghor. Arabs settled among the people, forming those families of Sayads that still maintain their distinctive status, tracing their descent from the Prophet and his tribe the Qoresh.

By A.D. 644 the flood had reached to Kabul, though it receded again, being more permanently established at Ghazni, whence it took many generations to roll on towards India. In 711, however, Islam came to India for a while from the sea, some 6000 Arabs under Qasim, nephew of the Governor of Basra, which we used to spell Bussorah, invading and conquering Sind. The effect of this conquest did not long endure, though the great resemblance between the Moslem boatmen on the Indus and the Tigris, suggests that the Arabs themselves for a while made the former river as much their own as the Tigris and the Shatt el Arab.

Except for this venture, Islam was concerned for the next three centuries in consolidating its hold on Seistan and Kandahar, Central Asia and the Mountains of Ghor, a task which kept the Arabs and their converts busy.

If India was invaded by Moslems from across the Indus before the end of the tenth century, Aryan chivalry succeeded in expelling the invaders. In 977, however, Sabaktagin, the Turkish slave-king of Balkh and Ghazni, initiated the series of invasions from Afghanistan and Central Asia, which lasted in some form or other till the coming of the British to the Sutlej at the commencement of the nineteenth century.

Sabaktagin commenced a series of raids on the Indian princes who inhabited the Indus Valley, and whose traces are to be seen in the many ancient ruins and castles on either bank of that river. High up on the hills, close among the rivers to this day stand the black limestone ruins of the 'Kafir Kots' the 'Castles of the Unbelievers.' They frown down from the Khaiber peaks black, dour, silent and haunted. The men of the hills, Wazirs, Afridis and the like, were being converted, and were already following these Turkish kings of Ghazni to the harrying of the infidel. The country-side to-day knows little of the story of the black ruins that stand among them. If you go into the Derajat the 'country of the tent dwellers,' the inhabited plains and riverine valleys on the right bank between the Gumal and the Kurram Rivers, you will find to this day on the Indus banks at the north and south ends of a precipitous razored line of hills known as the Ruttah Koh or Red Mountain, two Kafir Kots. The more southerly is the Kot of Rajah Bil, the northerly, that of Rajah Til. That is all the country-side knows. No, stay . . . there is one more fact that legend will tell you. Not about the Kot of Rajah Bil, the one in which Hindu carvings and idols still remain, but of the great, black, almost intact, fortress high up on a plateau that belonged to Rajah Til. At the foot of one corner where the terraced bastions come down to the river, stands an ancient temple, resembling the ruins of the smaller temples in Kashmir. It is known as the *Khanjari Kothi*, 'the house of the dancing-girl,' there the villagers will tell you, dwelt a dancing-girl who sold the garrison and admitted the invaders. That alone of a story of what must have been one of might and dominion, does the country-side remember through a glass darkly. Yet the coming of the Turks and Arabs and their henchmen of Roh must have been a very notable affair if the Hindu kings' hands could keep their heads at all.

It is said that when Sabaktagin re-crossed the Indus and returned to Ghazni with much spoil, Jeypal, king of the Punjab, Kashmir and Multan, assembled a vast array of Hindu chivalry, and himself crossed the Indus and advanced into the mountains of Roh. Overtaken by storms and snow he offered terms and was allowed to withdraw. On arriving back at Lahore he repudiated his promises, whereon Sabaktagin again invaded Hindu territory and took Peshawar. Advancing on India he met the forces of Jeypal, with whom were the armies of the kings of Ajmere, Kanouj, Delhi and Kalinga, one hundred thousand strong. Defeating them heavily he took all the plains west of the Indus to add to his dominions. Sabaktagin died, and after civil war between his children, his illegitimate son Mahmud – that terrible name of ill-omen – became king of Balkh and Ghazni.

Ere long the habit of invading India with hordes of wild hillmen became almost perennial. Mahmud, fiercest of Moslems and most relentless of inconoclasts, swept far down into India, enslaving tens of thousands of Hindus, forcing others to embrace the Faith at the point of the sword, carrying off with them thousands of girls that were comely, the boys as slaves to boot, and splintering the carven images that ornamented the Hindu temples both inside and out. The method incidentally was to heat them by bonfires and then dash water on the heated stone. To the Moslem the representation of the human form in stone is pure idolatry, while the Hindu carvings,

'The organs of sex and the circlets of bones
and the loose loves carved on the temple stones,'

were abomination thrice personified. So Mahmud laid the temples waste, as they lie to this day where he left them, and even destroyed the super-saintly temple of Somnath, carrying off to his fastness at Ghazni the great sandalwood 'gates of Somnath.' The roads and passes by which the British maintain the peace of the borders have seen these great comings and goings, the caravans of outraged Hindu maidens, the troops of orphaned boys, and the camels laden with the sack of cities.

At Somnath the great stone gods were broken, in search for the jewels said to be therein, lament the priests never so bitterly.

Ten times did Mahmud of Ghazni march into Hindustan, each time to lay waste some new district and return with its spoils, after rudely circumcising in the presence of the hosts those males who saved their lives by adopting Islam. In vain did the squadrons of the Rajputs gather to withstand him; in vain did the women of Hindustan melt down their silver and gold ornaments to fill the war chests. Never again, except in the fastnesses of the Rajputana hills and deserts, did the warriors of India resist with success the invaders of the North. In 1761 took place the last battle of Panipat, to be described hereafter. History has written fully enough of this, and as was that slaughter of Mahratha chivalry at the hands of the Afghans, so may we believe were the earlier victories of Mahmud.

Three-and-thirty years lived as sultan this fierce Mahmud, a faithful, cultured Moslem, who endowed Ghazni with all that he could wrest from the idolators of Hindustan. In 1030, before even Harold of England went down before the Norman, Mahmud was gathered with his fathers in the sixty-third year of his age, and has remianed ever since the hero of the Muhammadan historians, affectionately spoken of by his co-religionists in song and fable as *Sultan Mahmud Ghaznavi.* To his successors, both of his own dynasty and that of Muhammad of Ghor, who overthrew it, the use of India as a milch cow was not enough. They determined to conquer and rule. The Indian princes, too cruelly misused by Mahmud, put up little resistance, and then was set up that Muhammadan kingdom at Lahore which soon spread to Delhi, and gradually absorbed the greater part of northern India, while Moslem adventurers led forth bands of Central Asians to set up Turkish and Afghan kingdoms deep into India and far Bengal, and even away into the Dravidian kingdoms south of the Vindhya Mountains and the River Narbudda.

The story of the Tartar race has been outlined, and let it be said now that from the days of Mahmud of Ghazni in the year 1000, down to the rescue of the blinded Mogul Emperor from the hands of the Mahrathas in 1804, never did a Hindu dynasty rule, except in subordination, over the Hindus of India. For seven hundred years first Aryan India, and then the whole of the Peninsula, was a Moslem empire, and not only that, except for some forty years of Afghan rule, the dynasties that sat at Lahore and Delhi were Tartar. Some reference has been made to the wide psychological difference between Tartar and Aryan creations. If India has been persecuted and butchered for generations to make a Tartar holiday, she might well be somewhat more enthusiastic of what her fellow Aryans, the British, have done to save her from the state in which the break-up of the last great Tartar dynasty had left her.

§ 2

THE BEN-I-ISRAEL

The coming of Islam to the hill country that men call Afghanistan, but which India itself prefers to call Khorassan, brings us to the story of whence the name Afghanistan is derived, and what it means, and who are the Afghans whose name has been taken for the whole tract. It is as germane to the story of the North-west Frontier, as we know it now, as it was a thousand years ago.

This page of the story of what once was part of Aryan India touches, as does almost everything else, what William Bolitho calls 'those eternal contemporaries,' the Jews. Some little time, probably before the coming of Islam, there arrived in the country about Kandahar, a people who eventually made their home in the mountains of Ghor. From this tribe, one among the many who go to make up the inhabitants of Roh, the country became known as Afghanistan, the country of the Afghans. The tribe who were apparently among the first to embrace the new faith, describe themselves as the descendants of Afghana, a son of Saul of Israel, who was, they say, commander-in-chief of the Israelitish hosts. Their more recognizable progenitor they claim to be one Kish or Kais, eighteenth in descent from Saul, and the tribe, which has grown to a race, to this day calls itself *Ben-i-Israel*, the Children of Israel.

Because they were a tribe of prestige and vigour, and because they held some of the best part of what we now call Afghanistan, and because it was one of their chiefs who founded the Afghan power, calling it the Durani Empire, all the Moslem tribes, other than those of Turkish origin, claimed to be offshoots of the same race. Afghan genealogists were only too eager to oblige, so that every Pathan tribe claims to belong to this race, though it is certain, as has been explained, that many of them are of Jăt or Rajput origin. A study of the characteristics of the Rajput Moslem of the Punjab as compared with a Pathan shows clearly that, allowing for the effect of a mountain environment and freedom from any governmental control on the one side and the comparatively ordered life of the Punjab plains on the other, there is no great difference.

The whole of the Pathan people, Durani or otherwise, speak the ultimately Persian-derived Pashto, though language is no sure criterion. This is readily illustrated if we think of the Boers, very largely Huguenots (as their names show) and not Dutch, yet there are no French words in the Taal, which men now call Afrikans.

The claim of the Duranis to be descended of Israel may easily be true, using the word Israel in the sense of Hebrew. It would be still easier for them to be of the Lost Tribes, as a *trek* along the valleys from Persia would be nothing of a move. Equally possible would it be for them to be descended of some offshoot of the Babylonian Captivity. They have, especially in old age, the appearance which we call Jewish, and that really applies probably to Judah only, who acquired the Hittite profile by commerce with Moab. Israel appears to have blue eyes and among its characteristics red hair. But there is no sort of proof of the claim, nor is it likely that one can ever be forthcoming.

Their names are very Jewish, but so to a great extent are all Muhammadan names, yet perhaps the Biblical names do appear more often among them than among other Moslems, Joseph, Jacob, Jesus, Moses and Abraham, and heard more frequently among them than among other Moslems, in the form Yusuf, Yakub, Isa, Musa and Ibrahim. There is one custom of theirs that does give some colour to the story in that they alone of Moslems have a feast akin to that of the Passover.

At any rate they, the descendants of Afghans, have given a name to the country in comparatively modern times, formerly known as Kabulistan, Zabulistan and Korassan, and also to the whole Pashto-speaking people. How this race became predominant in Afghanistan will be told later.

§ 3

THE GRANDEUR AND ROMANCE OF THE MOGUL

To the varying Turkish and Afghan dynasties that wrought such universal dominion in India, and broke into pieces and rejoined again, there at last succeeded the greatest of them all. All the while that Lahore and Delhi warred and rejoined, and the Afghan kingdoms and provinces in lower India waxed powerful, and built mosques and castles and warred, eastern Afghanistan remained for the most part a portion of northern India. The mountaineers of Roh shot at the strong and slashed at the weak as of old, rode with kings to Delhi, but in their own fastnesses bowed the knee to no man. The roads *via* Multan to Kandahar, and the Khaiber route to Kabul, were kept fairly orderly so long as the writ from Delhi or Lahore was current. The intermittent periods were, then as now, considerable factors in keeping the tribesmen wild and untouched by Moslem civilization.

Out of Ferghana in Turkestan there arose one of the most fascinating characters in history, Baber the Jagatai Turk, who founded the empire that the world inaccurately calls Mogul. The young Baber was a Turk from the province of Jagatai, or Chagatai, which is the word used in India to describe anything Mogul. It is true that his mother was descended from Ghengis Khan, but he himself was sixth in descent from the great Lame Timur, the Tamberlane of Marlowe, and had no love of the Mogul connection; probably he and his successors suffered the appelation Mogul to their dynasty because it was a name of fear. The world quailed before it in shuddering memory. 'Names of Fear' have meant much in the ancient darkness of races and religion.

In 1504, Baber, whose father had been Governor of Kabul and King of beautiful Ferghana, possessed himself of the lordship of Kabul and Bactria, and conceived the idea of conquering India, to which, as a descendant of Timur, he considered he had a better right than the adventurer dynasties that had ruled of late years at Delhi. Especially did he feel capable of ousting the remnant of the Ghilzai dynasty, which had already lost most of its power. In 1519 and in 1520, Baber entered India, but on both occasions trouble on his Afghan frontiers called him home.

Finally Baber crossed the Indus on 15th December 1525, and being joined by local chiefs, rode on towards Delhi, where he met the Indianized Afghans and Pathans, on the already famous battle-field of Panipat. Ibrahim Lodi, the Emperor, and fifteen thousand Rohillas fell, and on 10th May 1526 Baber was proclaimed Emperor of India at Delhi. His son Humayun was sent on to Agra, which was captured, and northern India lay at his feet. Then was inaugurated this great empire which was gradually extended almost to the southern seas.

But before we glance at the great empire which he started, let us take some stock of the fascinating personality of Baber. Born in 1483, and brought up in the wonderful province of Ferghana lying at the foot of the mountains whence drain the Oxus and the Amu Darya, irrigated, gardened, tilled and vineyarded by help of the river known as Zar-afshan, 'The Gold-sprinkler,' its memory was always green. The hero of a hundred fights, the inspirer of countless horsemen, the warrior always fled before the poet and the gardener, whenever the hour was spare and the plan propitious.

Wherever he went Baber must have his rills and his fountains, his poplars and his cypresses, and as much as climate would permit, his upland home was reproduced. Sheikh Umar, his father, was a scholar and a poet, a lover of birds and of nature's sweet familiar things. When not a poet, the Sheikh was a mighty hunter and carouser, but he had seen that Baber was taught Persian as well as his native Turki.

So Baber, when not soldiering, would lie and enjoy

the drowsy splash of the fountain, or the mutter of water in the carved rills, and sport with those daughters of the south that shared his camp or the Turki maids who rode in saddle beside him. And as Baber planned and built in memory of Ferghana, so did his descendants carry on that tradition the length and breadth of Hindustan.

Six Moguls there were worthy of the name, though his son, Humayun, for a while lost it all for Akbar to recover. Their names, or rather in most cases titles, sing themselves in sonorous Persian cadence as they go – Baber, Humayūn, Akbar, Shahjehān, Jehangīr, Aurangzebe Alamgīr. After Aurangzebe, whose title was Alamgīr, the 'World-grasper,' the edifice began to totter by its own weight and the inferiority of the materials that made it and the hand that swayed it. Top-heavy and ill-balanced, it crashed with a mighty crash, and ere long there were none so poor as did them reverence. Then it was that the British merchant adventurers, humble lodgers in the Mogul ports, set about to pick up the pieces and rebuild the edifice.

Nevertheless, from the days of Queen Elizabeth to the days of Anne, the dynasty dazzled the world by its wealth and brilliance. Great are the monuments of the period, the gorgeous fort and palace of Agra, with the marble courts and fountains, the halls of splendour inlaid as they remain to this day with the semi-precious stones. The same at Fatehpur Sikri, the strangely forsaken capital of Akbar, where on the mosque of Chistie is written the striking sentence, so new and yet so like, that is quoted in Chapter Four

THE INVADERS' WAYS TO INDIA

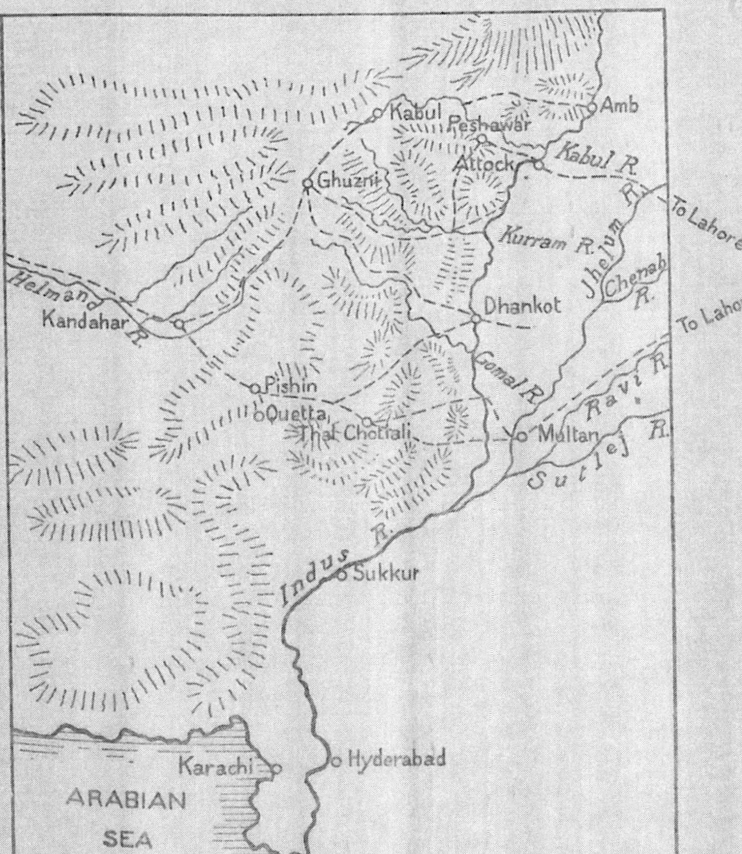

J. H Astle

for all the world to rejoice in.[1] Then again in the city of Shah jehan-abad, the Seventh City of Delhi, is the marble splendour repeated, and once again at Lahore. They marched in great moving cities, these Moguls, starting early from Agra, spending two or three months at Delhi, and a month or so at Lahore, judging the people and transacting business in the marble halls of Public and Private Audience, till the heat sent them on to Kabul or Kashmir, and always the same gardens and fountains, the ripple rills and the narcissi and roses all the way.[2] For long they were Central Asians first, and Indians afterwards, talking Turki and Persian in their palaces and with their wives. Kings and princes rode in their trains and their harems were filled with kings' daughters from north and south and from east and west. Akbar was the greatest ruler India had ever seen, and the *Ain-i-Akbar*, his code of laws and business, worthy to rank with the code of Napoleon. Akbar would heal the sores of strife and oppression which other Moslem rulers had kept raw. To do so he married over ninety daughters of Hindu chiefs, and undoubtedly for a while removed the bitterness which his successors, especially Alamgīr, revived by cruel and intolerant treatment.

At Agra stands, as all the world knows, that wondrous monument of man's grief and love for a woman.[3] Never, never, has so beautiful a monument been built

[1] See Chapter Four, p. 100.
[2] See the story of 'The Lost Garden,' in the next chapter.
[3] *The Taj-Mahal Bibike Rosa.* 'The Tomb of the Crown-of-Palace Lady,' which we know as the 'Taj-Mahal.' She, the thrice-beloved wife of Shahjehān, died at Berhampur, in 1629.

before or since; a monument to the sense of beauty that actuated these Central Asian rulers, and the grandeur of their architects and designers, the patience of their craftsmen.

With Alamgīr went the majesty and dominion of the dynasty, though its tradition and the veneration in which the mighty name was held long lingered. He died in 1707 and his son Muazim, who was then Governor of Kabul, succeeded him on the Peacock Throne at an age that was close on seventy, assuming the gallant title of Bahadur Shah, 'The Bravest of the Brave.'

For the five years that remained of his life, the prestige of Alamgīr, his father, held the empire. Then it fell to a series of palace murders and king-makers, as one puppet princelet after another was placed on the throne, and removed at the makers' will by dagger and poison-bowl. At last choice crystallized on the colourless Roshan Akhtar, grandson of Bahadur Shah, under the title of Muhammad Shah, who succeeded in reigning, for he could hardly be said to rule, for twenty-nine years, that were often periods of humiliation, during which authority waned and decayed and the distant provinces revolted. With the death of Muhammad Shah the Mogul Empire became little more than a name and a memory.

§ 4

THE COMING OF NADIR SHAH KULI

Once more, while the Tartar throne of Delhi tottered and faded, another great phenomenon was to take place in the passes that lead to India. A Turkish shepherd lad had risen to fame as a soldier, and eventually secured the throne of Persia, driving forth a horde of Afghans who had seized the power and dominated the Persians. Then he in his turn marched for Afghanistan, and appeared at Kabul. Thence he proceeded to invade India by way of the Khaiber and adjoining routes. The Mogul was already involved in a struggle with a race of half-bred Hindus known as Mahrathas, whose impudent claim to have for pocket-money a fourth of all revenues of India, the land was much concerned in resisting. Thus the loss of Kabul was accepted philosophically enough for the moment, and even when Nadir Shah crossed the Indus, only ineffective steps were taken to stop him. The swarms of Persian Turks with plenty of Afghan mercenaries and young Rohillas in their train, ate up the land like locusts, as they advanced in leisurely and comfortable fashion to Delhi. There Nadir Shah was bent on a 'squeeze' of Delhi, a bloodless squeeze if possible, and no one was man enough to try to stop him.

Barely a hundred years before the accession of Queen Victoria, on Valentine's Day 1739, Nadir Shah entered Delhi after being received outside by the Mogul. The squeeze was severe enough, and Nadir Shah got away with many millions sterling and also the Peacock Throne with all its encrusted jewels. Unfortunately a city riot, started, it was said, by a rumour of Nadir Shah's death, resulted in the Persians carrying out a three days' sack and massacre. Then restoring, as it were, the throne to his 'brother Turk,' as he called the Mogul, Nadir left him thereon with an empty pocket, hecatombs of dead and piles of heads in the capital to mourn. It was the last straw that hurried the empire to its fate; such loss and such indignity was not recoverable. Further Nadir Shah compelled his 'brother Turk' to submit and agree to the annexation of Afghanistan by Persia, which included Sind, Multan, and the districts in the Punjab near the Indus. And then the Persian host went back, this time by way of Multan and Dera Ghazi Khan, and the passes through the Baluch hills.

§ 5

THE RISE OF THE AFGHAN EMPIRE

Yet once more in this period was the kaleidoscope to rearrange its disc and glasses. Nadir Shah Kuli, the 'Slave of Destiny,' had grown more and more masterful and imperious as conquerors and despots are apt to do. They reach that dangerous frame of mind known as *Dunya-dar*, 'World-possessing.' Then their fate overtakes them. Nadir Shah was murdered in 1747, and his empire fell to pieces. Now it happened that among Nadir Shah's commanders was one Ahmad Khan of the Abdalli race, viz. of those Ben-i-Israel, who have been described, and whom we may consider the true Afghans since from them comes the name of the country and its people, the descendants of Afghana, son of Saul of Israel aforesaid. Ahmad Khan commanded ten thousand horse and also had charge of Nadir Shah's treasure chest, two useful appendages to him who would seek power. The Afghan determined to try and found an Afghan kingdom which had never yet existed, separate from India. His money and the force at his disposal made his fellow nationals of the clans of the Ben-i-Israel choose him without demur as the new ruler, though his clan, the Saduzai, was in itself among the least important. To the Afghans or Abdallis he gave the name Durani, 'The People of the Pearl' calling himself Dur-i-duran, 'Pearl of Pearls,' and turned the provinces that Nadir Shah had wrested from the Mogul into the Durani Empire. This included Sind as we have seen, Multan, Peshawar, Hazara and Kashmir, as well as Kandahar, Kabul and Ghazni, and as much of the country on the far side of the Hindu Kush to Balkh and the Oxus, and even beyond as he could hold.

But twice as big as France though it was, it was not enough for him. India soon became his ruling passion, and ten times did he lead his armies across the Indus. The decadent Moguls were quite unable to restrain him, and the Afghan colonists often sought his aid. Especially when the Mahratha half-bred races from the west presumed to try to wield authority behind the Mogul prerogative, did Ahmad Shah arrive near Delhi in his anger. In 1761 was fought the last great battle of Panipat, some fifty miles from Delhi. All the Mahratha chivalry were assembled, and many of the Moslems of India, to meet him. For some weeks the armies lay watching each other, and then hunger compelled the Mahrathas to leave their entrenched camp. After the most desperate battle they were completely defeated and almost destroyed.

The news of the victory went through India with a wail of despair. The way in which news circulates through India has always been something of a mystery, and the underground channels are many. This tragedy of Panipat swept through India by the bankers' channel, probably the most complete of its kind in the world. This is how it ran in bankers' metaphor. 'Two pearls of great price have been dissolved, twelve gold mohrs have been lost, and the silver and copper cannot be cast up.' It went like the wail for the field of Flodden.

The story of this tragedy, which however gave the Moslem power at Delhi a fresh lease of life, is sung in the famous ballad of 'With Scindia to Delhi,' by Rudyard Kipling. It is the story of a beggar girl, probably some lass of a gipsy tribe who had followed an Indian prince, wildly attractive, active and staunch. One of his henchmen tells of the battle, and of the flight. For a while the Mahratha chivalry drove the Afghan before them:

> 'The children of the hills of Khost before our lances ran,
> We drove the black Rohillas back as cattle to the pen.'

But the fortune was to turn, men said by treachery, and the Afghans chased them from the field with horrid slaughter, and the prisoners taken were all put to the sword. The prince with his maid on his saddle bow, rode hard 'from Panipat to Delhi town.'

But

> 'Lutuf Ali Populzai laid horse upon our track
> A swinefed reiver of the North that lusted for the maid.'

The race is not always to the swift. Scindia would not slay the maid who, tearing herself free to ease the failing mare, fell with a scream to the Afghan, while Scindia, one of the 'pearls of great price,' fell below the foundered mare he had himself stabbed, within sight of the protecting walls of Delhi.

'Lost mistress and lost battle passed before him like a dream in the restful oblivion of death. . . .'

'Two pearls of great price, twelve gold mohrs, and the silver and copper cannot be cast up'!

It ended the Mahratha dream of succeeding to the place of the great Mogul. When they tried again, another northern folk were protecting India from the shameless demand of *Chouth*, a fourth of the revenue, for their guerdon.

§ 6

THE AFGHANS ON THE FRONTIER

Ahmad Shah, the Durani Emperor, placed Mogul Ali Jowahar, with the world-famed title of Shah Alăm, 'King of the Universe,' back on to the throne that was no longer peacock, as a puppet in the hands of the Indian Rohillas, and fixed for his guerdon his own frontier as far south as the River Sutlej, where the British practically found it forty years or so later. Between Panipat and the battle of Delhi in 1803 when Lord Lake rescued the now blinded Mogul, blinded by a Rohilla minister in revenge, it was said, for castration when a boy, from durance at the hands of the Mahrathas, much water had flowed. The restless Ahmad Shah died in 1773 after repeated pourings into India, undertaken to preserve to himself the Punjab from the rising power of the Sikhs. Timur Shah, his son, reigned on his prestige, somewhat ineffectively, in his stead till 1793, and was succeeded by *his* son, Shah Zaman, the 'Ruler of the Epoch.' By now, Mogul and Pathan India was everywhere pressed by Mahratha or Sikh and British. Many were the calls to come down and save Islam, and though the Punjab was falling away, Zaman Shah came again in answer to an appeal from Tippu, the Afghan-descended usurper of Mysore. Trouble on the Oxus called him back, and he made the young Sikh baron Ranjhit Singh, governor of Lahore on his behalf, apparently in return for help in getting his cannon over the Chenab. However Ranjhit Singh might have observed this trust under other circumstances he was not likely to hold by a failing Afghan crown. Shah Zaman could not ride in the saddle of the Durani Empire, and Ranjhit Singh overcoming and uniting the various Sikh chiefs who had been forming into powerful cliques during the Mogul decay, formed his one-life Sikh kingdom, and steadily drove the Afghans from India, making their settlers his subjects. Multan and Kashmir, the beautiful summer home of the Moguls had long been Afghan territory, and now it became Sikh. By 1820 even Afghan Peshawar in the Afghan territory proper had fallen to the Sikh. This terror of the Afghan armies crossing the frontier of India and sweeping the Punjab bare was thus very real even in British times. Great was the relief to villages, long had mothers calmed their naughty children by threat of the Afghan, when first the Sikh and the Briton succeeded in placing a barrier at the foot of the Afghan hills.

CHAPTER FOUR

THE LOST GARDEN

BECAUSE this story of the past ages has been but one of marchings and slaughterings, and all that man unto man has done, let me for a moment bring a lighter vein, that will perhaps make the beauty of the gardens that Baber and his Chagatai brought from far Ferghana and mountain-girt Kabul live for us. It is a story of one of those hallucinations which Yoga, that mysterious power of the Hindu, can cast on one, especially when readings and musings have prepared the mind. A Hindu ascetic, simple, devout and wise beyond worlds, talked to me and I listened, as he led me up the hill-side in answer to my query as to where the Mogul garden lay, the lost garden that I wanted to roam in.

§ I

BELOW THE PIR PANJAL

Ever since mankind have searched for and pondered on the lost site of the Garden of Eden, the finding of an old site that once was a pleasaunce has always filled souls with delight. And there are so many places in the world to be found by those who look for them; some carefully tended, with ruins to match, so that they are not really lost, but only gone before. Others struggle with bramble and overgrowth unknown, a broken idol or an old-world fane amid the screen of creepers. I have met such round the world, and sometimes you find them in Ireland, lying to the soft, wet west wind, looking through the mullion of what once was a chapel window, amid the saxifrages and old-world things grown wild.

The East is perhaps where they strike you most, especially since Lord Curzon has had gardens planted round all the famous ruins of the Mogul days, too tidy perhaps for their purpose, but before his conserving hand came eastwards, you might ramble along among the ill-kept or forgotten *baghs*. The ruins and remains of Mogul gardens are the most fascinating things in India. They were great gardeners, those Turkish and Mogul princes. Somewhere in Central Asia the garden cult had excelled, making use of mountains and streams, and using for their purpose the fruit and the rose, the narcissus and the iris which grow wild. A Chagatai garden relied not on its wealth of flowers, but on the beauty of its layout.

Some years ago, chance willed that I should journey from the ancient bastioned city of Jammu at the Indian foot of the Kashmir Himalaya to Kashmir itself. But I was to have with me as furniture and recreation a newly raised mountain battery, formed under my supervision for the army of the Kashmir State. And we were to march to Gilgit, far away towards the tumbled mountains that lead to the Pamirs and the 'Roof of the World.' But as never a man had marched before, and few of them could even girth up a gun mule, which is a feat of strength, we were going leisurely so that the men should learn, far from the haunts of men and troops who might jeer. Also we were going by a route that no one knew, across the great Chenab at Akhnoor, all under the slopes of the Pir Panjal, and then into the little principality of Poonch and thus on to join the great highway into Kashmir and thence up the snowy passes to Gilgit.

So we marched by way of stony country paths along the foot-hills, past here and there a castle, some still garrisoned and some derelict, till we came to the level of the lower pines, the *longifolia.* The length and breadth of the Himalaya you will find the grouping of accurate Old Testament! The cedar, the pine, the fir and the box, *Cedrus deodaris Pinus excelsa* and *longifolia,* the Norwegian fir, the *Abies Webbiana* and *Taxus baccata,* and no doubt many another, always together, as wise old Isaiah chants, 'The cedar, the pine, the fir and the box.' But first and foremost, as you leave the plains and the hot plain air you come to the *longifolia* amid the sandstone hills. Then as we marched, we struck into the ancient way of the Mogul emperors when they journeyed from Lahore in May, as was their programme, right over the Pir Panjal, by a cobbled road which rises still to many thousand feet and passes out of the forest to the birch tree and the juniper bush, close to the great glaciers, and then down into the Happy Valley of which Tommy Moore sang so convincingly.

And the Moguls longed for their Central Asian gardens, and made them in miniature at every stage – and from Lahore to Srinagar is thirty-one stages – as they had made them at Agra and Delhi and Lahore aforesaid; walled serais with bastions round the garden, planted with peaches and plums, and with iris and flowering shrubs and little terraced rills and channels and fountains. When the hills begin then the Central Asian gardener could have his tiny waterfalls and fountains. Elephants and even guns, wives, eunuchs and courtiers, tramped up and down these mountain roads, spring and autumn, for a century and more, for the great emperors with their sonorous Persian titles, since on the ascension to the throne their names left them. They sing themselves as they go, as I have said before, Jehangīr, Shahjehān, Alamgīr, Shah Alăm. . . . Intone them aright as you would a Kyrie – 'The World - Holder,' 'The King of the Universe,' 'The World Encircler,' 'The Ruler of the World,' so let them go.

And their gardens, those in the great places rescued by a greater world-holder, George Curzon, the rest left to the dragon and the bittern and to some toothless old keeper, too old to keep the ivy from displacing the carved stones in the summer-houses. Here, marching from Jammu City to Kashmir, we struck into the first by the old castle of Rampur Rajaori on that good fishing river the Rajaori Tawi.

The battery camped outside the serai, and I went in to look and fell a-musing. The headman of the village brought me two gold coins in a handkerchief as *nazzar* to touch and to remit after the way of magnates, for was I not the supermaster of a battery of artillery and the only Angrez, for here they use the old forgotten name of the English, who had come this many a year. I found it all as Tavernier had said, the French chirurgeon of the Mogul, nearly three hundred years before.

It was a hot day, though within the lower hills, and there was little to do save spin for *mahseer* in the Tawi and explore the garden. The pattern of the serai seemed to be sealed, for one had seen the high archway and the bastioned corners, with the umbrella-shaped awning in red sandstone, wherever the Moguls had built their pleasaunces. But this garden was on the side of the hill, and water from a canal could enter it. Down the centre came the long stone water-trough, and the series of cascades each cut in stone in a different pattern, so that the water should ripple contrariwise in the sunlight, and fill the round breast-like fountain tops long dry and silent. Gnarled old apple-trees were still in blossom, and the almond-tree flourished hard by the husk of an arabesque pleasure-house. The iris and the Prophet's Flower peeped out among the gentle *banafra*, the spring violets that all the world use as *tisane*. The little pink tulips abounded among the paths and narcissi in crowded profusion sprouted in the side channels, and squirrels chattered among the pilasters. I looked for the canal that should bring the water in and heard it gurgling outside, taking the clear hill water to the terraced wheat-fields. It was easy to dam it and to turn it into the garden under an arch in the wall. It pushed masses of fallen leaves along and made its way to the masonried troughs and the channels which lead to the stone cascades; at last it got room to move and opened out over the fluted stone. Then began the music of long-parched rills and the water danced as it danced to the Mogul ladies. Beside me stood the gardener, toothless and doubled with age and rheumatism. One yellow tooth peered at me over a mouth so old that it was like a rotten medlar, fringed with beard and moustache dyed red, after the red hair of the Prophet.

'*Sahib*,' he said, 'it is forbidden, but who can compel the Angrez, though the Presence will certainly reward his faithful servant, who has not had wherewithal to smoke this twelvemonth,' and he fell a-mumbling that aforetime he was a man and a king's servant and carried a matchlock in a red baize bag behind a potentate, and now had not even a *huqah* fill, and so forth after the manner of ancient mariners and gardeners all the world over.

So while the battery rested, and when the fishing had grown dull, I brought my camp chair to the *chabutra* and sat among the ruins and watched the apple blossoms fall and smelt the sweet narcissi and wondered, for –

> 'I love the cities to whose ruined walls
> The ivied vesture of oblivion clings,'

and would fain have seen the Turkish ladies of the

marching train disporting on the sides of those mountain ripples.

And so the day just frittered itself away and the soft breezes blew, till 'boot and saddle' called us on our way. Then at dawn we swung out, the jinketty-jink of the gun mules sounding on the *pavé*, whose large rounded pebble-ways suited the spongy feet of our baggage camels. And we followed the ancient way for fifteen miles, till we came to the next stage, in a dark cool glen under a pine-clad hill-side, above which towered the snowy peaks of the Pir Panjal, and against the green background I could see the great arch of the serai, but the modern camping-ground lay half a mile back from it, alongside a Moslem burial-ground, with iris growing over the tombs. My Moslem orderly rolled out the Arabic greeting, '*As Salaam Aleikum ahl-i-kabool*,' 'Peace be with you dwellers in the tomb.' By a small white shrine, a dozen bamboos carried the fluttering rags that pilgrims leave, and near it grovelled a leper, who joined his arm stumps and sought largesse, in a cry forged on anvils hot with pain.

§ 2

THE SANNIYASI

Later in the day I strolled down to the serai to look for another tangled garden, and found outside it a Hindu shrine, of severe and very ancient style, standing by a sward of turf. Up and down the green walked the *sanniyasi*, 'The world renouncer,' the recluse in charge, apparently deep in thought, grave of *mien* and austere of countenance, as becomes one who long ago renounced in seven years of novitiate the pleasures and the pains of this world. I accosted him humbly and courteously, as a man should speak to a recluse. He halted in his pacing and looked at me for a second, and then he bowed. I smiled at him, and a flicker of a smile played across his smooth, lineless face in answer.

'My son, what seek you?'

'*Nahin, Baba!*' I seek nothing, I but eat the air after a long march, wandering hither and thither without purpose, but I would enter the old Mogul garden that must belong to this serai.'

'What brings you to the old garden?'

'Curiosity, father, and a love for old places. Especially would I call to memory the times of the Chagatai, and see their courtiers and their ladies a-marching to Kashmir.'

The *sanniyasi* nodded and smiled to himself. 'My son, you have spoken well. I too love to muse on things that have passed as well as on things that are to come. Perhaps I can help you in your quest. You will not find the garden by the serai. It is up on the hill, and the Chagatai put it there because of the *karez*, the water channel which runs out of the rock.'

'Indeed, *Baba*,' I replied, 'if you could help me or tell me some legend of the place that would be a great pleasure.'

'Come first with me.' And he led me towards the little shrine, a shrine of grey limestone carved outside with a curious pattern, something resembling the rose and portcullis of the Tudor period. The entrance was through a high pointed arch, and the darkness within for the moment was unfathomable. And then my eyes slowly recovered from the numb of the outside glare, and I could see that a tiny flat lamp, or *chirag*, flickered in front of an image. Then I saw that it was not the popular conception of Mahadeo, but the solemn, deep-browed Indra, another *persona* of the deity. The figure was cut of black basalt, dark and polished, and then the *chirag* flared as the *sanniyasi* dropped something over it. As it flared I could see the countenance of the carven image, and it was a countenance that betrayed calm and peace on a road untold, far different from the more common Hindu figures. The stone eyes seemed to watch and to follow one, with a look that would penetrate one's deepest thoughts. I looked at the *sanniyasi*, who smiled at me, and said, 'That is the great Indra who knoweth and maketh all. Yesterday, to-day and for ever are but one, and could you but see as those eyes see, you would know all that you want of the garden of the Turks. Now look at me.'

And I looked, and he passed his hands in front of my face, and the *chirag* flared again. Then we went out.

'Now I will take you to the garden.'

§ 3

THE GARDEN

Above the temple a cobbled stairway led up the face of the hill-side. And we climbed up, the Indian leading, on to a plateau which lay at the foot of a wooded hill-side, and below me lay the dressed lines of the battery camp. Thus we came by a clump of pine to the *Kaiseri Darwaza*, the door of the Emperor. To my surprise it stood in good order, complete in arch, and the polished plaster of marble surface intact instead of peeling. Over the inner gateway was a Persian inscription, and it was the inscription on the jasper-inlaid entrance over the Hall of Private Audience in the Mogul Palace at Delhi. Here it is in its beautiful Persian:

> 'Agăr Fărdous ba rue zămīnast
> Hămīnast! Hămīnast! Hămīnast!'

which may be translated:

> 'If there is a heaven on earth
> It is this! It is this! It is this!'

The Chagatai were famous for their inscriptions, and were students and lovers of Persian poetry, as were all the cultivated folk of Central Asia. But written on the great gate in the tomb of saintly Salim Chistie, in Akbar's wonderful city of Fatehpur Sikri, that is now deserted, is a more wonderful one still. Akbar would have founded such a religion as has been the despair of many great thinkers, that should combine the good of every creed regardless of the fact that no human mind could make the selection. But he culled what he could, and on the gateway of the Chistie's tomb is recorded the following in that beautiful flowing ornate form of Arabic, the *Khatta Kufi*: 'And Jesus said, the world is a bridge, you must not build on it.' Pass over, and build not tenements as men of old built on London Bridge. There it stands, a new message for Christendom, and for all the world, and now above me stood the words of different import, claiming that the garden within was a heaven on earth. And if you notice these things, you will see that the word used for heaven is *fardous*, not *behisht*. Now *fardous*, or paradise as the Greeks spelt it, means that thing of longing to Eastern potentates, a hunting-park, a New Forest, while *behisht* is the real heaven of peace, not of the slaying of game. Of all the beautiful names in the East, this is given to the water-carrier, the name that men so unthinkingly use, the *bheesti* or *bihisti*, the water-carrier, 'The man of heaven.' You can hear the cry going down the platforms of the railway-station on an Eastern day in midsummer. 'Oh man of heaven, bring water.' You can hear Dives calling to Lazarus, 'Touch my tongue with water, I burn.'

And here above me was the promised heaven on earth, and outside the gate a *bheesti* with his leather water-bag sprinkled water to lay the dust.

So together the *sanniyasi* and I entered the garden

laid them before them, while she that had the zither sang.

And she sang from the songs of Saadi that are written in the book *With Saadi in the Garden*, so that we too sat and listened, hiding behind a cypress hedge so that we should not trespass, and as we listened I must have fallen asleep.

And when I woke the Emperor and the women were gone, and the *sanniyasi* said, 'Come home, *sahib*, for the sun is getting high in the heavens,' and we walked once more on the cool turf to the door. But the plaster had fallen from the gateway, and the arch was broken, and I turned round to the garden. The cascades and the fountains were there, but dry and choked with dust. The fruit trees were old and twisted, though ablaze with blossom still; the cascades were chipped and lichen grew in the crevices as it did at Rajaori; the poplars were broken and only barely alive, and coarse grass grew where the lawns had been.

The *sanniyasi* said, 'Thus it is, my son, that the pomp and power of the Mogul are long dead, and there is little of what you seek. Many of the marble squares are stolen, and all is broken and desecrated.'

'But, *sanniyasi-jee*, where is the garden that I saw just now, and the maidens, and Jehangir and his consort that you showed me?'

'I, my son? Not I! Perhaps Indra may have brought before you things as they were, for to him time is nought. Yesterday, to-day and for ever. Here it is as you see it now, though perhaps you may rebuild it for yourself.'

But when I got back to the camp I found the Dogra commandant of the battery waiting to see me. It was slightly overcast, there being a cloud over the sun, and the poplars in the gully ahead looked dark, and somewhat menacing for the moment, as the breeze sighed through them, and the ruined serai stood up a black mass.

'*Sahib*,' said the commandant, 'the men would like to march on this afternoon, and say they are quite rested and the mules are fresh.'

'Why, Khajur Singh? What is the matter? Don't they find this a restful place?'

'No, sahib, they don't. Saving your presence, they say this place is haunted. There are *boots*[1] about.'

Boots or no *boots*, I was a little inclined to agree with them. The place perhaps was not quite canny. There were plenty of beautiful spots ahead, and, as he said, the mules were all right, despite their novice drivers. So march we did.

An hour later we left camp. I rode over to the *sanniyasi* to say good-bye, for I had been attracted by his grave, kind face, and I told him we were off. He expressed no surprise and merely said, 'Peace be with you, my son. Don't dwell too much in the past, for it is all one with the present and the future, and the world is *Maya*, a delusion.'

At the foot of the path up to the garden I halted, gave my horse to my trumpeter and climbed, for I felt I must see it again. There it stood, with its broken arch and its tangled trees and shrubs, and its dead

[1] *Boots:* ghosts, spooks.

water-courses. A peacock ran across my front, and for the moment I thought I saw the green and crimson bodices of the girls. I forced my way through a couple of peach trees, knocking off the blossom, but all was silence. Then I turned to go on my way, but as I turned, was it fancy? . . . a zither seemed to twang softly behind the rose bushes.

Below me the battery was closing up and I slipped down the path and mounted. I certainly agreed with the men that we had better go.

CHAPTER FIVE

THE COMING OF THE BRITISH TO THE NORTH-WEST FRONTIER

§ I

BRITISH POLICY

WE have just seen how the Sikhs in making their one-man kingdom had driven the Afghans over the Indus, had actually crossed that historic river, and occupying the fertile Peshawar Valley, had driven them through the portals of the Khaiber. They had also crossed into the Kohat and Bannu districts and had even overrun the Derajat; the country of the 'people who live in tents,' which lies between the Mountains of Solomon and the river, and which sweeps inland in a bay between Dera Ismail Khan and Tank. They had hunted the wilder tribes back into the mountains and their posts now stood where the ruins of the Graeco-Bactrian posts lay hidden in sand at all these gorges, where the raider will – not, as might be expected, enter the plains – but drive off the captured flocks and herds. The raider can arrive by any old spur but his loot can only go by a track that is accessible.

In 1808 the British started their policy of extending their trade and that of all and sundry to Central Asia, via the great waterways of the Indus and its tributaries,

A RECONNAISSANCE ON THE FRONTIER. THE TOP OF THE RAZMAK NARAI (PASS)

To face page 106

and also the even more essential matter of trying to block the plans of the Tsar and the Emperor Napoleon, which had been disturbing them for over ten years. Mr. Mountstuart Elphinstone, a brilliant young Indian civilian, conducted a mission to the Shah of Afghanistan in 1808, Shah Shujah, then holding his court at Peshawar, which the Sikhs had not yet wrested from him. This brought British officers into direct touch with Afghans and frontiersmen, whom hitherto they had but met as traders or mercenaries in Hindustan. While down in Sind, British officers sent to discuss the matter of transit dues on the Indus with the Amirs, were meeting the Baluch, Afghan and Pathan bravos who took service with them.

It was in 1820 that the Sikhs captured Peshawar and Multan, and crossed to the Derajat. Then followed years of warfare between Sikh and Afghan for the recovery or retention of the captured province, while Shah Shujah had been driven from his throne, and at first from the Punjab, and then from British India, had made attempts himself to return to Kabul. At last the British introduced their great policy, which was to end strife on the Punjab border, to bring peace to Afghanistan, now under the rule of Dost Muhammad, often torn by civil war, by the establishment of an Afghanistan which would put an end to any fear of Russian penetration towards India. The British, Ranjhit Singh, Maharajah of Lahore, and ex-Shah Shujah of Kabul signed the Tripartite Treaty up in a Simla garden, whereby in return for a friendly settlement of all outstanding disagreements between the three parties the Shah was to be restored to the 'throne of his fathers' as the Treaty somewhat pompously had it.

§ 2

THE JAUNT INTO AFGHANISTAN

Then began that most dramatic and astounding of episodes that was eventually to produce such tragedies, known as the First Afghan War. Not that it started by being a war. Not a bit. Shah Shujah was raising his own troops, at our expense, to regain his throne, while we and the Sikhs pushed in a friendly way behind.

The British frontier lay on the Sutlej River not far from the other bank where Alexander had erected his altars of disappointment. There at Ferozepur were the most elaborate meetings of friendship between Lord Auckland and the Maharajah Ranjhit Singh. Two Indo-British divisions in the full dress of Europe were there assembled. The Sikhs had hardly less troops, and reviews of each force were held. The British for the first time examined, somewhat disdainfully, the troops of their allies that ere long they were themselves to meet in conflict. The European troops of Her Majesty and the East India Company, the magnificent Sepoys of the Bengal Line dressed, like the Europeans, in red coats and white belts with chakos atop, gleamed and drilled with magnificent precision. Many troops of horse artillery galloped before the Sikhs. Then Lord Auckland must inspect the Sikhs.

A large staff accompanied him, amused at the bizarre and somewhat ragamuffin appearance of the American and European officers in the Sikh service, with now and then some cashiered British officer recognized by his quondam comrades.

The contingent of Shah Shujah was in itself a romantic and interesting formation. It was hastily raised by British officers lent to the Shah, and for a while was a sought-after service, offering considerable prospects in the great adventure on which we were embarking so light-heartedly. But the force was not to advance across our allies' territory via Attock to Peshawar and thence enter the Khaiber, despite the fact that the Afridis were very much attached to the Shah. No, the Sikhs did not want their allies in their country, so for this and various reasons the force, which was to be two divisions plus the Shah's troops, was to go to Kabul by three sides of a square, and march down the Sutlej and the Indus till it reached the island and fortress of Sakkar Bakkar, one of the world's river crossings, which we had, as paramount, insisted on being placed in our hands. Thence we were to march across the bleak desert of Kach Gandava up the Bolan and over the Khojak Pass to Kandahar, the Shah leading – an astounding distance and a roundabout road, as a glance at the map will show.

Light-heartedly the Army marched, leaving a division in reserve at Ferozepur – a long, uneventful march with some black partridges and some gazelle to shoot, the stores going by boats, and herds of transport camels being hired *en route*. At last the

'Army of the Indus' as it was called, in its full dress, with far too much baggage, reached Kandahar. Horses and men were weary from want of forage, want of water, and short of rations. They had also had their first experience of the frontiersman as armed robber and marauder. They had experienced what invading armies of the past must have undergone in the same passes. Raid and murder by night, and the cutting-off of stragglers, with devil a foe at all to tackle by day. Gradually they got handy at repelling them and turning the tables. At Kandahar, flowing with fruit, milk and honey, and plenty of grain, the troops recovered. Then they started on the great march through the valleys and passes between Kandahar and Kabul. Again all passed quietly, till the force arrived at Ghazni, still a walled city with a lofty citadel. This was held against the Shah, and was the scene of a glorious episode. The Bengal Engineers, under Captain Peat and Lieutenant Durand, blew in the gates, and the 13th Foot led the stormers.

After this storming of the stronghold of the dynasty that first overran Hindu India, Sir John Keane led the Army into Kabul. A few miles from the citadel the Afghan ruler had arrayed all his cannon, forty in number. Alas, his fickle army had fled, even looting his camp, and the guns met the eyes of the Army of the Indus standing arrayed and deserted on the crest of a rise. Harlon, the American adventurer, who had been with the Sikh army, and was present in Kabul, tells the tale.

§ 3

THE BRITISH IN KABUL

The Shah now re-entered his lost capital at the head of his contingent supported by a British army. Rank on rank of British Infantry and their imitators, the Bengal Sepoys, marched behind, chakos, scarlet and pipeclay, the imagery of power and precision, and the thousand marching as one. The lancer cap and lances of the 16th Lancers, the brass helmets and tigerskin rolls of the Bengal Horse Artillery, who in those days were expected to do what mountain artillery are used for to-day, made a glorious scene. It was set in the most beautiful scenery of its kind in the world, the gardens of Kabul, the poplars, the cypress, and the green of the mulberry trees, the grim outline of the old fortress of the Bala Hissar on the hill above the city. Behind it was the great massif of the heights and the snow-topped mountains around: a garden and a graveyard, and the handsome courtly king, with his flowing white beard . . . escorted to his palace in the Bala Hissar, amid the blare of British trumpets and the roar of British guns! He may well have said, as he gazed down from the lofty terraces over the city from which he had so long been an exile, as Lyall makes Abdur-Rahman say:

> 'You might think I am reigning in heaven,
> I know I am ruling in hell.'

But there was no sign of hell yet awhile. The people

had, it is true, shown no sign of enthusiasm at their rightful king's return; possibly the Afghan does not suffer them gladly, and at any rate, what the British spectators may not have known, to shout in the presence of Majesty is disrespectful. When King George rode through Delhi, you could have heard a pin drop. Last time they had seen a king ride by it would have been the bastinado for any man so rude as to shout. For the ways of the East are not those of the West.

In Kabul, while the Shah's troops moved to their stations in the districts, and a small mounted force chased the fugitive Amir Dost Muhammad, the Army sat down to enjoy rest and to fraternize with the Afghans, a people far more open in their ways than those of India. The Afghan gentry came in to watch the British horse-racing, to watch cricket, to be the guests of the officers' messes. The men strolled through the bazaar and bought and chaffered for the embroideries and the inlaid knives of Kabul and Central Asia. The officers, too, rode far afield to shoot and hawk with the Afghan gentry.

In fact, in this autumn of 1839, and all through the winter, the British were what they claimed to be, the troops of a friendly power who had but come to assist in restoring their rightful king, and with him prosperity. When the winter came, the Afghans slid with the British on the frozen waters round Kabul. But when the British officers set their artificers to make skates, and shot off across the ice, an art new to their friends, then the Afghans said, 'Wah, Wah, these people really do, as they say, come from a northern land.'

Such anxieties as there were, were soon countered. British columns moved with ease wherever they listed, and wherever any opposition to the Shah was found, it was soon dispelled. Sir William MacNaghten, the British Envoy with the Shah, controlled everything, and as the war was not a war, the soldiers merely lodged in their camps, little concerned, apparently, with the state of affairs.

Fascinating as this story is with the steady development of the drama, and its passing to tragedy, it is beyond the scope of this book, which aims but at bringing the romance of our inheritance of dead and gone empires into understanding.

So bright were the general prospects, so did Kabul but seem to be as India, that the wives of officers and of some of the British rank and file, were sent up, marching through the Khaiber some months after the Shah's womenkind, his zenana, had joined him. The garrison of the whole country was then reduced to little more than a division, stationed at Kabul, Kandahar and Ghazni, and Sir John Keane returned to India. The rest of the country was held by the Shah's troops and Afghan levies which British officers raised as fearlessly as ever, and for a while as successfully . . . and all the time there was not a railway line in India, and the Punjab was not even British. Yet the brigade in Kabul foolishly, at the behest of Sir William, left the forts and went into open cantonments as in British India. It was a fool's paradise beyond belief. Embassies were sent into Central Asia to influence the khans, and Sir William and his entourage dreamed of a great game to be played, in their zeal for England, half-way across Asia.

So 1840 passed into 1841, and English flowers bloomed in upland cantonment gardens, and English vegetables prospered and delighted the Afghan people, who took to them readily, and all seemed amazingly quiet. The Dost had returned and secured adherents, but just as he seemed likely to make headway, he threw up the sponge, and came in and surrendered himself to Sir William MacNaghten, who had met him coming alone to the capital. To Calcutta he was sent in all honour, profoundly relieved that his eyes would be safe with us, and for ever grateful for his kindly reception and accommodation in Kabul, a gratitude which stood us in good stead in the troublous times of the Indian Mutiny.

§ 4

THE PASSING OF THE DREAM

The British dream of a settled Afghanistan and an untroubled Punjab was to pass, not, perhaps, because of its inherent failings, though those were many, so much as by the blight in execution that ensued. Among the troubles was the policy of the Shah. When the good King Charles of pious memory was restored to the English throne of his fathers, whatever his failings were, want of flair was not. He was too wise a man to antagonize those he was to rule over again, by reinstating, at the expense of those in office, the friends who had supported him in misfortune, and bitterly was he reproached therefor, but he kept his throne and brought peace to the land. The Shah not only made a refugee supporter his chief minister, but one singularly unfitted for the purpose, and his rule, bolstered by British bribes and troops, became more and more unpopular. Because the country was crying aloud for good government, the political officers tried to rule, and that way, in such circumstances, can have but one result.

Just before Christmas 1841, Sir Alexander Burnes, who was appointed to succeed Sir William MacNaghten as envoy, was murdered in his house in the city. Hostility of all the nobles against the Shah and against us was acute. We were staying to keep an unsuccessful ruler on the throne of a kingdom we were ruling for him, and then, with the appointment of an aged and gout-ridden general to command in Kabul, our doom was pronounced. The Envoy himself was quite unfitted to ride a storm and rule rough men. A few weeks after, MacNaghten was murdered at a durbar by excited chiefs. The military authorities, instead of at once seizing the fortress and making themselves secure, stayed to be enveloped in their futile cantonment, treated for leave to go under escort, quarrelled among themselves, would not abandon their baggage, and were caught by winter. Setting forth late they were destroyed under the most pitiful scenes of a massacre of half-frozen Indian troops. The 44th Foot and the Bengal Horse Artillery struggled on as soldiers, only to perish in their turn after scenes of great gallantry and despair. Thousands of followers were massacred, followers who so crowded on the troops that they could not fight. Many of the followers and Sepoys were carried off as slaves. The aged general and the ladies were surrendered as hostages, and this had the merit of saving their lives. Among them was the redoubtable wife of General Sir Robert Sale, an old campaigner, who had already expressed her opinion of the follies in no measured terms. Her published diaries tell the story of their captivity and how they were eventually spirited away far over the Hindu Kush to Bamian. At first very harshly confined, they were eventually collected together with certain captured officers and a soldier or two, and at the instance of some of the many of our genuine friends among the Afghans, received much better treatment.

The picture by Lady Butler, 'The Last of an Army,' is well known. It represents Surgeon Brydon on a broken-down pony riding into Jalalabad, and a few mounted men coming out to meet him. He was the only survival of Elphinstone's Brigade, a force of four battalions, guns and horse, save the captives referred to, the slaves carried off to Central Asia, and the frostbitten remnants of a few Indians who dragged out a miserable existence as crippled beggars in Kabul, and had once been Rajput soldiers.

But just as folly, worse confounded, had destroyed this fine brigade, which well handled could have defied half Afghanistan, so at Jalalabad, at Kelat-i-Ghilzai and Kandahar, the Indo-British Army was worthy of itself. At the former, Sir Robert Sale, who was taking back a relieved brigade, and who had been chastising Ghilzai marauders *en route*, conducted a memorable defence against the Afghans, sitting, as it were, in the winter residence of the Afghan Court. The prolonged defence, chastened by a severe earthquake, which had hurled down the old walls of Jalalabad in which they sheltered, gained for the Brigade the name of 'The Illustrious Garrison,' coined in one of Lord Ellenborough's flowing periods. At Ghazni a strong Bengal regiment had let itself get into a state which compelled it to surrender. At Kelat-i-Ghilzai there was a famous defence for which, as for Jalalabad, special medals were struck. At Kandahar Major-General William Nott, with a force of Bengal Sepoys and some irregulars, maintained his force and his prestige with ease, by being wise and stout-hearted.

Both the Indian and Home Governments had long tired of the imbroglio, and the fact that the king they had set up could neither remain without them nor rule with them. The expense for several years had been enormous. Now that there had been disaster no one, save only the indignant Army, seemed to care what happened. As a matter of fact the shock to our prestige had been great, and Lord Ellenborough, who had succeeded Lord Auckland as Governor-General, found that troops were hard to come by. At last, at Peshawar, an avenging army was assembled under Major-General Pollock. Undisciplined and dumb, cowed Sepoy corps had to be disciplined and heartened, and it was many weeks before the avenging Army set forth to relieve Jalalabad. Then General Nott was authorized to withdraw via Kabul and General Pollock to go there and meet him. There was no very great plan for extricating the prisoners, but the generals rose to the occasion. Nott advanced from Kandahar, Pollock forced the Khaiber, and found that Sale had relieved himself by a stirring victory over his besiegers. Together they swept on to Kabul, driving the Afghans like dogs before them. There, too, came stout and somewhat difficult old Nott, while the captives under Eldred Pottinger had released themselves, now that British prestige was able to get helpers. Sir Robert Sale himself went to meet them on the Bamian passes, to find his stout-hearted consort and his daughters well, and most of the captives in Afghan dress and in good case, after many weary months of anxiety.

After some punishments and the unsuitable destruction of the famous bazaar in Kabul where MacNaghten's body had been exposed, the troops returned at their leisure to India, telling the Afghans that they must now choose their own king, for they had murdered the Shah and installed a puppet son. Ere long the Dost was invited back and went with the British blessing, a chastened spirit.

One more scene may be presented. The Governor-General, always enamoured of gallant deeds, was now waiting at the Sutlej to receive the returning Army, as they marched out of the Punjab. A large force had been there assembled as an army of reserve. Triumphal arches had been erected wound in rainbow muslins of the colour which the Viceroy had chosen for the ribbon of the war medals. First marched Sale's Brigade, 'The Illustrious Garrison,' now a name of fame, but for long a subject of chaff, followed by Pollock and Nott, amid salutes and ceremonies, though the war-worn troops were in no particular mood for functions.

That, in outline, gives the story of the first great events which brought us to the hills and passes which we know as the North-west Frontier. Our two routes had been the Khaiber and the Bolan, with an excursion to and storming of Kelat, and on the southern line our officers had learnt much of the Baluch and Brahui, tribes of the passes. In Peshawar, where the great General Avitabile ruled on behalf of the Sikhs – a gallows at each corner of his garden and an Afghan tassel usually thereto – the frontier tribes of our own day were duly met, and in the Khaiber, then Afghan territory, the political officers dealt with the Afridis and raised a corps of *Khyberrees* in the diction of the day.

But as Pollock marched down and the last Briton left the frontier, once more the old law went on, an eye for an eye, and a tooth for a tooth. The Sikhs had given us little real assistance, though a few Sikh corps came to Kabul with Pollock to reap the harvest.

§ 5

SIND

The abandoning of Afghanistan by the Khaiber left us withdrawing the troops in Kandahar and those that guarded the road up from the Indus. The British regarding Sind rightly enough as either part of the Durani Empire of Kabul, as arranged by Ahmad Shah, or as part of the Mogul Empire before Nadir Shah dismembered it, insisted at the time of the move to Kabul that passage to their own troops and to the Shah of Kabul's contingent should be given as related. Sir Charles Napier, then recently appointed to command the troops in Sind, and conduct the withdrawal, was directed to obtain from the Amir the observance of their treaty obligations, and to enforce a new one. This latter was to embody certain new points especially as regards transit dues for goods on the river, moving either to the British at Ferozepur or the Sikhs on their rivers, points which incidentally had long been matters of enmity between Ranjhit Singh and the Amirs. The Amirs had gradually been assembling a large armed force of the Baluch of the hills, and who openly talked of serving the small force as Elphinstone had been served at Kabul. As Napier was in full charge, he took liberty to disbelieve the reports of his political officers and accept those of his own Intelligence staff, that very large gatherings were present. He moved down the Indus from his position at Sukkur, and found many thousands of tribal forces about Hyderabad. With them were fought the two extremely severe battles of Meeanee and Hyderabad or Dubba, against overwhelming odds and great fury, after which Lord Ellenborough, under orders from Home, added Sind once again to the body politic of the Mogul Empire. Whatever opinions there may be as to the treatment of the Amirs – and the provocation they had

SIR CHARLES NAPIER PURSUING THE ROBBER TRIBES. THE CAMEL CORPS CAN BE SEEN ON THE RIGHT

(From an old print)

To face page 122

given was great – there was never any question that Sir Charles Napier was right and that huge armed forces had been collected unknown to Major Outram, the political officer, and that with the intention of falling on Sir Charles. He characteristically preferred to do the falling, rather than be 'caboolcd' as the phrase of the day went. The annexation of Sind brought us into close touch with the tribesmen of the Baluch border and lower Suleimans, some years before that took place farther north. Sir Charles Napier found himself concerned with protecting the inhabitants from the hitherto uncontrolled and relentless raiding of the hill Baluchi, studying as to how best to repel them and at the same time gain influence over them. His experiences were dour but successful, and he experienced sharp fighting in the stupendous gorges which allow the mountaineers to debouch into the valleys. During the years that the Afghan Wars had lingered the protection of convoys and the desired friendliness had set political officers in touch with the tribes. At this time arose the Irregular Horse, afterwards known as the Sind Horse, which attained much fame under John Jacob, who after many years on the frontier, rose to the rank of brigadier-general. For years he did from his cantonment and famous house at Jacobabad 'put the fear of God' into all raiders' hearts. His two regiments of horse held the whole border, and the men who did it were what we should call 'Hindustanis,' mostly the descendants of the Rohillas already described, now too far removed from wars to retain the old martial spirit, but in that generation still famed as horse-soldiers, though, under lesser leading, already losing some of their daring. With such men to protect them, the work of civilization as well as of the taming the hill men went on steadily.

The whole of the Baluchistan hills owed nominal allegiance to the Khan of Kelat, and with him and them, the frontier officers had plenty of dealings. The Baluchis came under two very distinct categories; those who are cultivating in the Indus, and who are '*le tuman*,' that is to say without *tuman* or clan, and are generally spoken of as the 'broken' Baluch, *i.e.* those whose clan organization had long been broken, and the 'hill' Baluch who were most severely and effectively tribal, and who lived the purely tribal and warrior life of the frontier hills, but tempered with tendencies somewhat less ferocious and ruthless than the Pathan tribes farther north.

Their ways and country will be more full described in dealing with the North-west Frontier to-day.

§ 6

THE SIKH WARS

It is not possible to place ourselves logically back on the frontiers which now in 1842 we had left apparently for good, unless we have in our minds some outline of the Sikh Wars, which brought us to the Indus for keeps. Our ally, Ranjhit Singh, had died on the 27th July 1839, before ever Ghazni fell, without the pleasure of seeing the trouble the Tripartite Policy, as he had probably hoped, would involve us in. And he went to his God in state, this swartzreiting baron who, after the Indian fashion for strong men, had carved himself a throne, with his wives and concubines burning around him, to the horror of Her Majesty's representatives who would not go in attendance.

When he went, the Lahore throne fell into terrible trouble. The old 'Lion' had left no heir that could hold a throne. His early deeds of derring do had given place to the last word in Eastern debauchery. The Sikh Court was steeped in every evil that imagination can fancy, and the spirits of the stern old Sikh fathers must have stirred in their horror. Murder and counter-murder removed all heirs to the throne and all the figures of influence, save only Gulab Singh, Rajput of Jammu. Dignity and prestige had left the scene, and the famous disciplined army of Ranjhit Singh having murdered or driven forth its Europeans, delivered itself into a soviet system which aimed at making the forces the supreme power in the State. Many indignities had any leader to submit to if he would still remain in even nominal command. Then the effete junta at Lahore, the timorous but intriguing Durbar, bethought itself of British bayonets. They would settle the army goose, so the army was encouraged in its half-baked idea of invading British India, born of pride and ignorance and the memory, perhaps, of Elphinstone's disaster and its aftermath. There is a pleasing story of the child telling her version of Elisha and the bear that ate the children, how 'he had said to them if you tease me again I will tell my bear and he will eat you . . . and *they* did, and *he* did and *it* did.' So is the story of the great army of the Khalsa.

It would threaten the British frontier and cross the Sutlej nudged and hypnotized by its own Durbar. *They* suggested, *it* crossed the Sutlej into British India, and *it*, in the shape of Sir Hugh Gough and the British Army, fell on them. But it was no mean antagonist, this army dressed in some imitation of the Indian Army. Four desperate battles ensued in which the European troops had to bear more than their share – Moodkee, Ferozeshah where Kipling's Snarleyow was off-lead of No. 3 gun in G Troop, 2nd Brigade Bengal Horse Artillery, and the 'Driver's Brother' with his head between his heels – Aliwal, and the great and completing victory of Sobraon and . . . the Sikh army died.

Then did the British try and rebuild a tutored Sikh throne with the child Dhulip Singh, the very putative son of the aged and debauched Ranjhit Singh, as a minority ruler. The Sikh frontier was at the foot of the frontier hills, and the famous frontier names now come on to the stage. Henry Lawrence was Resident at Lahore and his assistants were posted through the land to establish a system of government and revenue for the boy King, and set better counsellors in the right path. John Nicholson and Herbert Edwardes in the Derajat with a few Sikh troops holding the border and getting as a matter of routine, revenue that the Sikh governors only got at the head of an army. That was the Waziristan border, George Lawrence and Reynel

Taylor were at Peshawar; Abbott in Hazara; Herbert at Attock.

At once on this border, especially on the strip known as the Derajat, already referred to as meaning the country of the 'people who live in tents,' which runs along the Indus, between the river, the Waziristan Hills and the lower Suleimans, the presence of the British officers began to be felt. Inland from the Indus, up the Kurram, lies the fertile highly irrigated plain of Bannu, a beautiful emerald spot among the mountains, where Greek settlements have waxed fat in days of old. The Bannuchis included the descendants of the scum of countless invading armies marching to India, via the Tochi route from Ghazni or the Peiwar route from Kabul. Every sort of crime was rife among the descendants of pimps, pandars and swashbuckler settlers. Ere long they had been reduced to order and to the paying of their revenue, while they were even persuaded to pull down their towers and live as citizens.

§ 7

THE DRAMA OF MULTAN

The attempt to set up a Sikh rule in perpetuity, with the boy Dhulip Singh as ruler, was not destined to last. Henry Lawrence, the Resident at the Lahore Court, worn out by two years of astounding labours, had gone Home for a while, and a rising broke out, which spread to the whole of the existing Sikh army, to which also the old soldiers flocked. The arrogant Sikh soldiery, despite the memory of Sobraon, were at heart out to try their luck once again. Multan, the erstwhile Afghan city and provincial capital, was the scene of the first outbreak. The Governor, one Mulraj, irate at being called on to render certain sums, asked to be relieved. Mr. Vans Agnew, one of Lawrence's political officers, with a couple of Sikh regiments, attached to which was a Lieutenant Anderson, accompanied the new Governor to see to his installation, arriving at Multan on the 18th April 1848. An excited mob attacked and wounded the British officers outside Multan. A little later the wounded officers were attacked in their camp and destroyed, the escort of a Gurkha corps on the Sikh service failing to protect them. The retiring Diwan, or Governor, Mulraj, who had been riding with the British officer, identified himself with the disturbers, and declared himself in rebellion against the Durbar at Lahore. The officers' bodies were beheaded, and the heads treated with great contumely.

Now comes the truly dramatic situation. Agnew when first wounded had sent word to Lieutenant Herbert Edwardes in the Derajat, telling him of the occurrence and asking for help. The moment Edwardes got this he crossed the Indus with Sikh troops which failed him. Returning, he assembled a force of frontiersmen and of the Afghan colonists in the Derajat, usually referred to as 'Multani Pathans,' and set forth to cross the Indus accompanied by 'General' Van Courtland, a European gentleman in the Sikh service, and who acted under his orders as British representative, bringing a most reliable corps of the Sikh Government as nucleus.

It was now the middle of the Punjab summer, and the Derajat was, of all places, the hottest of the hot. Edwardes crossed the Indus, and in sweltering June, defeated large forces sent by Mulraj to meet him at the battle of Kineree, and approached Multan. The Nawab of Bahawalpur, a frontier state on the river between the Punjab and the Sind, always protected by the British from being absorbed by the Sikh power, sent levies, led by Lieutenant Lake, the political officer. The former, who had been joined by a large and hitherto loyal Sikh force under Imam-ud-Din, now defeated Mulraj at Sadusam. Edwardes, properly elated, wrote to the Resident at Lahore that, given a battery of heavy guns and Major Napier the Engineer officer, he would take Multan, but in Simla and Calcutta some hesitation reigned. The Commander-in-Chief was very averse to sending European troops at that time of the year, and the situation was allowed to develop and deteriorate.

In July when the rains had begun and the fierce heat was at times less, a force from Lahore was sent down, but by this time, what was a local trouble had become widespread. The Durbar had sent a large force of its own troops down to Multan, which was assisting Edwardes in blockading the city. This, with the Lahore force under Brigadier Whish, proceeded to invest Mulraj in the stronghold of Multan, which with its vast mud bastions was comparable with Bhurtpur, that had proved such a nut to crack to the

British Army. It was not till the beginning of September that Brigadier Whish appeared before the city, and by the 7th the battering train got to work and the Sikhs were driven within the walls. Then General Sher Singh, commanding the Sikh contingent of the investing force, declared himself, and marched off to join his father, Chattar Singh, who was also in rebellion farther north against the Durbar and its advisers. Whish was fain to draw off and await more troops from Sind and it was not till the end of December that the siege began again. The city walls were first breached and stormed and the big guns turned on to the citadel. Just as the breaches therein were practicable Mulraj hauled down his colours and surrendered unconditionally. Then, so deep an impression had the murder of Vans Agnew and Anderson made on British minds, that their exhumed bodies were carried into the fort, not by the gates – oh no! – up the rubbled slopes of the battered breaches of remembrance.

That is the drama of Multan, the 'inner key of India,' so far as the British are concerned, remarkable, in the purpose of this book, for the share which the fierce tribesmen and Afghan colonists of the frontier districts took in this war with the hated Sikh, and the influence that Herbert Edwardes had acquired over their minds.

§ 8

THE BRITISH REACH THE FRONTIER

Long before Multan fell, the rising of the Sikhs *en masse* had come about, and the Indo-British Army was once more called in. Sir Hugh Gough led his divisions over the Chenab to the fierce drawn battle of Chillianwallah, where Alexander had beaten Porus, and the 'Crowning Mercy' of Goojerat. Down the Khaiber curiously enough had come, as friends and perhaps hoping to recover Peshawar, five thousand of the ancient enemies of the Sikh, in the shape of a body of Afghan Horse led by Sirdar Akram Khan, one of the Barakzai brothers. That contingent did little to distinguish itself save an attempt to get behind the British line at Goojerat, and was hunted back by Sir John Gilbert, scuttling into the Khaiber with the British on their heels, as their allies said, 'like dogs.' And that was the last time that an Afghan invader put his nose inside British India till 1919, when young Amanullah thought he saw sufficient feebleness of purpose to make an invasion of India a good proposition. He soon learnt better, and probably in his Italian exile, ponders on what on earth led him to break the worth-while friendship of forty years.

So because the Sikhs would not accept their medicine and allow the British to build a better kingdom for them, they lost it all, for Lord Dalhousie and the British Cabinet in January 1849 declared that the lost Mogul province which Ahmad Shah had wrested from Delhi should once again be added to the parent. The Sikh frontier which British politicals were nursing now became the British frontier, and speaking generally, as it was then so is it now.

CHAPTER SIX

CLANS AND TRIBES ON THE FRONTIER

§ I

THE FRONTIER MOVES TO THE INDUS

We have now seen the British frontier move to the Indus and beyond, to wherever the Sikh rule had traced it, and then begins our own story of the tribes and how to deal with them, and a story of romance, devotion, and disappointment it has often proved to be. Before tracing the story of it all, and that rough-and-tumble life that our soldiers have led during the last seventy years, it will be well if we look at the clans, tribes, and races as they stand to-day. We shall then be the better equipped to follow it, we shall see how true is Mr. Kipling's *Frontier Arithmetic*.

> 'A scrimmage in a Border Station,
> A canter down some dark defile,
> Two thousand pounds of Education
> Drops to a ten-rupee Jezail,'

and duck our heads to

> 'The flying bullet down the pass,
> That whistles shrill, "all flesh is grass." '

ROAD-MAKING ON THE N.W. FRONTIER
(Note the piquet on the right)

To face page 132

The whole story has a note of pathos in it, that is dwelt on later in the 'Story of Martyrdom,' for all that has been done in the endeavour to bring some other rule of life than 'an eye for an eye, a tooth for a tooth' has met with no great success, although those who have been many years on the border can recognize the working of the leaven even if through a glass darkly.

§ 2

THE PATHANS

It has been explained in chapter three, that the tribes of the frontier and of Eastern Afghanistan, while claiming to be Durani, are in many cases nothing of the sort, but that among them, however, are sandwiched clans that are truly Durani, *i.e.* of the Ben-i-Israel, while here and there, as with the Turis of the Kurram, there are tribes of Tartar origin. It has also been mentioned that all talk the Persian-derived *Pashto*, or *Pakhto*, there being two general methods of pronunciation, soft or hard, one prevailing in the north and the other in the south, and that it is these Pakhto-speaking folk of whom the Alexandrine historians speak as Packtyae. The word Pathan really applies to the speaker of Pakhto, and in that sense any of the Pakhto-speaking folk, be they of Durani or non-Durani origin, are Pathans, and they will be so spoken of here. Occasionally also non-Pathan clans will be referred to, and that will mean tribes who are different in origin from the normal speakers of Pakhto, and either of

Dard or unknown origin. Incidentally it may be mentioned to those who are inclined to pronounce Pathan as 'Paythan' that the correct pronunciation is more like 'Putarn' with the 'r' silent.

But though this word is applicable to the whole of the eastern Afghan folk, who speak this language, the Englishman in India uses it generally to denote the tribes of the frontier hills with whom he has to do.

The story of the Afghan tribes, those who call themselves the *Ben-i-Israel*, has been told, and how many have tacked themselves on to a bogus genealogy because it was the fashionable thing to do. It has also been related that most of the tribes from the Kohistan behind Kabul, down to the Indus, calling themselves Pathan, are really but the descendants of the old Aryan colonists who remained in the hills and grew harder and fiercer with years of rugged mountain and fierce snowy winters and internecine strife. As the centuries rolled on came Islam, which appealed to their fierce natures, so that they readily embraced it and followed the fanatical Arabs who bore the standard of the Prophet over half the known world.

Now let us examine them in their own glens and plateaus and see them by sept and clan.

§ 3

THE YUZUFZAI

A good deal has been said in the earlier chapters of this book, in general terms, of the descent and origin of the frontier clans, and it is now time to specify them by those names under which they appear in frontier news of to-day and in accounts of operations of the important works of peace in their land. We may begin at the far north, where the frontier hills run up into the great whorls where no man will live and in which at most he may graze his flocks as the snow melts from the hill-side and the young grass springs anew. Before the Indus leaps from its deep-cut gorges into the plain for a while at Attock, it cleaves its way through the great hills known as the Cis-Indus and Trans-Indus Kohistan *litt*, 'hill-country.' In the far north the tribes are non-Pathan, and of no great fighting proclivities, inhabiting the Shinaka and Kohistan Republics of Tangir, Darel and Jalkot, with the Kohistan Kandia. Below these on both sides of the river are the Pathan clans of the great Yuzufzai group, the clans of the 'Sons of Joseph.' Cis-Indus is the tract once famous as the 'Black Mountain' and the scene of many expeditions to prevent its tribes raiding into the peaceful districts of Hazara. Here the bulk of the clans all belong to the big sub-group of the Izazai, but with them are three of non-Pathan origin, known as the Gaduns, the Swatis of Allai, and the Tanawals.

On the other side of the Indus outside the British border are the Yuzufzai clans of the districts of Swat known as the Utmankhet group and those of Buner, Dir, Bajour, Jandol, generally known as the Tarkanri group, the Mohmand clans and the like, who belong to four main sections, viz., the Izazai, the Iliazai, the Malizai and the Allazai. It should be noticed that the non-Pathan tribe who gave their name to Swat now live on the hither side of the Indus. The Mandan group of clans of the 'Sons of Joseph,' live within the British border on the Yuzufzai Plain. It should be noted that this plain is now one vast cornfield, owing to a great British scheme of bringing the waters of the Swat River under the Malakand range of hills and spreading it out on the former arid Yuzufzai Plain. The Yuzufzai clans spread down to the Khaiber, those immediately north of the Kabul River, on both the British and Afghan sides of the border, being usually known as Mohmand clans. The Yuzufzai, the people of the Kingdom of Jhandara, of which Taxilla was the capital, are said to have been originally of Rajput descent, to have trekkėd to the vicinity of Kandahar, and then after the passage of many generations and after years of inter-marriage with the Duranis who inhabit the vicinity of Kandahar – a name which some claim to be but another Alexandria[1] . . . to have returned to their present situation.

§ 4

THE AFRIDIS

When we come to the Khaiber we come to a people who are now universally admitted to be of Aryan and probably Rajput origin, viz. the group of clans who are called Afridi, and who, as has been explained, must be those Aparoetae of whom the Alexandrine historians

[1] But more likely derived from Ghandara.

speak of in the Khaiber. They are divided into several large tribes whose names are well known, such as the Malik Din, the Khamber, the Kuki, the Jowaki, the Sipah and the Zakha Khel. Those that live in the Khaiber Pass and its neighbourhood are responsible for the protection of the route by levies now known as *Khassadars*. Until Amanullah's wanton invasion, they enlisted into that fine militia corps, the Khaiber Rifles. That corps practically deserted when the Afghans attempted to enter the Khaiber, and the corps has not been raised again. Further, several Afridis deserted in France and Mesopotamia from the ranks of the Indian regiments, and therefore, since 1919, have not been enlisted to anything like the same extent, though one of them did actually receive the Victoria Cross in France. The fact that few are enlisted and that there is no militia is having a very serious effect on the tribes. Further, the number of pensioners drawing that civilizing element, a British pension, is growing less and less and there are no new claimants coming on. Their unrest is largely due to economic reasons. No longer can they hack their way to power and wealth in the train of the Afghan and Turkish invaders of India. Their stony hills, terraced carefully as they are with much fostering care of the water of the mountain streams, do not yield enough food. Therefore it was that in the year of grace 1930 we saw a few hundred of these hungry lads bought by the Congress seditionist to come down and shoot up Peshawar, Nowshera and Attock and generally raise Cain within the border. Incidentally it is amusing to learn that they were not prepared to fire a shot more than they were paid for, breech-loading cartridges being expensive things.

It will probably be better to forgive them their sins both for the excitement of 1919 and the desertion in France. It has been said that the latter was due not so much to inherent unreliability, serious though that may be, so much as the fact that the destruction of a whole company of, say, Khamber Khel, as might have happened in France, would upset the whole balance of tribal politics unless other clans were to lose equally heavily. The clans quarrel so much with themselves, and fight out their quarrels so bitterly, that the loss by one clan of more men than another would be unthinkable. To most British officers the jaunty, vain, light-hearted, reckless young Afridi appeals irresistibly, as indeed do most of the border clansmen, for, like Saul of Israel, they are choice young men and goodly, if dirty.

§ 5

THE TRIBES OF KOHAT, MIRANZAI AND KURRAM

Between the Afridi Tirah and the long valley of Miranzai lies the Orakzai Tirah, also a desirable upland, inhabited by the various clans of the Orakzai, of whom the Khanki Valley is the main habitat, a valley which opens into Miranzai not far from Kohat itself. Between the Orakzais and Mianzai lies the great knife edge of the Samana. The Orakzais are a very similar folk to the Afridis, but curiously enough a section of them, at some enmity with the rest of their neighbours therefore, belong to the Shiah sect of Islam, as do the Turis who are described in the next section. How a few of the clans come to be of this sect is something of a mystery, possibly some wandering mullah as far back as the days of Persian Nadir Shah may have been in the country. Quite lately they, who have always wanted to be annexed, have been attacked by Afridi young men out of a job. One of the Afridi mullahs suggested that to raid them would be less costly than raiding into British territory. In the Orakzai tribes there is a curious division of politics whose origin is hard to trace. Some are '*Gar*,' the rest are '*Samil*' and bitter is the difference, though in just fact it is little more than 'Oxford' or 'Cambridge' in a boys' school, but blood runs often enough over the division.

Within our border in the hills on both sides of the Indus below Attock, are the famous Khattak clans, all within our border, who serve very faithfully in many corps, and beyond them in Miranzai and round Kohat are another somewhat similar folk, the Bangash, who are equally welcome in the Indian Army.

The Khattaks (over 40,000 men) are divided into two main groupings, Sagri and Akora, the former dwelling on both banks of the Indus, south of the Kushalgarh crossing, and the latter close to the Kabul River near its junction with the Indus. The Khattak may be said to be the ethnological link between the Pathan of Rajput origin and the Punjabi Moslem who still know themselves as Rajputs, and in style and appearance they are half-way between the two. Indeed it is an interesting phenomenon to watch some of the lesser Pathan clans on the bank of the Indus below the Khattak's country becoming Punjabi Musalmen *tout simple*, such as the Niazai, the Khutti Khel and one or two others, of whom some live on the left bank of the Indus round Mianwali. In fact it is not too much to say that on the Indus he is a Pathan when he wears the loose Pathan pyjamas, and a Punjabi Muhammadan when he dons the *chaddar*, that is to say, the towel round his waist and legs. He then becomes a *Jăt* or cultivator and perhaps drops his *Pashto* for the *Jătki* of the Indus Valley.

Far up the Miranzai and in the Kurram are two more tribes, numbering several thousand fighting-men, the Chamkanni and Zaimukhts, Pathan but probably not Durani. In the conflagration of 1897 the Chamkannis took part and earned chastisement, but the Zaimukhts, largely owing, it was said, to the influence of the local Rob Roy, Chikai the Freebooter, held aloof, to their own advantage and the considerable convenience of the British Government who had quite enough on their hands already, and who did not want to have more enemies in distant Kurram.

One other people in this direction, of great interest and also of importance, are the Turis, a people entirely '*alag*,' that is to say, 'apart' from their neighbours. They are a people probably of Tartar extraction sandwiched in, by some unremembered movement, among Rajput and Afghan races. It is even possible that they are some relic of the Yueh-chi hordes that established the Kushan dynasty in Kabul and Northern India after the Graeco-Bactrians. They have always been at enmity with those round them, partly, no doubt, from racial dis-affinity, to coin an expression, but largely because they, in common with the large race of the Hazara, another Tartar folk beyond Ghuzni, belong to the people of the great Schism in Islam known as the Shiah faith. All those round are most uncompromisingly and ignorantly Sunni or orthodox, save, as related, that among the Orakzai clans near Kohat there are some who are also Shiah.

The Turis have been within our borders since the Treaty of Gundamak in 1878. General Fred Roberts, after his victory over the Afghans of the Peiwar Kotal, promised the Turis British protection, and this was implemented in the subsequent treaties. Since when in addition to finding two battalions of admirable militia for the defence of Kurram and the frontier, their conduct has always been excellent. Colonel Roos Keppel, the well-known Chief Commissioner on the Frontier Province made his name among them, and had the greatest affection for this part of the frontier, in which he had spent many years.

§ 6

WAZIRISTAN

We have now reached that part of the frontier which had given us the most trouble of all – that of Waziristan. This tract lies between the Miranzai Kurram route to Kabul, and the Gomal route from Ghazni. The

Waziris are divided into two great groups – those of the Darwesh Khel, generally spoken of as the 'Wazirs' and the Mahsuds. They, too, are probably of Rajput origin, with perhaps some Durani infiltration. The Tochi route from Ghazni to India via Bannu and Kohat, or via Bannu and the Tangdarra to the Kalabagh crossing of the Indus, passes through the Darwesh Khel country. The protection of these two important routes down which the Ghilzai clans from Ghazni conduct a vast trade had long been an intention of the British, in the general advancement of civilization in pursuit of world obligations. It was started in 1894 when a delimitation commission escorted by a force of all arms was making the newly agreed-on Afghan boundary known as the Durand Line. This force was camped in Wazir country in the upland plain of Wana, and was fiercely and unexpectedly attacked at dawn by the local tribes, chiefly Mahsuds, who actually penetrated the camp. The Mahsud country is a powerful and turbulent enclave within the Darwesh Khel, and with a view to the protection of the Gomal route and watching the Mahsuds, a force was for a while kept at Wana. Later in the season of 1894-95 the opening of the Tochi Valley was undertaken, and since those days while the Darwesh Khel have, as a whole, acted up to their obligations, the Mahsuds have been in constant bitter and entirely unnecessary collision with us. The efforts of the mullahs stirred them during the World War and the invasion of India by the Afghans in 1919 disturbed them greatly. In 1920-21-22 there were constant operations against

THE ROAD TO RAZMAK ON CHRISTMAS DAY

A MAHSUD FAMILY COMES TO TOWN

To face page [illegible]

them and eventually order was only restored by forming at Razmak in the Wazir country, but close to Kaniguram, the Mahsud centre, a large military cantonment connects with Bannu and Tank by a circular motor road. This has produced such civilizing results as to give us new ideas for humanizing the whole country-side.

The endeavours made to civilize these tribes and improve their economic status have been many, and will be referred to under this question generally.

Between Waziristan and the administered districts of Bannu and Dera Ismael Khan, are certain less important tribes, notably the Bhittanis, a tribe who are dominated by and driven into evil ways by the Mahsuds, whose 'jackals' they have been called, while in the country between Bannu and Pezu are a pleasant Pathan folk, the Marwats. Many of them live in the plains and rotting sandhills and are known as 'sand' Marwats. They have a habit of sitting ruminating in circles, turning over the loose sand with their huge splay feet and prominent toes. A very few enlist in the Army, but more serve in the local levies. Round Bannu and in the lower Tochi are folk known as Dauris for whom little good has ever been said, but on whom British rule and example has produced distinct advancement. The fertile and beautiful Bannu Plain watered by the Kurram River has a varied and mixed population. In the past, as the armies moving from Ghazni to India stopped in this valley of ease and rest, all the concomitants of moving armies, more vile even than in Western armies in the Middle Ages, must have made Bannu the centre whence they preyed on the troops – pimps and pandars, harpers and whores. As the generations rolled on the name of Bannuchi, or man of Bannu, was a by-word among men, and it was here that among green fields and poplar and mulberry groves, every farmer and peasant lived in his own towered house, his hand against every man, trusting the word of none, till John Nicholson taught them otherwise.

§ 7

THE GOMAL TRIBES

The Gomal, the great river of Ghazni side, has long been a famous highway, as has been related, coming into the horsehoe plain of Tank at Jatta, the roadway leaving the gorge and crossing the Gwaleri Pass, moving high to avoid the flood levels. It is largely in possession of the Wazirs and the tribe of Sherannis, whose main habitat is the valleys round the *Takht*, the Throne of Solomon, which towers above, 15,000 feet high.

The Sherannis are probably a Durani clan but sandwiched in between Baluch and Mahsud are of no great quality, though tiresome enough withal. Over on the other side of the plain which lies between the *Takht* and Sheikh Budui are one or two small Pathan tribes. Round Paniala, famous for its hot springs and its dates that have grown, men say, from the debris of Alexander's camps, is a small clan, Pathan in origin, owning the name 'Baluch,' but having no connection with the Baluch race.

Another small tribe owns the border town of Tank, which has a nawab of its own. Below the Sherannis are two more Pathan tribes, the Ushteranas and Khetzans, and between the *Takht* and the plain within the line, are several small clans of Ghilzai origin, placed there, perhaps, by the Ghilzais of old time to block the raiding paths from the hills.

§ 8

THE GHILZAIS

Here we may profitably discuss one of the most interesting of all the frontier phenomena, the Ghilzai clans of Afghanistan who, residing though they do in Afghanistan, yet spend six months of each year in the more hospitable regions of the British frontier. Each year the Ghilzai clans come down the Khaiber, the Tochi and the Gomal in many thousands, with their families, their ox and their ass, and everything that is theirs. They come down in strict and rigorous order, by sept and clan marching off by tuck of drum.

The Ghilzais, with the Duranis, form the two main races of eastern Afghanistan, and hate each other cordially. They are the one important folk of Afghanistan against which the Durani race have had to contend, or who they have had to square, and for that reason they have often been on the side of the British. Abdur Rahman, the *Amir el Kebir*, found that he and they could not lie down together and a bitter struggle occurred which was not ended till he had broken the Ghilzai chiefs who opposed him. Tradition has it that he broke them more often by foul means than fair. Lyall sings of it thus, in the ballad of 'The Amir's Message.'

I

'Abdurrahman, the Durani Khan, to the Ghilzai Chief he wrote,
God has made me Amir of the Afghans but thou on thy hills are free,

. . . . . .

I look for a wise man's counsel and I would that Afghans were one,
So choose thou of all thy liegemen or choose thou of all my host
One true man, loyal-hearted, whomever thou trustest most,
Whom thy tribe has known and honoured to bring thee in safety and peace,
Thou shalt ride unscathed to Kabul, and the feud of our lives shall cease.

II

The Ghilzai Chief wrote answer, "Our paths are narrow and steep,

. . . . . .

High stands thy Kabul citadel where many have room and rest

The Amirs give welcome entry but they speed not a
parting guest.

. . . . . .

Shall I ask for the Mullah in Ghazni to whom all
Afghans rise,
He was bid last year to thy banqueting, his soul is in
paradise."

. . . . . .

The night shade falls over Kabul, dark is the down-
ward track,
And the guardian hills ring and echo, of voices that
warn me back.'

And so forth. . . .

The Ghilzais have given the Lodi dynasty to Delhi in the past and we find the latter Ghilzai clan perpetuated in the name of Ludiana or Lodiana in the Punjab. The term Ghilzai is said to mean the People of the *Kalej* or sword and to be of Turkish origin, but it is likely that only their leaders may have been of that race in the old time afore. The folk themselves are many of them of distinct Semitic appearance and more likely of Arab descent, or any rate descended from the Jăt and Rajput stock to which so many of the Pathans belong.

It is a brave sight to see them come down the Gomal, the jolly olive-tinted girls on the camels with their bright red cheeks and their enamelled plaques, ready to laugh and chaff with all. There are old ladies tramping alongside, carrying perhaps a samovar, and the bright young things lolling in the camel-*kajawahs* little reck of the days when they too must trudge alongside, and get up o' nights to catch the loose and grumbling camels, for the frontier does not make much of its old women. The great clan to come down the Gomal is the Suliman Khel from Ghazni, as with them Kharotis, Nazirs and the like. They form huge camps on the Indus Valley and in them the men leave their families and female camels, and sally forth to earn a living in Hindostan, penetrating all over the land, trading, bullying, lending money, domineering. Years ago many would take their camels to the Australian gold-fields, aye, and perhaps bring back a strapping Australian wife, to lord it in Ghazni, if she could hold her own. The roads on the frontier run close to the camps, and you will meet as you drive by dozens of rosy-faced children who will turn cartwheels for you, shouting '*Paisa Wachawa*,' which being interpreted is 'Chuck us a copper, guv'nor'! Perhaps if you are lucky to come by a Kharoti camp you will see the girls a-tent-pegging with merry shouts, which turn to dismay if a strange male comes on the horizon. It is on record that in the year of the Mutiny of the Bengal army, many of the Ghilzais who usually return in April stayed down at Delhi and Lucknow because of the rumours of coming trouble that were current.

They park their arms in the frontier police posts and draw them again when the times comes to flit, and guard their way through the country of the frontier tribes. It is a strange sight to see them all assemble at the mouth of the Gomal or the Khaiber for their return, when they march off again by tuck of a giant drum, sept and clan as before, each in their allotted place. While the wealthy camel-owning clans come down the main passes, humbler clans, donkey or bullock folk, come down some of the less-known routes where roads are bad but good enough for the likes of them, for even in free Afghanistan each man loves to lord it over his neighbour.

The small tribes of Ghilzai descent long settled in the Derajat, referred to, under the shadow of the Takht-i-Suleiman, are the Gandapurs, Babers, Mian-Khel, and Kundis, and are a relic of old invasions. They have long served in the best of the cavalry regiments. The Nawab of Dera Ismael Khan on the Indus, at present (1931) in London to protest against handing over India to the Hindus, is a Saduzai, an Afghan of the old Royal clan of Kabul.

High up on the hills above the Gandapur country is an enchanted castle, some ruin of the Kafir days, a Kafir Kot like those described in the Khaiber, but with the difference that the hill folk are so afraid of the ghosts that none will take you there. And at the foot-hills watching the passes, are the ruins of the Graeco-Bactrian posts referred to, that guarded the same ways of the raiders almost before time was.

§ 9

THE BALUCH

And now as you go down the frontier below the Ushteranas and Khetrans, in the great wall of the

Suleiman hills which now come nearer the Indus, the racial venue changes. We have left the Pathan country and come to those of the Baluch, often, as explained, spelt Belooch. This is a vast race claiming some form of Arab descent, orthodox professors of Islam, living for the most part under a more definite system of chiefs and more under their control than is the case among the democratic Pathans. They are far more readily managed and controlled by these chiefs, and for many years have given little trouble. In the first few years of frontier life, however, they gave our frontier force more to do than ever did the Pathan tribes. The Baluch generally owns some allegiance to the Khan of Kelat, especially in those tracts south of the Bolan, and it is through his agency generally that the tribes are kept in control. But between the Gomal and Quetta itself lies the district known as Zhob, and this, which is part of the Baluchistan Agency, is inhabited by two Afghan tribes of Duranis known as the Khakars and the Tarin, who are sufficiently under control of chiefs to be managed through them, so that the latter can be held responsible for their good or bad behaviour. The country of this part of the world is profoundly mountainous though it has level valleys between the ranges which makes it more accessible and thus easy to maintain order in. Amanullah's wanton invasion, however, did destroy the pacifying and civilizing work even in Zhob that had been at work for forty years.

The Baluch tribes with whom our officers have had most to do are the Maris, Bhugtis, Domkis, Legharis, Rinds and others. They do not take to military discipline and cleanliness, and we have never been able to enlist many even in the so-called Belooch battalions. Their Muhammadanism is orthodox, but far less fanatical in its expression than with the Pathans. They wear long locks parted in the centre and without their head-dress would make admirable models from which to paint the 'Last Supper.' In fact, their likeness to the traditional scriptural type is most marked. Among them are a most interesting race ethnologically, the Brahuis, who speak a Dravidian language and who are probably a relic of a very ancient people.

The Brahuis are divided into two groups of clans, the Highlanders (Sarawan) and Lowlanders (Jhallawan).

The Baluchis do not speak Pashto but a separate language – Baluchi, an Iranian tongue, however, derived from the same stock, the old Medic Aryan.

The foregoing is but the briefest description of the races of the North-west Frontier with whose names everyday happenings make us familiar, running from the ancient Dard stock of the states of the Pamir edge in the far north down to the Baluch in the south, but with the Pathan folk as the predominant factor.

§ 10

THE STRANGE STORY OF KAFIRISTAN

In this chapter may well be included the story of the Kafirs, one of the most fascinating of all the stories of the mountains or the frontier.

In the great gorges that came down to the south-west from the Roof of the World lies the inaccessible region known as Kafiristan, 'The Country of the Unbelievers.' Caffre, our word for the natives of South Africa, is but the Arabic word *Kāfir*, which to the Moslem Arab applies to all who are not *Ahl-i-Kitab* or 'People of the Book.' To the Moslem, on the other hand, Christian and Jew are *Ahl-i-Kitab*, 'People of the Book,' those, who have a revealed and written Book of Sacred Law. Only very ignorant and fanatical Moslems dare call Christians 'Kafir.'

Up till somewhere about 1892, popular legend and belief peopled Kafiristan with a Macedonian pocket, some remnant of the C.3 men whom Alexander had left in India. Those who remember that most wonderful of Kipling's stories, *The Man who would be King*, know that that story is built on a strange white people inhabiting the mountains to the north of Jalalabad. Alas, in 1892, Sir George Scot Robertson, as he was later, when British Agent at Gilgit, entered the country twice, on the latter occasion making a prolonged and adventurous stay, visiting several of the valleys and staying at the villages. He made a close study of their language, habits and traditions, and it cannot be said that he found them a pleasant people, despite much that was romantic and inexpressibly ancient. His reports quite dispelled the idea that they had any Macedonian origin that at any rate showed itself by outward signs or relics of the past. He found that the people were tall and handsome, of an Aryan type, with the exception of certain lesser and subject tribes. It seemed to him that some of the inhabitants of East Afghanistan may have been driven up the valleys by the coming of Islam, and had impinged on some of the older Dard race which is to be found in all adjacent Himalayan pockets. In the old classical maps indeed this country is shown containing the *Daradae*. Robertson's theories, however, do not quite tally with history and known facts. Any Aryan inhabitants of eastern Afghanistan at the coming of Islam, must have been Hindu or Buddhist, and some trace of their faith would remain. As it is he found them practising some pagan worship of a head-god Imbra, and a war-god Gish. As Peachy Carnegan says in the Kipling story, they had some yarn of relationship with the English, which Robertson relates (this *after* the date of the story), and had many strange but not very informing rites. The women were comely enough, and the men tall, handsome and active, but rude and disagreeable, subject to great outbreaks of temper. Rough gold and turquoise formed their ornaments, and a short stick of silver with a horse's head was a much-prized possession among the women. Our connection with Chitral, from whence Robertson had entered the country, brought us into some touch with Kafirs who came to Chitral and Kila Drosh. For unknown centuries almost untouched by the outer world, this mysterious people had lived on, not being the better therefor. Timur, or Tamerlane, had turned aside from Anderab near the Kabul River to invade the country but had been roughly handled for his pains by the Kator and Siahposh Kafirs, two of the principal tribes.

In the general clear-up of the political status of the statelets bordering on the Pamirs, Kafiristan was lamentably, from a humanitarian point of view, placed within the Afghan sphere of influence, in the year 1895. Abdur Rahman then invaded the country and carried out a fierce and cruel conquest, carrying off many girls and boys as slaves, forcibly converting all on whom he could lay hands to Islam, the old folks in the glens, however, fiercely clinging to their old faith. Kafirs, now as servants and labourers, are often to be seen in Kabul. Once the quite unnecessary misery and agony of the conquest was over, it is possible to argue that this brooding, world-forgotten people may have been much the happier for their forcible induction into a modern world and a 'revealed religion.' Incidentally a good deal has been lost, for had they remained within the British sphere, some more developed study of their ways and origins would have been possible. Indeed, *The Man who would be King*, gives us a realistic account of the country and its gorges and a reasonable presentment of the people who crucified poor Carnegan, and gave him Michael Dravot's head, still wearing its gold crown, to bear away as a memento.

CHAPTER SEVEN

THE FRONTIER IN BRITISH HANDS

§ 1

THE FAMOUS FRONTIER OFFICERS

THE Afghan War of 1839-42 as we have seen, brought the British soldier to Afghanistan, and his drums and fifes to awaken the Afghan glens from north to south. In Kabul and Ghazni, in Kandahar and Jalalabad, the reveille had raised the sun, and the tattoo by the regimental bands had sent him below the horizon. Chakos and crossbelts, frock-coats and epaulettes, cocked hat and plumes had swaggered at Kabul as in Paris. The sun of victory had melted the memory of the disasters, and to the shades gouty Elphinstone and ineffective MacNaghten, the Indo-British Army had shown that it only wanted leading to be triumphant. The Afghan disasters had, however, made one point clear, and that is that the Army must not be dominated by young political officers, whose perverse folly so often endangered its safety. Where troops were in an enemy country, there the responsible authority must be the military commander, with a political officer with him no doubt to advise him, but not to hamper him. The case of war on the frontiers, however, has its difficulties, in this connection, as had war in India itself. It was usually desirable to avoid hostilities by negotiation, so that there was in its first conception some reason for the arrangement too often allowed to develop into folly and disaster. Happily those days are past, and until the recent happenings in the Peshawar Valley, one would have said past for ever, and that when the guns begin to shoot the soldier is the responsible official.

When the Sikh rule came to an end, a division of the British Army in all its bravery marched up into the Peshawar Valley. Akram Khan and his scampering horsemen had gone, and the administration of all the frontier tracts was taken on by a most remarkable generation of frontier officers, taken from both the civil and military services, but chiefly from the latter. These officers were at once intimately concerned not only with the tribesmen within the administered boundary, but with men of similar race in the hills beyond. This condition of affairs was and is, especially noticeable when dealing with a big clan such as the Mohmands, who are permanently settled within the border and have also large bodies of their clan outside it. The first thing to do, was to equip the frontier officers with force sufficient to repel the hill raiders, and to stimulate the local people themselves to repel the smaller raids. But the question of arms presented a difficulty. We have always been anxious to disarm the country-side, as the first condition of law and order, but on frontiers such as this, the possession of arms was a necessity of life.

§ 2

THE PUNJAB IRREGULAR FORCE

The Regular Army at Peshawar was much too big a hammer to use for lesser semi-police work, and almost at once was formed a force that is still famous, at first known as the Punjab Irregular Force. This afterwards became the Punjab Frontier Force, whose regiments, merged in the Indian line, are still famous for their handiness and activity in frontier fighting, and preserve both name and tradition in their titles. In 1846 as part of the penalties for the wanton attack on India, the Sikh Government suffered the loss of the districts known as the Jullundhur Doab, always an unruly tract, disturbed by the quarrels of the Rajput chiefs in the hills and by the invasions of the Gurkhas. An Irregular Force was raised at once, chiefly from the disbanded troops of the Sikh army, consisting of horse, foot and artillery. This force was in 1849 transferred to the Afghan frontier, and to it were added some six battalions of infantry and several corps of cavalry and artillery, also raised from the armies of the Sikh Durbar. Those who look into such things, will be interested to see that this irregular force consisted of the 1st to the 4th Sikh Infantry, and the 1st to the 6th Punjab Infantry, as well as a Gurkha corps. These cumbrous numberings remained till the days of Lord Kitchener, when the whole Indian Army was brought on to one roll and numbered in consecutive order, the Force having come under the Commander-in-Chief some years earlier. The meaning of the term Sikh as used in the first four regiments of Sikh Infantry, colloquially referred to as 1st Sikhs, etc., was misunderstood in Lord Kitchener's time, and an inaccurate nomenclature has existed since. Whereas the Sikh corps such as the 14th and 15th Sikhs of the Indian Line, meant that these corps were racially composed of Sikhs, the term Sikh Infantry merely meant that they were formed from the disbanded and runaway soldiery of the Sikh Durbar, an army that was largely Muhammadan, and which enlisted both Gurkhas and Hindustanis of the same classes as the Bengal army.

The meaning of the term 'Irregular' in this connection should be understood. In the years when the British Army had earned such renown on the Continent, no better model could be looked for, and the Line of the Indian armies was modelled on the British Army, which it copied with picturesque slavishness, even to the matter of grenadier and rifle companies, fur caps, brass helmets and the like. The appearance of a long line of troops in scarlet and white belts overawed the large armies of the Indian states, many of whom so disputed our supremacy. This army was a magnificent force for battle, but was growing far too formal as the years rolled by and was losing its readiness. There were also many corps raised for rough and ready local work, with Indians in important positions, and a few carefully selected British officers, and these were known as 'Irregular.' The drill and methods of these corps were on guerrilla and rough-and-ready lines. They appealed to a very good class of fighting soldier, and they were by no means merely *bashi-bazouks*.

The Punjab Irregulars were the finest of this class of troops, and their discipline and precision, which was maintained without losing their rough-and-ready attributes, made them *corps d'élite* of a very special kind. This Irregular Force was under the orders of the Government of the Punjab and not part of the regular standing army maintained and commanded by the Commanders-in-Chief of the Presidency. Its cantonments existed all along the Indus on the right bank, with the exception of the Peshawar Valley, whence came the main exits from Kabul and in which as now a large force of the Regular Army, British and Indian, was maintained. But the Indus beyond Peshawar ceases to be the main frontier, and comes straight out of the frontier hills, so that there is a portion of the North-west Frontiėr, lying cis-Indus, but inhabited by Pathan tribes, between that river and Kashmir. This too was garrisoned and defended by the Irregular Force, their principal cantonment being Abbottabad in the beautiful upland valley of Hazara.

The cantonments of the Irregular Force were not only the names so well known to-day which are still frontier stations, Kohat, Bannu (of which the official name is still Edwardesabad after the Herbert Edwardes of Multan fame), and Dera Ismael Khan, but several others of equal importance now forgotten that run down the Derajat to the boundary of Sind. These were Dera Ghazi Khan, a well laid out and popular cantonment on the frontier side of the city of that name, which during the last twenty years has disappeared into the Indus, and Rajanpur. When this frontier was first taken over a large cantonment for a force of all arms was constructed at Asni, but that proved so destructive to horses that it had to be abandoned.

The dress of the Force was a serviceable one, chiefly of grey, or rifle green in the case of the 1st Punjab Infantry, still famous as Cokes Rifles, or in army parlance the 'Cokies' (pronounced 'Cookies'). The officers in their full dress, especially in the cavalry, inclined to an elaboration and fineness typical of irregulars of the age, paralleled in that love of baldricks at which Gustavus Aldophus made such a set, but in their workaday kits they were like the men. In the 5th Punjab Cavalry, the officers in service dress wore a red helmet with horsehair plume to match the red *lungies* worn by their men, but with something gorgeous in brass or silver for gala occasions. That did not prevent their being remarkably fine rough and tumble frontier soldiers, who captured the imaginations of the hard cases in their ranks.

This force was long isolated by the Indus and vast stretches of wild country from the ordinary come and go of military life, developing a cult of its own, on which the rest of the army looked with good-humoured admiration. It took its holidays in Kashmir, with half a keg of rum to fill with morella cherries and bring back for Christmas, and when it could not go to Kashmir, it took lively holidays in a small hill station of its own at Sheikhbudin on the Nila Koh, the 'Blue Hills' between Bannu and Dera Ismael Khan, from which the outlook was on to such twisted, torn, up-ended strata as could only be drawn by a Gustave Doré. The disturbance of the frontier which has come about of late years has rendered it unsafe within a few miles of the Waziristan border. Folk said too that the fakir who lived in the shrine had lost his prestige, having taken to allowing lady visitors to amuse his pilgrims, the which had added perhaps to his perquisites, but – to the credit of Islam – had lessened the fear of his curse. So Sheikhbudin, with its silhouette like some Tibetan *jong*, was now deserted, deserted as the old haunted Kafir Kot on the way to the Takht-i-Suleiman across the valley to which no local guide dare show the way.

But fifty and sixty years ago the band played on the roller rink, and the Piffer played Paradise, in the happy days before handsome Tam Edwards left his bones in so forgotten a place.

So gradually some of the glory departed, and the Frontier Force was numbered with the Line by Lord Kitchener, and took its ways at times at stations other than the frontier, which pleased the younger generation and their wives at any rate. Nevertheless, the corps keeping after their name the magic letters P.F.F., the successor to the original P.I.F. (Punjab Irregular Force), have retained most of their old prestige as *corps d'élite*, and happily, to belong to a *corps d'élite*, is still the soldier's pet ambition. The British soldier at any rate takes leave to dub and to make his own corps such, and if that be not possible, to transfer to one that is.

§ 3

THE DRAMA OF PESHAWAR, 1857

There was now to appear on the scene of this eight-year-old British frontier an entirely new phenomenon. Peshawar, the Afghan city in which Mountstuart Elphinstone had interviewed Shah Shujah – Peshawar for whose possession Sikh and Afghan had battled so bitterly – was now a huge British garrison town. There were several corps of the British Line, and there were also, in close imitation of the same, dressed also in scarlet coatees in a head-dress resembling a chako, and wearing the white buff cross belt, several corps of the magnificent if somewhat pampered corps of Bengal Infantry. In the spring of 1857, the garrison of Peshawar consisted of H.M. 70th and 87th Foot and the 21st, 27th, 51st and 64th Bengal Native Infantry. There also were the 5th Light Cavalry of the Regular Army. At the outposts were the Khelat-i-Ghilzai Irregular Regiment, and the 24th Bengal Native Infantry. In the Yuzufzai Plain, twenty-four miles west of Peshawar in the supporting cantonment of Nowshera, were the 27th Foot, the 10th Irregular Cavalry and the 55th Bengal Native Infantry. A few miles farther off was the already famous Guide Corps at Mardan. The 17th and 18th Irregular Cavalry were also in the district.

There were several troops of horse artillery, who in those days took the part that is now performed by the mountain artillery, namely, lightness, mobility and go-every-where-ish-ness. In the First Afghan War they had actually crossed the Hindu Kush, crossed it in their brass helmets and tigerskin rolls, and dress jackets, for all the world to marvel at.

To Peshawar in the spring of 1857 had crept up this strange rumour concerning the Bengal army, of mutterings, of the greased cartridge trouble, which seemed so trivial in front of those fierce frontier hills – of the army being uneasy. With the mass of Bengal regiments clustered in and round Peshawar for the defence of India, anything wrong with them would be unthinkable. But the unthinkable, the absolutely unimaginable was happening, and happily at Peshawar and in northern India were some stout hearts who could face dangers. John Lawrence was in control of the newly annexed Punjab, with the pick of the young officers of the day, civil and military, helping in the administration, and they had happily hypnotized the people of the Punjab. Major-General Reed, an old Peninsula soldier, commanding at Peshawar, was elderly but understanding. He was switched off to a newly made post as Commander of the Troops in the Punjab, when the outbreak at Meerut and Delhi showed what the danger really was. Colonel Herbert Edwardes was Commissioner of Peshawar and Brigadier Sidney Cotton commanded the district on the translation of Reed. As the stories of the mutinying army came north, much exaggerated, the tribes of the frontier hills and the Afghans in the Kaiber, pricked up their ears. Now was the time. Were these infernal, adventurous, masterful and attractive English to go under?

Huzza! What larks! and Abdul Haq Rafiq sharpened up his knives, and looked to the priming of his matchlock. In the bazaars of Peshawar city the tribesmen and their cousins within the border were gossiping and lobbying hard. Here in this mountain-girt enclave poked out unto the tribal hills were a few British with a huge rebellious native force. Abdul Haq licked his lips and thought of the Hindu traders the British made so much of. In Ali Masjid, in Jalalabad, in Kabul, men urged the Amir Dost Muhammad to strike for the lost province of Ahmad Shah, at any rate to get Peshawar before those misbegotten Sikhs could recover them. But the Dost was very mindful of all that had been done for him, of the kindly friendliness shown during his exile in Calcutta, and held his hand. Had he not a year or so before come down and hobnobbed with John Lawrence, and sworn again his friendship? At worst he would wait, and it was time the British wanted. Edwardes had the Sepoys' letters opened. Phew! what a game was in progress.

The first step taken by the Punjab to help the Commander-in-Chief, now, alas, dying of cholera at the head of the column marching to Delhi, was to send the Guides to Delhi, securing the fort at Attock from the hands of Bengal Sepoys *en route*. A part of the 55th had mutinied at Nowshera, and with this open sign that the trouble at Meerut and Delhi was equally likely to be fermenting in Peshawar, Cotton and Edwardes decided to go the whole hog forthwith, and disarm the bulk of the regiments at Peshawar. It was done forthwith, despite the protests of the British officers of the Sepoy Corps, some of whom threw their own swords and spurs on the heaps of their men's arms. To this Edwardes has written the fitting epitaph, 'How little worthy were the men of such officers who could nearly mutiny for their sake.' Taken by surprise in front of the European corps and the guns with portfires lighted, three Sepoy battalions and the regiment of light cavalry laid down their arms quietly enough, and all the frontier side applauded. Many were the congratulations that poured in from the frontier chiefs to the Commissioner, and loud now were the offers of assistance. Huzza for the top dog and the masters who could rule! The 21st, always an exemplary corps, were not included in the precaution, the Kelat-i-Ghilzie regiment, that corps which as the Shah's Infantry had defended Kelat-i-Ghilzie in 1842, was also exempt, and its staunchness never doubted. The unstable 64th, which had been sent to the actual border, was left awhile. A force was now sent off to Mardan where the main body of the 55th had been sent to release the Guides, to disarm that corps, after the behaviour of its detached companies. As the column approached, the excited regiment broke into mutiny and marched off to offer their services to the Akhund of Swat, then a bitter enemy of the British. Their colonel took his own life in grief and chagrin at his regiment's behaviour. Pursued by the famous John Nicholson with mounted police and the 10th Irregular Cavalry, many were cut down and 150 captured. The remainder dragged their colours across the border, but, coldly received, were hunted and slaughtered by the tribesmen for the value of their arms and accoutrements, until a few survivors escaping into Kashmir were handed to the British. The 150 prisoners were taken into Peshawar, tried, and sentenced to death. Lawrence reprieved the less culpable and the younger soldiers, but forty were blown from guns, that awe-inspiring but entirely merciful form of execution, on a parade of the disarmed regiments and Europeans, the men of the frontier looking on and applauding. The danger on the frontier was over, and the tribesmen flocked down to enlist in the corps that were being raised to take the place of the Bengal Sepoy. The capture of Delhi with the British, appealed to the heart of every border loon, and to Delhi all would go.

That is the story and glory of the stiff upper lip, and the men who would have no mutiny, enacted under that rim of Afghan snows and frowning cliffs, in the valley where once the gentle philosophy of the Buddha held sway.

§ 4

FRONTIER EXPEDITIONS

Almost from the moment of the arrival of the British frontier at the line claimed by the Sikhs, commenced that series of punitive expeditions, which to the despair of all wise heads have continued to this day. Punitive expeditions, however, are by no means deserving of all that the name implies. They are punitive in the sense that they would not be undertaken

NORTH-WEST FRONTIER TRIBESMEN

AN AFRIDI WITH A HOME-MADE MARTINI RIFLE

A WAZIRI WITH A STOLEN SERVICE RIFLE

To face page 166

had not the resources of civilization been exhausted. The invitation to 'Come, let us reason together' had been spurned, invasions and inroads, the carrying off of peaceful persons and holding them to ransom, murder of frontier officers, outrages on women, had all totted up on the debit side of tribal behaviour . . . the day of reckoning had come. But the expedition even then would be far more humanizing than punitive. It would march to some central and revered spot in the tribal lands, and if opposed it would fight its way. Having got there terms would be propounded. A fine in money and arms to be paid, some hostages handed over as earnest of good faith, a good deal of expostulation and reasoning; a suggestion of education for the chief's sons, something better and fuller than Arabic texts by rote, would be made; a hint of medical assistance forthcoming. Some offer of mediation in disputes with a neighbour would perhaps sum up the British terms. The tribal council would be warned that it must keep its young men in order lest worse befall, and then a promise of some work in roadmaking, some allowances in return for protection of trade routes would be offered. It has always been recognized that much of the trouble is economic, that the young men tread on each other's heels, that some outlet is needed. So if the tribe behaved itself, there might be more openings in the police and militia, or even in the Regular Army. In the matter of allowances, it has always been the fashion in some quarters to speak of them as 'Dane-gelt.' But if Dane-gelt they be, it is Dane-gelt for a purpose. From time immemorial

Highlanders who have been lucky enough to live on a trade route, have gained pleasure and profit from blackmailing merchants, in other words, for protecting them, for a sum down. If the British were to insist on the routes being inviolate and that the levying of such should cease, then they must give compensation. The giving of a tribal allowance for some service, even if nebulous, meant that the tribes had a credit against which authority could operate, something from which to deduct fines for outrages. This is how the system would work. The political officer on allowance day would attend with his money bags and an assemblage of the tribal elders.

'Here are the allowances for the Bhoosa Khels, 15,000 rupees.'

A member of the council of elders might say, 'I thought it was 20,000?'

'So it was, but then there are some deductions. Let me see. . . . Ah! There is that case of the murder of the corn merchant in the bazaar at Tor-sappa. The offenders have not been given up. There is 2000 rupees for his widow. Then there were two rifles stolen from the border police at Ragstone Tower – a thousand rupees. Three hundred sheep were driven off from Malikh End, that is a thousand more, for in spite of my representations the Council have done nothing.' The Council nod their heads. Then perhaps comes a bombshell. 'Further, I am to announce to you that you are not abiding by the terms of peace. Your young men are not being kept in order. The Government will pay no more allowances if there is a single cause for complaint in the next six months.' And such like, and so forth.

During the first fifteen years there were innumerable small expeditions necessary to make the tribes have some idea of the authority and would-be friendly authority that had now come to be their neighbour. The Pass from Peshawar to Kohat was opened and a road made, the Mohmands were taught a thing or two. The Mahsul-Waziris had their tails twisted.

During these pow-wows or during a punitive expedition the tribesmen would be encouraged to state their grievances. They would generally consist of complaints against the salt levy, small enough; or the fact that wives who had run away, usually to save their amorous noses from being cut off, were not given up if in British sanctuary.

The so-called 'Frontier Medal,' which is in reality the 'India Medal of 1854,' and has clasps for '*Pegu*' and '*Persia*,' has many clasps for operations on all the frontiers of India. Those for the North-west, which took place for the first ten years, were all embraced by a general clasp for the '*North-west Frontier*,' and this covered many small operations, and constant raid and counter raid, some of most dramatic occurrence, when the tribesmen and the Frontier Force were learning each other's equation and value, and developing a rough affection for one another. And all the time, while the story tells of raids and counter raids, yet the attempts at friendly settlement and the bringing of some measure of assistance to people whose hand was as hard against nature as it was against their neighbours were continually in progress. Perhaps the most interesting phenomenon of all was the bringing to our side of innumerable landowners, chiefs, nobles and the like, settlers from the hills whose land tenures varied from Imperial grants, to sheer seizure and squattage. They too readily came under the influence of our remarkable frontier officers, and they too often had influence with the clans across the border as with their own tenants. These were the men whose sons brought their retainers to the Irregular corps that flocked to the taking of Delhi in 1857, or watched the disarmed Purbiah troops throughout the Punjab.

For much of the humanizing that has gone forward and some of the missionizing, De Pennel's book, *Among the Wild Tribes of the Afghan Frontier*, may well be consulted, a maze of human interest, and also of despair.

The India Medal of 1854 has clasps for '*Umbeyla* 1863' to commemorate the extraordinary frontier fighting in Yuzafzai in that year, when Government set out to root up the colony of Hindustani fanatics at Sitana near Mount Mahabun whose denizens had molested the border in 1857. This colony had originally been founded by a refugee Pindari chief from India, one Amir Khan, and had many a struggle with the Sikh troops in the days of Ranjhit Singh. To it had always been attracted some of the Wahabi zealots who had their hand against every man in Patna. They succeeded in raising a *Jihad* for their defence, with the result that the army, hardly recovered from post-Mutiny reconstruction, had a most desperate war on its hands. The clans from far and near hastened to help the Bunerwals to block the Umbeyla Pass to our troops. Eventually the tribes themselves agreed to root out the fanatics and admitted a British commissioner to see them do it.

The expedition against the Jowaki Afridis in that tongue of independent country between Kohat and Peshawar in 1877 earned a medal with clasp '*Jowaki*,' and the Black Mountain tribes on the cis-Indus produced clasps for '*Hazara*' in three different years, while the Pamir troubles, described hereafter, earned a clasp for '*Hunza* 1891.' The demarcation of the Durand Line occasioned the attack on the escort at Wana in 1894, and the campaign that followed, already referred to, was rewarded with the last clasp awarded for this medal, viz.: '*Waziristan* 1894-5.' In 1891 the opening up of the Samana gained a clasp '*Samana* 1891.' After this came the '*Indian Medal of* 1895,' inaugurated with its first clasps, '*The Defence of Chitral*,' and '*Relief of Chitral*,' and this medal served for the campaigns of the great Rising of 1897, when clasps for '*North-west Frontier*,' '*Samana*,' and '*Tirah*' were given.

There was some delay in settling the design for this medal and an amusing story was current. On the reverse was a picture of an Indian cavalry soldier holding a flagstaff with the Jack in one hand, and his lance in the other. The original design showed a pennon to the lance, but flying in the opposite direction to the Jack. It was said that when the design was presented to Her Majesty for approval she noticed this, and remarked, 'Faith! 'tis a mighty queer wind ye have in those parts,' or words to that effect, and that the design had to be altered.

§ 5

THE SECOND AFGHAN WAR

In 1878 the ordinary life of the frontier was to be greatly stirred by the Second Afghan War, and from that date began the era of what used to be known as the 'Scientific Frontier,' when we secured control of the routes to India sufficiently to enable us to make a better 'show' if India were invaded. The Second Afghan War arose from the same cause as the First, viz.: the necessity of having a peaceful, prosperous and friendly Afghanistan as neighbour, which would respond to our influence and not that of Russia. A Russian mission had been received by the Amir, and Great Britain demanded that a British mission should also be received. The Mission, under General Sir Neville Chamberlain was, however, refused admittance to the entrance of the Khaiber. Britain then made war, and a British force advanced to Gandamuk above Jalalabad, fighting an action at Ali Masjid, also to Kurram, storming the Peiwar Kotal, and in the south to Kandahar. Peace was then made, the Khaiber and the Kurram were recognized as within the British sphere, and Sir Louis Cavignari with a small escort was received at Kabul as British resident minister.

The storming of the Peiwar Kotal by General Roberts was a dramatic episode, amid the deodar forests of the Peiwar, while the return of the troops after a terrible epidemic of cholera is told most pathetically and dramatically by Kipling in *Love of Woman*. He shows us the Highlanders coming out of the Khaiber 'swinging their rumps like buck rabbits,' the Rifles carrying their dead colonel at their head and playing 'Saul,' and interwoven the pathetic story, 'Die here Egypt,' that touches the very *lacrymae rerum*.

But the war was not to end so easily. In a very few weeks the Cavignari Mission at Kabul had been most pitifully exterminated by mutinous Herati soldiery and city mob, defending themselves heroically, and Lord Roberts led his force in the Kurram to Kabul fighting the battle of Charasia *en route*. This march into the host of Afghan troops and tribes is one of the most memorable feats the British Army has ever carried out. It was followed by the punishment of those responsible for the massacre, and then Roberts was besieged in his cantonment at Sherpur by vast hordes of Afghan tribesmen who had risen in wild fanaticism. Sir Donald Stewart led up a division to his support from Kandahar, fighting the battle of 'Ahmed Khel' *en route*, a battle which will long live in literature because of Kipling's wonderful story, *The Drums of the Fore and Aft*, the dramatised elaboration of one of the episodes.

The Amir Yahub Khan had abdicated, and the British offered the throne to Abdur Rahman, a prince long exiled with Russia. Down in the south the ex-Amir's brother, Ayub Khan, had defeated a British force at Maiwand, and General Roberts then marched the pick of the Kabul Force on his famous march to

Kandahar, defeating Ayub Khan handsomely and relieving the beleaguered garrison of Kandahar. That was the end of it, and with the end came the occupation of British Baluchistan and Zhob and the establishment of a first-class British *place d'armes* at Quetta on the great plateau of Shawal.

Wars in Afghanistan have always been a romantic if not always successful memory to the British Army, and there is hardly a pass or a stone not sacred to one of the many corps who have served there in the two great wars. The induction of Abdur Rahman to the throne was to commence a great season of prosperity and development under the 'Great Amir' with British support. This was not upset, even in the World War, till foolish Amanullah, his grandson, elected to invade India in 1919 at the behest of Indian sedition mongers, and to terminate a profitable alliance of over nearly forty years, sowing thereby the seeds of his own ignominious expulsion.

After the Afghan War, the policy of the British Government has been to live up to its responsibilities and gradually pacify and humanize the trade routes to Kabul via the Khaiber and Kurram, and the route to Ghazni and Kandahar, fighting where necessary the frontier tribes who opposed our action.

§ 6

THE STATELETS THAT FRINGE THE PAMIRS

By 1892 a most interesting state of affairs had arisen. By arrangement with the Amir of Kabul we were engaged with his officials in marking out the actual frontier between British India and Afghanistan, that Durand Line already referred to, showing where Afghan and British responsibilities began and ended. Besides the more hackneyed part of the frontier – Baluchistan, Waziristan and the Afridi Tirah, which was being delineated, and north of the latter – we begin to come to that group of statelets which ran under the high mountains and the big whorls that edged the Pamirs.

Some disturbance had of late been born in northern India. The rumours of the 'grey coat' guard on the Helmund Ford were about again. The loom of the Bear that had died away for a while was now being cast forward once again. What had happened was this. Enterprising Cossack officers with stray sotnias of Cossacks had poked their noses across the great passes from the Tagumdash Pamir, Gromchefski had come over into Hunza and disturbed the minds of the Kanjut robber clans, and Colonel Yanof by the Dorah into Chitral. Now Hunza and Nagar, little states whose rulers claimed descent from Alexander, were subject to Kashmir, as were also a ring of states that nestled under the shadows of the great surging mountain tops into which the Himalayas surge. It was most desirable that Kashmir should now see to it that its control of its feudatories – the lesser fleas of our great feudatory – should be sufficient to ensure that neither the Amir of Kabul nor the Russ from the Pamirs should come a-meddling. Further, the Kanjuti robbers had quite got out of hand and the Thum of Hunza was not doing his duty as chief.

The Amir had been compelled to admit that neither the Khan of Dir and Jandola, nor the Mehtar of Chitral could by any stretch of imagination be claimed as within the Durani Empire, and when Ghulab Singh, the first Maharajah of Kashmir, and Runbir Singh, his son, used their considerable armies to extend their influence over these queer statelets they were certainly not poaching in Afghan waters. In view of the Russian filibusterings, arrangements were made between Great Britain and Kashmir that a joint Indo-Kashmir Mission and force should occupy Gilgit and work therefrom. The first result of this policy was the 'Campaign on the Roof of the World,' that of Hunza-Nagar, dramatic by reason of the remoteness of the scene, the altitude of the terrain, and the interest of the races involved.

§ 7

CAMPAIGNING ON THE ROOF OF THE WORLD

In expansion of what has already been said of the process by which the British shut the far mountain gates of the Pamirs against strangers, and gradually brought under a simple system of control the statelets far up in the Kohistan, there are two dramatic occasions connected therewith which are worthy of more attention. They involved peculiarly thrilling and adventurous travel and fighting amid stupendous passes and gorges. The first is the War on the Roof of the World, otherwise the Campaign of Hunza-Nagar in 1891, the other the Defence and Relief of Chitral in 1895.

The states of Hunza and Nagar, two statelets rather than states, face each other on the Hunza or Kanjut River, which runs into the Gilgit River, and up which lies the track to the Killik Pass leading on to the Pamirs, extremely lofty, and only open to travellers for a very short period each year by reason of the snowfall.

The Thum of Hunza lived in isolated pride, confident in his unassailable descent from Alexander of Macedon, and at this juncture was defying his own Suzerain. Gilgit was the headquarters of an outlying province of Kashmir, where also the British Agency for frontier affairs had recently been revived. Hunza and Nagar were vassals of Kashmir. So far back as 1848 the Thum of Hunza had annihilated a Dogra force of the Maharajah of Kashmir.

In 1866 the Kashmir fort of Chalt, thirty miles from Gilgit and thirty from Hunza, had repelled a Kanjuti attack, but in 1888 the Kanjutis, the people of Hunza or Kanjut, had captured it. The troops of the Kashmir Durbar were now being remodelled and trained by British officers for Imperial Service, and in the beginning of the 'nineties, service at Gilgit, long deemed the last word in horror and exile, was wearing a very different aspect. The difficult question of food and transport, much neglected in the Kashmir army, was now in the hands of British commissariat officers, and the troops of the Kashmir army smiled again. Mention has already been made of the incursions of Russian colonels with cossacks into Hunza and into Chitral. Two British officers exploring on the Pamirs had been unwarrantably arrested by Russians in May 1891, while the Kanjutis had been for some years the terror of traders on the high passes.

The British Government were now in a position to assert their own authority and that of Kashmir on these distant confines. Lieutenant-Colonel Algernon Durand was appointed British Agent at Gilgit, and with him, training the Kashmir troops, were several British service officers. A summons to the Thum of Hunza to desist from his defiant behaviour and restrain his unruly people was rejected scornfully. 'Potentates like myself and Alexander of Macedon answer no summons and acknowledge no rule.'

As the two statelets assembled a force of some five thousand men, it was decided to settle the matter once and for all. A small British force was marched up from the Punjab, consisting of two hundred men of the 5th Gurkhas under Badcock and Boisragon, and two guns of No. 4 Hazara Mountain Battery under Lieutenant Gorton, with a small party of Bengal Sappers and Miners under Captain Aylmer, the 3rd Kashmir Rifles and No. 1 Kashmir Mountain Battery. With them also were a few men of the 20th Punjabis, forming the British Agent's escort. On September 1891 this little force started for Nilt, a fort higher up on the cliff closing the gorge and entrance to the Nagar Country. Opposite on the other side high up on the top of an apparently unscalable cliff lay the position and fort of the men of Hunza, ensconced behind stone sangars.

The roadways were closed by what is known as *paris*, a stone slide from above, down which an avalanche of stones would sweep away all who tried to pass along the path cut in the side of the cliff below.

The force approached the unscalable fort of Nilt on 2nd December. The mountain guns could make no impression on its walls. Then Aylmer and his sappers under heavy fire clambered up to the gateway and blew it in, and the troops rushed in to take possession from the now frightened garrison.

The Hunza position was not to be tackled so directly. At last Lieutenant Manners Smith, an expert cragsman, fancying that one of the crevassed funnels in the cliff side might be escaled while someone diverted the attention of the garrison, volunteered with a few Gurkhas and Dogras of the Kashmir Rifles to attempt the astounding feat. Sure and certain death from an avalanche of stones was the only prospect for these audacious mountaineers, had their presence on the cliff face been suspected. Nevertheless steadily and steadfastly did they face the adventure, breathlessly watched by their companions, and covered by such fire as could be brought to engage the attention of the defenders. The God of Battle was with the scalers, and after a prolonged and eager watch, those on the opposite height saw Manners Smith and his gallant pug dogs arrive on the top, and hustle out from their defences the surprised Kanjutis. Never were decorations better earned than those awarded to Manners Smith and his merry men. The *Sahib* received the Victoria Cross, as did Aylmer and Boisragon – the

Bargeen *Sahib* of his regiment – the heroes of Nilt, and the Indian heroes, the Order of Merit. Sir Fenton Aylmer will be remembered as the commander condemned without artillery ammunition, and without hospitals, amid the Tigris floods to attempt the Relief of Kut. So does a career begun in glory sometimes for duty's sake end in disappointment.

With these gallant little operations the statelets returned to their allegiance, and indeed Nagar had been half hearted in its recalcitrance, while the Thum of Hunza made off to the Killik Pass, his brother being installed in his stead. That once and for all settled matters, and the country-side has been content and orderly ever since.

Among the interesting side incidents was the share taken by a firm of engineers, Spedding and Company, who were making the Gilgit Road fit for pack traffic. Two hundred of their Pathan workmen were enrolled as combatants and armed under the young European assistants of the firm, most of whom had some military training. They ensured that excitement on the long road to Hunza on the part of other statelets and tribes should have no untoward result.

§ 8

THE DRAMA OF CHITRAL

One more little bit of history is needed to finish off the story of making good the Pamir fringe, necessary, as has been explained, owing to Russian penetration and the talk that grew therefrom, and also, be it said behind the scenes, necessary to forestall Afghan attempts to extend influence in contravention of agreements as to respective British and Afghan spheres. Along the great slopes, gorges, and water-courses which run down from the Pamirs beyond Gilgit, are several other small states, and petty chiefs, then subject like Hunza to Kashmir, and Kashmir officials supervised by the Gilgit Agency, were making their liaison effective through Yasin, Mastuj and Kila Drosh towards Chitral.

The non-Pathan state of Chitral ruled over by a prince known as the Mehtar – which is but a Persian word for prince – that word used in India to denote the domestic scavenger in that spirit not of sarcasm but of kindliness, which calls the tailor the *Caliph*, and the water carrier the *Behishti*, or 'man of paradise.' To settle affairs and current business with the Mehtar, and generally express the goodwill of the British and Kashmir Governments, as well as settle the question of the border and Russian visitors, a British political officer, Lieutenant Gurdon, with a few soldiers of the 14th Sikhs, had proceeded to Chitral by the long, difficult gorge road of two hundred miles, a road often scarped and galleried on precarious logs out of the cliff side – a road of which the mere memory would keep men awake in their beds.

Then quite unexpectedly, as things do befall in out-of-the-way and ill-balanced tracts, on the fringes of empire and borders of civilization, war, raw red war, came to Chitral.

While Lieutenant Gurdon was there the Mehtar, Nizam ul Mulk, was murdered by his brother, Aman ul Mulk. The news of this typical occurrence reached Gilgit, over two hundred miles distant, on the 5th January 1895. To follow what happened let us look at the most unusual and phenomenal geography of this land of mud, mountains, stone shoots and snows. From Gilgit the road to Chitral runs almost east along deep river gorges and at the side of galleried cliffs, past Gakuch and Gupis and Ghizr, for over 128 miles, till it crosses the Shandour Pass 12,000 feet, into Chitral territory. From the Shandour the road runs north for twenty miles into Mastuj, a Chitral fort on the Yarkkun River, a branch of the Kunar River of Afghanistan on which Chitral itself actually stands. At Mastuj was a political officer and detachment of the 14th Sikhs. From Mastuj the road runs south-west to Chitral down the Kunar River. The passage of the Shandour and the marching by the river gorges and rough cliff galleries are hair-raising experiences.

As soon as the news reached Gilgit, fifty Sikhs from Mastuj under Subahdar Gurmukh Singh were ordered on to Chitral some sixty miles, to strengthen Gurdon. But so serious was the happening with all the intrigue that lay behind it, that the British Agent, Major Scott-Robertson, decided to go there himself in some strength. Taking one hundred men of the 4th Kashmir Rifles under Captain Townsend (the defender of Kut), and picking up forty more of the 14th Sikhs at Mastuj under Lieutenant Harley, he arrived at Chitral on the 31st of January. By this time a pretty intrigue was in hand. Afzul ul Mulk, the Mehtar's uncle, claimed the throne under Moslem custom, always obscure, and persuaded one, Umra Khan of Jandol, who was probably little loath, to help him. By the beginning of March, Chitral was surrounded, but before this had happened, two more parties of the 4th Kashmir Rifles, each one hundred strong, had reached Chitral, so that the force with the Agent which was commanded by Captain Campbell of the Central Indian Horse was augmented to one hundred of the 14th Sikhs and three hundred of the 4th Rifles. Captain Townsend and Lieutenant Baird led out two hundred of the Kashmir men to meet the Afghans who were escorting Sher Afzul. A sharp fight ensued in which the Kashmir force was heavily outnumbered, and forced to retreat, with severe loss, including Lieutenant Baird, severely wounded. The fort was now closely invested, the young prince being inside. It was a tall, high-walled, four-square erection, with a lofty tower at each corner.

Meanwhile disaster was to follow. Lieutenant Moberly at Mastuj, not knowing how serious matters were, sent on a convoy of ammunition, with sixty rifles under two British officers. Getting as far as Reshan they were attacked and surrounded by Umra Khan's Pathans and Afzul's Chitralis. After they had defended themselves for seven days till supplies were exhausted, the enemy announced that peace had been settled at Chitral and invited the officers, Lieutenant Fowler and Lieutenant Edwardes, to come and watch polo. The officers, hoping to succeed by bluff and confidence, did so. In the middle of the game they were seized and bound, and their men massacred, save a few Moslems. In the meantime Moberly, representing the British Agent, hearing some rumours, ordered Captain Ross with Lieutenant Jones, with one hundred of the 14th Sikhs, to follow and see that all was well with the convoy. At Buni, seventeen miles from Mastuj, Ross left forty of his men and pushed forward to succour the convoy with the remainder. On the way, they were set on in a defile by men rolling stones on them, 2000 feet above. Then after heavy losses, he tried to return to find a bridge cut behind him, and the hill tops sangared.[1] Under a heavy fire the survivors succeeded in reaching some caves, where they sheltered without water for two days. They then decided that there was nothing for it but to try and cut their way back. An attempt to scale the mountains was brought up short by a precipice. Ross was shot through the brain storming a sangar, and eventually Jones managed to reach Buni with fourteen survivors out of the party of sixty that Captain Ross had led forth on his desperate mission. Here at Buni the Pathans attacked them, when Lieutenant Moberly from Mastuj appeared with fifty rifles and took them off forthwith, his own party having marched thirty-four miles without a halt, including a fight with the enemy. The enemy followed him up and proceeded to invest Mastuj when all communication between Mastuj, and incidentally Chitral and Gilgit, shut down. At Gilgit, shut off from India for the winter by snow, the greatest anxiety prevailed. The force in Gilgit was

[1] *Sangar*: a stone wall parapet.

always a small one, though fortunately the 32nd Pioneers under Colonel Kelly were there concerned in road work. But already Chitral and Mastuj had absorbed close on a thousand of the available Rifles.

In India the news of the various disasters had also created alarm. It was impossible to reinforce Gilgit, for the only route lay through Kashmir, and between Kashmir and Gilgit the passes were entirely impassable from snow. It was therefore decided to send a force through the almost unknown road via the Malakand and Dir from the Punjab.

While this was in progress, Colonel Kelly also decided to make the attempt to get through from Gilgit, and it must be remembered, in considering efforts of this kind, that in Gilgit transport for food and ammunition was always a serious difficulty. The roads, as explained, were execrable and extremely easy to block, while the snow on the Shandour and other passes would be hard to cross, and unless the troops were well equipped with goggles, sure to bring on snow-blindness. Nevertheless, Colonel Kelly and his four hundred Pioneers started forth in great heart, picking up at Gupis, sixty-five miles on from Gilgit, the famous Lieutenant Cosmo Stewart of the Royal Artillery with two guns of No. 1 Kashmir Mountain Battery.

All went well till Ghizr, 125 miles from Gilgit, was reached, and then the difficulties of the snow became very great and the Kashmir gunners displayed great endurance in getting their guns over. The details of the adventurous march need not be repeated, suffice it to say that Mastuj was relieved, and two important actions fought in the gorges at Chaklewat and Nisa Gol, this side of Mastuj and beyond it. Then Colonel Kelly triumphantly led his Pioneers and guns into Chitral, relieving the siege on that sore-pressed post on the 30th April, Sher Afzul having evacuated the town the day before. The garrison had had a bad time, and were close to their last gasp. From 3rd March till 19th April the strain had been continuous, and those who love gallant deeds may well seek the detailed story, and especially read of Lieutenant Harley's sortie from the water tower against the Pathans making a mine. Captain Whitchurch of the Indian Medical Service earned a Victoria Cross on that day, the 3rd of March, when the force sent out against the approaching Pathans with Sher Afzul, on 3rd March, had been so severely outnumbered and handled, suffering sixty casualties.

So ended this strange and romantic series of happenings so far away from the ordinary ken. It will have been noted how small were the forces with which the British authority was maintained, and how severe the risks they were called on to run. The defence of the fort had largely been the doing of Captain Campbell, assisted by Townsend. Campbell had been wounded at the commencement, but was a more important factor in the defence from his bed than popular accounts gave credit to. Signor MacStinger, the 'Man in the Sangar,' otherwise Townsend, was naturally a prominent feature.

In the meantime a division from the Punjab was forcing its way up, the tribes in Swat having disregarded the appeal of Government to let the force pass through their territory unmolested. Sir Robert Low had forced the Malakand, and had a severe fight on the Panjkora. Then hearing that Kelly had reached Chitral, a small brigade under the famous General Gatacre marched over the Lowari Pass to penetrate to that goal also.

Ever since then, a British garrison has remained in Chitral and has been undisturbed, save during Amanullah's attempt in 1919 to set the frontier in uproar, and each year the reliefs march up and down in peace, save during the great blaze of 1897.

CHAPTER EIGHT

THE GREAT FRONTIER RISING OF 1897

§ 1

THE TREACHERY OF MAIZAR

THE story of the North-west Frontier now unexpectedly in 1897 gives forth a different note from the comparatively humdrum advance of the *Pax Britannica*, and the civilizing influences that were quietly at work. In June, the season when the heat has quietened the lads of the border villages, and when the holiday season is in full swing, the yeomen peasantry, who form the bulk of the Indian Army, are enjoying the largest possible amount of leave among their holdings, and many officers are shooting in the Himalayas, commenced a series of frontier risings which had something quite new about them. It was not unlike on a gigantic scale some of those fierce attempts of Picts and Scots to force the garrisons of Hadrian's wall in our own history, and it had far-reaching effects. As drama and romance it is a subject well worthy of our interest, and had it not been for the absorption of the Boer War in the next year, would have remained an epic in our military history.

A sequence of events and developments had been taking place which independently of one another had

THE LONG ARM OF RETRIBUTION. THE BURNING OF THE MAHSUD WAZIRI STRONGHOLD OF MAKIN AS A RETRIBUTION FOR A LONG SERIES OF RAIDS AND MURDERS

To face page 188

tended to disturb and inflame the tribal minds. Some of those events were of our own seeking, others were from entirely outside sources. The policy referred to, of opening up and protecting those portions of the trade routes for which we were responsible, the series of minor frontier wars and troubles resulting from our attempts to secure the passes of the Hindu Kush and the Pamirs from Russian penetration, the quietening of the Kanjut robbers, the Defence and Relief of Chitral, all gave rise to a thousand rumours. In Europe, Turkey and Greece had been to war, and the Crescent had triumphed over the Cross. To the ignorant and fanatical mullahs of Afghanistan and the frontier hills, the news had come as a brainstorm. They had yelled and beaten their drums. 'Rub-a-dub, rub-a-dub,' '*Ya Allah! Ya Allah!*' 'Glory for all and heaven for those who bleed!' And the frontiers answered to the call, and the *shahids*, the witnesses to the faith, seized their swords and grasped their banners. Up and down the glens wandered the mullahs, piled prayer on prayer and text on text, texts in the Arabic that they did not themselves understand, but the clansmen yelled approval, and the number of *shahids* swelled mightily.

Earlier in the summer had occurred one of those unnecessary and disconcerting episodes which drive soldiers to despair of their own kind and still more of political officers, and yet touch men's hearts with glory till they weep. One of these, escorted by some three hundred Rifles of the Frontier Force, a few sabres, and two guns of No. 6 Bombay Mountain Battery, had come from the cantonment in the Tochi Valley at Datta Khel, established as part of the British policy of protecting the caravan route to Ghazni, with the object of arranging for a militia post at Maizar, five miles from the Afghan Frontier. Colonel Bunny was in command.

The summer was at its height and though the altitude was considerable, the weather was more than hot, that 10th of June. The political officer had been settling the trivial matter of a fine for murder, and had just ridden back into the village in which, surrounded by loop-holed watch towers and village walls the escort rested, void of every precaution save that the arms had not been piled, but were in the men's hands. The two mountain guns stood in action, the ammunition boxes off the mules, the mules nuzzling their nosebags, for it was past high twelve. The village was friendly and had brought in wood for the midday meal and fodder for the mules and horses. Because we were in the midst of a strange folk, by one of those acts of aberration, with which apparently the gods afflict those whom they wish to destroy, there were but a pair of ammunition boxes – sixteen rounds – per gun, and but twenty rounds of rifle ammunition with the infantry. Think of it, ye frontier lads! But Colonel Bunny of the 1st Sikhs was a frontier soldier, and had learnt so much of the game that he seemingly had forgotten it nearly all.

The midday wore on, the pickets were out looking for distant enemies, and the troops were amusing the villagers by playing their bagpipes for them. All was peace in the midday haze. Suddenly it was noted that the villagers were drawing off. Before anyone could dream of trouble, every tower and house began to fire into the resting troops, at any distance from five to a hundred and twenty yards. The firing was at first directed on the officers who were lounging apart from their men. As they sprang up to go to them, Colonel Bunny fell mortally wounded and two more were hit. The gunners rushed to their guns and poured case shot into a rush of approaching swordsmen. The infantry fired as best they could. Captain Browne and Lieutenant Cruikshank of the battery were both severely wounded, the latter killed a little later. Havildar-major Muhammad Ismael took command of the guns, and with Havildar Nihal Singh, a Rajput from Oudh, kept the fire going. The situation was hopeless from the loss of officers and the exposed position. The guns were ordered to limber up and get away, no easy matter under such a fire. Then took place one of the most gallant of acts in the memory of the frontier. Subahdar Sunder Singh and ten men of the 1st Punjab Infantry, the famous 'Cokies,' charged the enemy behind a wall to give time for the guns to be packed on the mules' backs, and all gave their lives that the guns should get away . . . the memory of which on the forefinger of time sparkles for ever.

Colonel Bunny was able to give the order to retire, and as best it could the force withdrew, a slow, dogged movement, to the edge of a sloping plain three miles away. Here at 5.30 p.m. a stand was made, and here Colonel Bunny and Captain Browne of the Artillery, a son of the famous original 'Buster,' otherwise General

Sir James Browne of frontier memory, succumbed to their wounds, game to the last. The three remaining officers, Higginson, Seton-Browne and Surgeon-Captain Cassidy, had all been wounded more than once (the latter to die of his wound later), and the force encumbered with its wounded and almost without ammunition, stood its ground to die as game as it could. But happily help was on its way, hot foot. Troopers had galloped back to Datta Khel and Lieutenant De Bret of No. 6 Mountain Battery had come nine miles in one and a half hours over vile roads, to bring them ammunition and a small escort. When he arrived the force had not five rounds per rifle left and, of course, no gun ammunition. Like wolves, the enemy were gathering to make a rush in force, and finish off their helpless opponents. But the arrival of ammunition and a few fresh men altered the whole complexion of the day. The weary force took heart of grace, hugged their smoking rifles once again, and drove off their tormentors with steady rifle fire, though it was midnight before all were safely gathered in Datta Khel. Among the heroes of the day was little Salutri Kewal, the farrier of the battery – narrow-chested and full of mangled Latin drug names – but with a heart of gold beneath his leather farrier's apron.

So fiercely had the drum ecclesiastic of Islam been beating the last few months, that even some of our own Muhammadan soldiers down in the peaceful Punjab were wondering. In fact after the repulse of the attack on the Malakand now to be described, rumour said there were Punjabi lads licking their wounds in many a village as far down even as Rawal Pindi, and wondering whether the Glory of God and His Prophet was worth while.

In the force in Datta Khel was a fine Moslem soldier, a Syad, a descendant from the family of the Prophet, and he too pondered long and deep. But as he went out next day, to recover some of the bodies of our men which had been abandoned, all doubt left him as to whether or no the war in progress was a Holy War. These whoreson tribesmen had cruelly and horribly mangled the corpses of the slain, those who were Moslems as well as those who were Hindus. That tore any idea of a Holy War. Dog does not eat dog, and true Moslem *shahids* do not mutilate their fellow Moslems. A division under General Corrie-Bird was now hurried across the hot plains to re-establish the *Pax Britannica.*

§ 2

THE ATTACK ON THE MALAKAND

It was not long before this danger signal, more or less unconnected though it was with the rest of the unrest, met with response. The hot season being in full swing, as already explained, officers were on reduced leave from the trans-border garrisons, but in India, on ordinary summer leave, while the young soldiers were all in the hills as usual out of the heat. The Indian soldiers were on furlough at their homes in large numbers.

On the Malakand Ridge, overlooking the Swat

Valley at the top of the old Buddhist Road, the garrison established since the Chitral commitments, was drowsing, reasonably alert in the shimmering sun and haze. Down in the Swat Valley, amid the deep green of the cultivation, was the outlying post of Chakdara. A proportion of officers and men were away on leave, and though there were, as was often the case, some rumours of tribal gatherings up in the inner hills, there was nothing that the Brigadier, Colonel Meiklejohn, or Major Deane, the chief political officers, found unduly alarming, or from the soldiers' point of view, at all likely to afford a 'show' that would enliven the routine of the hot weather.

On the 26th of July 1897, some six weeks after the occurrence in Maizar, and while a division of the Army was concerned in combing out that affair, the garrison on the Malakand was concerned, in the more normal course of affairs, in playing its usual game of polo down on the flats at Khar below the Malakand in the Swat Valley. The game passed, and as the officers returned to camp, they heard that the remote gatherings were getting more interesting and actually moving nearer, and that the movable column, a portion of the garrison, would move out that night at 9.30, and march a couple of miles to the Amandarra Pass, the 'Door of Safety,' which, while blocking the road up to the cantonment, would afford support to the garrison of the post in the middle of the rice-fields at Chakdara. The force on the Malakand was not inconsiderable, and consisted of a squadron of the 11th Bengal Lancers, No. 8 Bengal Mountain Battery, the 24th, 31st, and 45th

Bengal Infantry, the first two of mixed Punjabi constitution, the latter the famous Rattray's Sikhs. With the force also was the 5th Company of the Madras Sappers and Miners, Christians, untouchables and other humble races from the south, famous as builders and workers, with some reputation for putting up a stout fight if need be.

As the preparations for the morning's march were completed, the officers were coming to their messes about nine of the evening, an officer broke into one of them and gasped, 'They are coming up the graded road.' As the words left his mouth the assembly sounded in the 45th lines, and firing broke out at the same moment.

§ 3

THE DEFENCE OF THE MALAKAND

And now was to commence a series of wild attacks by thousands of tribesmen. The rumours of the Mad Faqir with seven hundred men was, contrary to the usual thing, far short of facts. The tribesmen, coming faster even than the wings of rumour, had gained the Amandarra and swarmed in the first dusk up through the polo ground and round the bazaars, the camps and the perimeter. The tribal tactics that were looked for had been an assault at dawn, but tribal tactics had changed. They were on the defences like the surge of a spring tide, in the darkness all round and everywhere. Fortunately the orders for the midnight march had put every one on the alert, or the surprise might have been disastrous. Even as it was the night developed into one long, fluctuating soldier's battle, with platoon and company fighting for its life. In the wire, among the mules, over the stone walls and sandbags, rifleman and swordsman, jabbing knife and bell-mouthed pistol, rushed the tribesmen. Fortunately the troops were some of the finest in the Indian Army, discipline prevailed, and ordered commands were possible. Here a battalion would clear a square with the bayonet, there a sortie would drive the tribesmen from some galling coign of vantage. From 9.30 at night till 3.30 next day, when the cool breeze of the false dawn began to herald the morning, did the hand-to-hand fighting continue. Then it slackened and the swordsmen drew off, carrying some of their dead, but leaving more in the unbelievers' hands than they had ever done before. Then too, the pickets who had equally been struggling, had breathing space, and the headquarters, among whom the swordsmen had been busy, had time to take stock. It was not till 4.15 that the hostile sharpshooters withdrew to the heights which stood some half a mile from the centre of the camp.

As soon as it was daylight reserve companies began to clear the bazaar at the point of the bayonet, and search the scarred ravines. The brigadier now hoped that he had got his attackers cold, and ordered the 24th and 31st Punjabis with four guns and a squadron of the 11th to follow up the enemy and see how Chakdara had fared. The squadron actually got through, but the gathering opposition was so great after passing Khar that the main body was recalled to camp. All that could be done was to drive out smaller bodies from the adjacent heights and evacuate that detached portion of the station known as North Malakand. This was a wise precaution, as all day long the roads from the north were crowded with clansmen pouring into the 'divarsion' from the villages and valleys in that quarter. Banners topped the hill from far and near, banners blessed by the Hadda Mullah and the Mad Faqir (or Mullah), banners so sacred that they guaranteed immunity from the bullets of unbelievers to all who did not doubt it.

By 6 p.m. the force was all concentrated in the main camp, known as the *Kotal* or 'Hill,' and late that afternoon also marched in from below, in eight hours from the time that Colonel Meiklejohn had summoned them, the magnificent cavalry of the Corps of Guides. The entire force was now collected in one area and had had the whole day to improve its position and defences, with the exception of the garrison of Chakdarra, reinforced that morning by the squadron of the 11th Lancers.

It was fortunate that this was so, for at dusk the enemy, now numbering many thousands, came streaming up the Buddhist and 'graded' roads, banners waving and planted on every hill top. Then commenced a determined musketry attack with the swordsmen creeping up to every point of vantage. As on the previous night the fanatical courage of the attackers brought them into the defences, and as before, occurred sharp fierce hand-to-hand struggles, rifle butt against sabre, and sabre on bayonet and locking-ring, the combatants writhing in each other's grip in the dark. Now and again through the night some space into which the enemy had penetrated would be cleared by the disciplined advance of a reserve company, as they brought their bayonets to the charge with a grim slap of hands in the tightened rifle sling. As day dawned on the 28th it was now evident that the *kotal* was virtually besieged on all sides on the hills round, banners waved and breastworks stood up against the skyline. The deeds of daring by individual officers and men are too many to recount; whether it was Lance Naik Sewan Singh of the 24th, or Lieutenant Costello earning a Victoria Cross, or Lieutenant Climo leading that magnificent battalion whose seniors had been stricken down, or the mountain gunners answering to every call, matters not. The defence amid these yelling hordes was steady as a rock, and lucky that it was so, for there was plenty more to come. The day of the 28th was largely spent in repairing damages, improving the defences, and giving the men as much rest as possible.

During the day, too, more accessions of tribesmen had been seen trooping in, but while heretofore they had been dressed in the ordinary white and grey of the frontier, it was now seen that the black-shirted tribes from Buner were arriving in their thousands. Such a sight had not been seen since the great conflagration of 1863. By 8.30 p.m. the battle recommenced, but by 7 p.m. further reinforcements had arrived, in the shape of the welcome Guides Infantry, who had been marching steadily in the great heat of the Yuzafzai Plain below since 1 a.m. on the 27th. It was necessary to put them on to the outer defences the moment they came in, and by 8.30 the tribesmen began again. All during this night too the new arrivals tried their luck at other parts of the perimeter and likely corners and gorges, especially on the western face of the *kotal*. The exciting internal struggles of the first two nights, however, did not occur, and by 3.30 in the morning the attack died away, and the 29th dawned quietly enough till midday, when some activity sent the garrison to its alarm posts. That night, the eve of Friday, was a holy one, and the day also of the new moon, and the tribes were likely to make their best combined attack thereon. Soon after sundown a heavy fire opened, and from 8.30 p.m. till 1.30 a.m. the now frantic tribesmen yelled and surged and endeavoured to get the Afridis of the 24th to come over to them. The Afridis promised that if the enemy came over they would let them in and give up their rifles. The attackers were foolish enough to comply, with the result that the Afridis punished them very severely. The assault died away somewhat earlier, and the news came that Colonel 'Jock' Reid was at Dargai below the hill with the 35th Sikhs, the 38th Dogras, and some detachments of the Guides, but that so severe was the heat that twenty-one of the Sikhs had died of heat stroke.

The 30th passed quietly enough, and several officers returning from leave managed to get through. At night the attacks were renewed, but for the last two nights our casualties had been few and that of the tribes severe. On the morning of the 31st the two battalions referred to fought their way in with no great difficulty.

§ 4

THE DEFENCE AND RELIEF OF CHAKDARA

While the attack on the Malakand was in progress, the little outpost down in the plain, with its garrison of two weak companies of the 45th Sikhs was having the thinnest of times. Its only gun defence was one 9 pr. R.M.L. post gun manned by a detachment of that celebrated body, the Punjab Garrison Artillery, affectionately known as 'The Blokes,' to which the tired mountain gunners were posted as they grew older. Lieutenant Rattray, returning from the polo game on the 26th with difficulty, got through a press of tribesmen who had sprung as it were from the ground. In his absence information had been received and telegraphed into the Malakand which, as we have seen, put that place on its guard. Till the 2nd of August, this little post was attacked by 10,000 tribesmen, though on the morning of the 27th the forty sabres of the 11th came in to their assistance after an exciting ride, having run the gauntlet of riflemen and cut their way through swordsmen. Then the fog of war descended, and the garrison fought for its life surrounded by the finest marksmen in India who endeavoured to make even the loopholes untenable. Communication between the Malakand and the *kotal* was supposed to be maintained by a signal tower, but the small garrison therein, who were without water, could not even get a message through till the 1st, when with great gallantry a Sikh signaller under heavy fire slipped out and set his helio up, and got the words through, 'Help us.'

It was too late to organize a sally to their aid that day, but the cavalry might succeed.

The force had also been augmented by the remainder of the 11th Bengal Lancers, and they and the Guides Cavalry made a splendid gesture. Being ready saddled they hurried down towards the plain, lance and sabre in hand, amid a heavy fire from all directions, supported by the 24th Punjabis. It was a grand display of daring and the masses of tribesmen, thinking the cavalry were given to their hands, swarmed down from the heights in vast numbers, reckless fanaticism still, burning fiercely, led by those 'adjutants of doom,' the dancing mullahs. The charge of the cavalry into these masses over difficult and broken ground was one of the most thrilling episodes of Indian military history. Like the waves of the sea, the clansmen rushed and swarmed round the galloping cavalrymen on their active horses, lance and sabre rose and fell, and gradually the *élan* of the horsemen's impact sent the tribesmen fleeing before them and over a hundred bit the dust – 'Tread light o'er the dead in the valley.' Lieutenant-Colonel R. B. Adams, of the Guides, who was in command, had his horse killed under him, and many an officer and man was wounded, but their supremacy was complete. As, however, further huge masses of tribesmen were approaching, Colonel Reid ordered their recall, and it was too late to try and get through to Chakdara that day.

That evening General Sir Bindon Blood, commanding the Rawal Pindi Division, had arrived, and as with the accession of force the safety of the Malakand was assured, the incoming troops rested from the strain of heat. Next morning, the 2nd of August, at daybreak, the force marched out to relieve Chakdara and take the offensive generally.

To this end, a thousand rifles with one hundred and fifty sabres sallied forth, supported by four mountain guns, while two columns from the *kotal* attacked the tribesmen on the hill-tops that flanked the road to Chakdara. Surprised, the enemy fled from the high ground, but collected by their thousands to battle with the relieving force on its way to the valley. At the Amandarra the tribes again made a desperate stand, and as the shrapnel spattered along the hill-tops were driven forth at the bayonet's point. Then the troops, urged on by the sound of heavy firing from Chakdara, emerged into the open to find the road bridges destroyed and progress in the flooded fields most difficult. As they reached the Swat Bridge, which was intact, swarms of tribesmen round the fort broke away, and were pursued by horse and foot across the plateau beyond, the garrison, yelling vengeance, joining in. The week in Chakdara had meant almost day and night of ceaseless attack. Again and again rushed on the swordsmen and the heapers of incendiary grass, supported always by concentrated rifle fire. The careful loopholing and sandbagging had kept casualties down, and it was intense fatigue more than losses that had brought the garrison, and especially the signal tower, who had no water, almost to their last gasp. A moment's relaxation meant a successful escalade or an attempt to pick out the corners of the enclosure. The fury of the tribesmen was happily their own undoing. Their mullahs had blessed them, and the Mad Mullah had explained that the faithful were immune to bullets. 'Those who fall by your side are the doubters. On! On! believers! and the world is yours. *Ya Allah! Ya Allah!* Heaven for all and glory for those who bleed!' Twelve hundred tribesmen, it is said, lost their lives before the maxims and the well-served rifles within, and far and near were widows a-keening. Captain Wright, of the 11th, who had led his squadron to the reinforcement on the 27th, had taken over the command, and wonderfully had he and Rattray, who was severely wounded, heartened their men against the yelling hordes outside.

§ 5

THE SUBSEQUENT OPERATIONS

The Government of India were now thoroughly aroused, and troops were being mobilized and poured up. It was the first time that a modern mobilization scheme in India had been put into effect, and it was working marvellously. Down from the Himalayas, pony and tonga were bringing the officers on leave and the young soldiers in the hill depots, while out from England the usually empty steamers were crammed with those hurrying back, on their own, or in response to recall.

The tribal forces round the Malakand were still in being, and on the hills across the valley the standards waved on every hill-top, and enthusiastic clansmen still danced defiance. The political and intelligence officers were now able to probe the extent of the rising, and it was found that the clans from the remotest valleys had answered to the call of Islam, while undoubtedly the officials of our good friend and ally, the Amir of Kabul, who sat chuckling at our troubles, were taking a fairly active part in whispering evil. It was even said that a very pretty trade in Afghan ammunition was in progress, and the clansmen had sent missions to Kabul craving the Amir's blessing, and even leadership. The successful defence of the Malakand, however, naturally made His Highness deaf to any such improper suggestions, though, as has been said, many a jolly Moslem lad within our own border was licking the wounds he had illicitly received for the faith. The loss of the Malakand might have seen half the Moslem Punjab in arms, and the cry '*La illa ha, Ill illah ho!*' responding from all our own mosques.

§ 6

OPERATIONS IN THE GRAECO-BACTRIAN VALLEY

It is not part of the purpose of this book to trace again the history of the campaigns that followed, but only to dwell on the high-lights of the drama, among which the events amid the ruins of Graeco-Bactrian villages are undoubtedly to be numbered.

Now that Chakdara had been relieved, General Blood was directed to march up the Swat Valley and disperse the tribes, as well as try and settle the whole trouble. A force of two infantry brigades with plenty of artillery, and two cavalry regiments, had by now been assembled, and on 16th August Sir Bindon Blood marched with a portion of his force for Upper Swat. Two short marches up the valley brought the force up to the 'Gate of Swat,' the Landaki Pass above the river gorge. The tribesmen and their banners danced defiance among the Graeco-Bactrian ruins on the hill-side, but the shrapnel spattered up and down the ridges, and the troops pressed up the height under its cover.

Then in the ancient valley where the causeway had been cut away, occurred an action ever famous. After the pass had been captured with little loss, the Guides Cavalry, eagerly pursuing the fleeing enemy, found themselves in the midst of a host of tribesmen in fanatical despair, a group of officers and a few men being in advance of the main body of the troopers. Some doubt has always existed as to what actually happened, but three officers were killed, and in riding to their assistance, Colonel Adams and young Lord Fincastle earned the Victoria Cross in a desperate conflict with terrible odds – a riot of chargers and revel of blows – before the bulk of their own men came up.

After these actions political arrangements were completed, and Blood returned in time to move east and south to take part in certain expeditions against the Mohmands, of which the origin must now be described.

The march up the valley beyond Landaki for a few miles was the sum of operations in Upper Swat, for the penitent jirgas were coming in from all tribes within our reach, offering all and any reparations possible. It had been, however, a romantic adventure in this beautiful valley, once the home of an extended Graeco-Bactrian civilization, which up to the sixth and seventh century at least, flourished and was known to the civilized world. The country-side was full of Buddhist monasteries, round the remains of which our troops were fighting, and of which the famous itineraries of the Chinese pilgrims give a full account in the fifth and sixth centuries. With the coming of Islam began the downfall of the humanities, and these gentle civilizations gave way to the wild fanaticism of the savage tribes which overran the country-side.

Were Swat and the adjacent valleys under British or other civilized rule, the wealth of archaeological material to be explored would be very great.

§ 7

THE INVASION OF THE PESHAWAR VALLEY

While the force under Sir Bindon Blood was assembling on the Malakand, for such further operations in Swat as might be necessary, another and quite unexpected outbreak was to take place a little to the south, and still further astound the Government and

public of India. Almost due north of Peshawar, across the Kabul River, stands the old Sikh fort of Shabkadr, with the frontier bazaar of Shankargarh full of Hindu merchants close by. There had been some talk of disturbances in the Mohmand hills, across the border, which the civil authorities had neither probed nor taken much notice of, although the notorious Hadda Mulla was said to be on the move. In the afternoon of the 7th of August several thousands of Mohmand tribesmen crossed the border, attacked Shabkadr, burned Shankargarh and massacred any Hindus who had not fled to the fort. Fifty Border Military Police held the post, and did so resolutely. That night a column under Colonel Woon was sent out by General Elles at Peshawar to their aid. Consisting of seven hundred infantry of the Somersets and 20th Punjabis, with four field guns of the 61st Battery and two squadrons of the 13th Bengal Lancers, it marched the eighteen miles from Peshawar by night, to the glow of the burning village. As the troops approached the Mohmands withdrew to some hills a mile or so away, while the tired column rested after its march in the heat. On the morning of the 9th Colonel Woon moved out to the attack, but his seven hundred infantry were too few, and they were soon hard-pressed by several thousand Mohmands. General Elles had now arrived with a troop more of the 13th, followed by a wing of the 30th Punjabis. The General, seeing how severe was the tribal pressure, ordered the 13th under Major Atkinson to charge the Mohmand flank, and this they did, collecting first in a nullah, actually effecting one of the most brilliant cavalry actions in Indian history. In spite of broken and stony ground, the squadrons scrambled out of the nullah, formed line, and rode hell for leather at the flank of the tribesmen with astounding effect. The whole of the Mohmand line, over a mile long, was rolled up, breaking and fleeing before the relentless lance points. The battle was over, and the gasping infantry were able to reform and draw breath. Pursuit was out of the question, for you now could not see the Mohmands' heels for the dust, their losses being over a thousand, including, it was said, thirty-two of their maliks or leaders.

By now rumours of trouble in the Khaiber itself were coming in and three reserve brigades had been formed in order to support the Malakand at Nowshera and Rawal Pindi for general use, in case worse should befall.

§ 8

THE MOHMAND EXPEDITION

After the attack on Shabkadr, the excitement grew intense in the Khaiber region, and the Afridis, under circumstances to be detailed in the next chapter, caught the prevailing disease and seized the Khaiber.

Whatever the situation in the Khaiber, however, and whatever policy the Government might evolve for itself, it was felt that the Mohmand situation must be cleared up. Moreover with two brigades already across the frontier and 'in being' with transport in Swat, there was an exceptional opportunity to explore the whole

Mohmand problem, to ascertain the causes of the trouble and to exterminate the fanatical nidus which, if not the only cause, was certainly the principal stimulant thereof. Also there was another matter to clear up, for among the Mohmands were gentlemen in Afghan uniform!

There were by now close on 12,000 men in the Peshawar area. The Khaiber had been lost and, while the Afridi question was still under consideration, General Elles was ordered to take Westmacott's and McGrigor's Brigades into Mohmand-land as soon as may be. There he would co-operate with Sir Bindon from the north, and put it across all and sundry who had infringed their obligations and their traditions of neighbourliness in so outrageous a fashion. General Blood was now fain to summon his merry men all, and the reserve brigade under Woodhouse was moved across the frontier to take the head of the spear. On 8th September he marched across into the Panjkora Valley and up the Useri Valley to Nawagai, followed by the 2nd Brigade under Brigadier Jeffreys as far as Khar. This force not only put a barrier between hills and valleys to the north, known collectively as Bajaur, still throbbing with excitement from the events on the Malakand, in which many of its clans had taken part, and the Mohmands, but also put Sir Bindon Blood's brigades in a position whence they could co-operate, as was intended, with General Elles in the chastisement of the Mohmands. Events, however, and severe fighting, were to decide otherwise. By the 14th, the 3rd Brigade had penetrated to Nawagai, and from there had operated southwards towards the Bedmanai Pass. The Mohmands had *more suo* followed up the withdrawing troops into their camp on the 20th, and on that night made a severe attack on General Blood and the camp of the 3rd Brigade, in which, among many casualties, the brigadier, Woodhouse, was severely wounded. The tribesmen, however, whose onrush was lit up by the firing of star shell, suffered severely, and in view of the difficulty of inflicting loss on tribesmen in their own hills, the mere fact of provoking them to attack your defensible camp, must always be considered a tactical triumph. In this attack, as at the Malakand, the Ghazis, the fanatics, vowed to die, penetrated the camp and fought and died at the defenders' hands, and gave rise to many gallant deeds on both sides. Before the attack on Nawagai, however, the 2nd Brigade had turned up the Watelai Valley into Bajaur to visit the Mohmand country after the latter's share in the attack on the Malakand. On the 14th General Jeffreys was at Inayat Kila below the Rambat Pass, and on that night he was subjected to a very heavy attack in which, though our losses were not negligible, the clansmen, as at Nawagai, suffered severely. Next morning his cavalry sallied forth to see if they could find the enemy, and had to be extricated from a hornet's nest. On the morning of the 16th, the brigade also went forth in three parties to visit and punish various villages in the neighbourhood for their attacks, and all the banners from Bannerville waved on the hill-tops – the Mohmands were out 'good and proper!' This resulted in close hand-to-hand struggles, and one party, with which was the brigadier, after very severe fighting at close quarters in the village of Shah Tangi, was compelled to stay where it was for the night with many wounded, the mountain guns being immobile from heavy losses to gunners and their mules. Next morning part of the brigade came to the rescue, and all were brought in, but the troops themselves and the Army generally, were, however, very critical of the way they had been led and handled. The attacks on these two brigades had prevented their moving up to time in the general operations against the Mohmands, though no doubt their presence did contribute sensibly to the capture of the Bedmanai Pass against which General Elles moved on 15th September from Shabkadr, via the long Gandab Valley. On the 24th he was at the foot of the pass which he stormed with his two brigades next day, the able handling of the brigades and battalions by their commanders obviating serious loss. On the 26th the screen for the first time was lifted from the inner recesses of the pleasant Mohmand uplands, troops penetrating through the deepest gorges and burning Jarobi the immune, and especially the nidus of the Mad Mullah. On the 27th and 28th minor punitive visitations were carried out, and on the 2nd the force withdrew. On the 22nd General Woodhouse's brigade left Nawagai to support General Elles, and General Blood with a cavalry force marched to Inayat Qila to join General Jeffreys, who had been 'getting his own back' from the Mohmands in his vicinity. The 1st Brigade from the Malakand had now been summoned to his aid by General Blood, who now carried out severe visitations, accompanied by destruction of tribal towers and fortified villages. October was well advanced before he returned to the Malakand, after experiencing further brisk hostilities before the tribes made their submission.

In the rewards to the troops for their very gallant exertions in the Nawagai and Mohmand fighting, in addition to many orders of merit to gallant Indian soldiers, Lieutenants Watson and Colvin of the Royal Engineers received well-earned Victoria Crosses for a desperate affair at Shah Tangi.

By now Government had made up their minds as to how to cope with the Afridi invasions of Kurram, Miranzai and the neutral ground of the Khaiber, and a large concentration of troops was in progress, to which Generals Elles' and Blood's forces were to contribute.

Buner and the Bunerwals, those old friends of 1863, who had come down thirty odd years after, in their black shirts, might stew in their own juice till the Afridi fog was finished.

But the drama of the lifting of the Afridi Veil merits a chapter of its own.

CHAPTER NINE

THE WAR IN THE TWO TIRAHS

§ I

THE CRISIS IN THE KHAIBER

WHILE the excitement of the Malakand outbreak spread into the Mohmand country, and the Peshawar Division was engaged in threading the country of those tribes who had so wantonly thrown themselves into the plains of British India, an entirely new crop of troubles was breaking out. Already had the suddenness of the previous outbreaks upset the orderly mobilization and concentration to plan, by necessitating the dispatch of units to a danger spot that had suddenly appeared where least expected, but the events of the ensuing few weeks were still more to produce this effect.

In describing the Afridi clans mention has been made of the numbers of mullahs of an extremely ignorant type who dominated the country, supported by many disciples, who frequent the country shrines and form nuclei of every sort of intrigue and evil. The Afridis, in addition to their well-paid services in protecting the ancient way of the Khaiber, had drawn handsome allowances from the British Government and sent many men to the Indian Army. They had no grievances all this time, and though now and again fanatical priests and irresponsible firebrands had endeavoured to embroil them with the British Government, they had always stood firm. When, therefore, news was received that the excitement was spreading to the Khaiber tribes, the Government of India showed very great concern, and in its desire to avoid an Afridi war, succeeded in making itself an object of derision to the whole world of men, while even the mice shouted scorn. By a set of intrigues which are fully set forth by Sir Richard Warburton in his memoirs, one of the lesser mullahs, Sayad Akbar of Waran, seems to have been the one to carry the fiery cross, and raise the cry of the 'Faith in danger,' '*Ya Allah! Ya Allah!*' The mullahs and *talibs*[1] took up the cry with such fervour that all sense of proportion left the tribesmen, and the wise heads, of whom there were many, could not get a hearing. In those days the Khaiber was held by the Khaiber Rifles alone, and the nearest troops were in Peshawar. Captain Barton was then political officer in the Khaiber, and as such in charge of the Khaiber Rifles, a militia corps furnished by the various Khaiber clans at British expense, to maintain order on the route to Kabul. When the Shabkadr trouble broke out, he proceeded to the big post of the Rifles at Landi Kotal, as the most important point, from which to watch affairs and steady the corps and the Afridi clans generally. He brought up the garrison to 350 Rifles, sent up 50,000 rounds of ammunition, and saw that all the forts were completed with reserve water. On

[1] *Talibs* : religious students and learners.

the 17th of August he learnt that the Afridi clans meant to rise, and he asked the commissioner, Mr. Udney, in Peshawar, that he might have four regular companies, and two guns sent him, for Landi Kotal was a large place, and needed a garrison of at least one thousand.

To his surprise he was ordered down at once to Peshawar. Never doubting he would be back next day to conduct the defence and Afridi affairs, and never for a moment doubting his men, he hurried down. It would be three days, he knew, before any attacks on the posts could be made. Then to his horror he was not allowed to return. His Rifles were to fight alone! And his face blackened before all the clansmen he dominated! To anyone knowing the character of Barton, one of the very highest type of frontier officers that the British throw up, the order was gall and wormwood beyond belief. While Barton was thus forced by a timorous Government to disgrace their name, the Afridis were flinging themselves on their own brethren, who had eaten the White Queen's salt. Landi Kotal held its vast perimeter for over twenty-four hours, killing a hundred of the attackers. Five native officers were inside, of whom two were wounded and ten of the defenders were killed, before the ties of kinship took precedence. Even then the Mullagori Subahdar got his company out and led it down to the British Frontier intact, with all its arms. All along the line the posts held out. A large British force lay at the mouth of the Khaiber and behind it by now, and was not allowed to help. A few rounds at long range were fired at the attackers of Fort Maude. The Subahdar who defended Landi Kotal had two sons fighting with the attackers and one with himself inside. As the Mullagori Company, forty strong, having lost four killed and three wounded, marched into Jamrud, the troops, the bitter, scornful, hand-tied troops, cheered them wildly. A little later two Shinwari companies of the Rifles also marched in from Landi Kotal with their subahdar badly wounded, playing their own band, to be received with equal enthusiasm. The garrison of little Fort Maude, as it too marched in intact, spat as they passed the British troops, of whom there were now close on 10,000 near at hand. It was a day of shame and humiliation for every Briton and loud were the curses called down on Lord Elgin and his twopenny Council, and on Udney the Unready, as the troops dubbed the chief civil authority.

That for the moment was the end of the situation, and all the years of work in pacification of the clans had been torn up. The Afridis, having burnt and sacked the posts at their ease, now turned their attention to another quarter, while Government were trying to make up its faltering mind.

§ 2

THE FIERY CROSS IN MIRANZAI

The mischief in the Khaiber, in modern metaphor, 'fairly tore it.' The fiery cross now sped across to the

Orakzai Tirah that lies south of the tumbled Afridi lands. South of the Orakzai Tirah lies the long alleyway to the Upper Kurram Valley and the Peiwar Kotal, that General Fred Roberts had stormed in the first phase of the Second Afghan War, and beyond which lay the Pass of the Camel's Neck, over which next year he made his sensational march into Kabul, after the destruction of the Cavignari Mission. Miranzai is a long, open valley leading up to Thal, where the alley enters into the valley of the Upper Kurram, from Kohat, the frontier station, with the old grey Sikh fortress. This is reached from Kushalgarh on the Indus, where in those days the railway from Rawalpindi stopped. North of Miranzai runs for many miles the great up-ended mountain barrier of the Samana Range, which since the operations of 1891-92 has been held by the British, for the protection of the important route to Kabul and all the trade that lies along it. The major portion of the garrison of a line of mud-built fortlets were frontier militiamen, but at Fort Lockhart on the wider portion of the ridge, was the headquarters of a regular battalion, at this period the 36th Sikhs, with a strong detachment of 130 rifles at the outpost of Fort Cavignari or Gulistan, four and a half miles farther along the ridge. Because a crag of the mountain intervened between the two posts there had been built a stone post thereon for connection of the two by visual signalling. This post was known as Saragarhi, and had a garrison of twenty-one men of the Sikhs.

At Kohat was the best part of a brigade, with cavalry

and artillery, sufficient for the normal requirements of that part of the frontier.

North of the Samana lay the Orakzai Tirah, and beyond it south of the Khaiber, the tumbled gorges, mountains and plateaus of the Afridis. Thus Orakzai and Afridi touched one another, and the various mullahs were in close liaison. South again of Miranzai were the mountains of Waziristan, inhabited by the clans of Darwesh Khel Wazirs, already busy enough with the force of two brigades, exacting retribution of the Maizar treachery already described.

Up in Kurram were, as explained earlier, a very different folk, a large tribe of Turkish or Mogul origin professing the Shiah as distinct from the Sunni or orthodox Moslem faith, they were entirely apart from their neighbours. Taken under the protection of Great Britain by the provisions of the Treaty of Gandamak, in 1878, they formed a valuable outpost of order and reliability, and were foremost through the militia that they furnished in maintaining the peace of the road and long alley. Against them in Kurram the Orakzais and neighbouring tribes to whom the excitement spread could do very little. But, stirred by Sayad Akbar and all the howling ecclesiastics that fanaticism had set loose, the Orakzai lashkar poured over the Samana into Miranzai, and lapped round the various military police and militia posts, both in the plain and on the Samana, most of which opened their doors or else surrendered after a mere show of resistance, and all government for a while was at an end in British Miranzai and Kurram. Kohat itself was even threatened, while Thal, the Government centre, where the Miranzai Valley opens up to the Kurram, was invested, and such movable troops as Kohat could spare were marching all they knew in intense heat from one threatened point to another. The fort at Sadda was desperately attacked, but relieved by a cavalry force under Colonel George Richardson. The defence of the small post at Balish Khel within sight of Sadda is typical of the loyal work that some of the frontier militia and levies were capable of. This post had a tower and courtyard garrisoned by twenty Kurram militiamen. An Afridi was in command, and his friends who attacked the post called on him to come over with his arms. Hurling defiance, the twenty faced 1500 outside. At midnight when ammunition was running low and fire slackened, the enemy hacked in the iron-bound door with their axes, and the garrison retreated to the tower. Then, as the last round had almost been reached, fifty tribal levies from Sadda came to the rescue and the attackers, believing it was a large force, made off. Not far behind were fifty more Kurram militiamen under a British officer, also throwing themselves with magnificent disdain unto the troubled and seething country-side.

General Yeatman Biggs with his reserve brigade was hurried up to Kohat, taking post at Hangu below the Samana, and still more cavalry was being sent up to help keep the alleyway to Kurram safe.

§ 3

THE DRAMA ON THE SAMANA

Now was to be enacted the drama on the Samana, a drama complicated by the great heat below, where the reinforcements were assembling, and the fact that no considerable body of troops could remain on the ridge for more than two days without completely exhausting the water supply. Up on the ridge the Orakzai lashkar, swarming from the valleys below the Samana Sukh, surrounded Gulistan, and commenced a heavy rifle fire. Here was Major Mickey Des Voeux and one hundred and thirty of his Sikhs, the situation being complicated by the fact that Mrs. Des Voeux was expecting her confinement, and was there with three other children and her nurse, Miss Theresa McGrath, who, having been allowed to remain for the summer, could not now be removed when the trouble threatened. Colonel Haughton from Fort Lockhart brought over one hundred and fifty men, and with the garrison attacked the lashkar and drove it off, while General Yeatman Biggs brought his brigade up to the ridge of the hills and threw a convoy of provisions into Fort Lockhart, and helped clear the tribesmen away. Leaving some guns on the top the water shortage compelled him to return to the plain. On the way down he saw a large force of tribesmen below advancing as if to threaten Hangu. Marching towards them, he had a severe engagement, and succeeded in diverting them, getting to Hangu, very weary, on the 12th. But the situation was not to be solved so easily. The Afridis, now realizing that they were fully committed, and that in the Peshawar Valley the British were too strong to be lightly attacked, decided to come over to assist the Orakzais capture the Samana forts and even threaten Kohat. A large lashkar of 10,000 men marched into the Khanki Valley on the farther side of the Samana, and swarming up with the Orakzais, again threw themselves on little Gulistan. At the same time they attacked the signal post of Saragarhi with the most deadly determination, despite the fierce defence, eventually picked out a corner of the tower under cover of a mantlet of earth on a native bed, and rushed in on the survivors, killing all save one. Him they burnt alive in the post, cruelly and horribly mutilating the slain after their custom, roasting alive also two non-combatant cooks whom they secured. Then they swarmed and swirled round Gulistan, while Des Voeux and his Sikhs defended their post and their precious charges, under the most deadly and continued fire, fighting daily to preserve the hornwork.

Fort Lockhart could no longer come to their assistance, but a message from Hangu that relief was coming was received by helio, and once more General Biggs' troops set out to climb the great mountain, despite the fact that they had only just got in from a very trying engagement and rearguard fight.

It was on the 13th that the news of the fall of Saragarhi came through. At midnight the force struggled out of Hangu, and by noon of the 14th September, General Biggs and his men were looking in grim anger on the ruins of Saragarhi and the mangled, mutilated bodies of its defenders, after having had a sharp fight with Afridis round Lockhart, and having relieved the post of Sangar, whose little garrison of Sikhs proudly paraded with a captured tribal standard in their hands. There were masses of tribesmen on Saragarhi crags and on every spur and sky line, but the shooting of the Derajat mountain battery, and the rush of the troops brought the relieving force to Gulistan by 2 p.m., which was a more than fine performance. Pressing on against the tribes, the latter promptly vanished from the hill-tops.

With the Samana again cleared, the situation was in hand. A considerable force of cavalry and field artillery now dominated the more accessible portions of Miranzai, and authority was duly restored, while the tribes stood by and waited to see what their behaviour would merit at the hands of the British Government.

General Yeatman Biggs maintained his headquarters at the point of vantage at Lockhart, with the mass of his troops as high up in the coolth as water would permit.

§ 4

THE TIRAH CAMPAIGN

While the occurrences just described were in progress, five brigades of the Army were at work in the Mohmand country and the Swati hills as related in the last chapter, and it would not be possible to undertake further operations until some, at any rate, of these troops could be available. The situation in the Khaiber and Miranzai was in hand, and during the Mohmand operations the Government of India was able to study its policy as regards the Afridis and Orakzais. After much debate and much out-pouring of contumely on the part of the public, stirred by the spectacle of the abandoned Khaiber Rifles, the Government of India, who were not quite so much to blame as generally believed, made up their minds to grasp the nettle danger with the hand of courage. They decided that they would once and for all, in the picturesque frontier metaphor, 'lift the *purdah*,' that is, 'raise the veil,' of the two Tirahs, the highland homes of Afridis and Orakzais. A glance at the map will show that the long ranges and valleys which form this country all run more or less parallel, towards Peshawar, or towards Kohat. To advance up them would mean a long and tedious business, with every step hotly contested. On the other hand, it should be possible under cover of the Samana range to collect the force at a point in Miranzai, actually Shinawri, below the great Samana Sukh, and ascending the Samana range cut across the three principal valleys where their head waters approach one another. Thus in three short marches we should cross the Khanki and Mastura Valleys and arrive at Bagh and Maidan in the very heart of the Afridi Tirah, a strategical conception of whose transcendent merit there could be no two opinions.

If the force involved was well equipped with pack transport and accustomed to mountain warfare, the ascent of the Chagru Kotal out of Miranzai should be a simple matter.

It is not proposed to describe the long and important campaign in Tirah at length, but to endeavour to give the colour by describing the sensational and dramatic opening, the Storming of Dargai, Dargai being a high cliff overhanging the gorge down which the troops must descend from the Chagru Kotal into the Khanki Valley.

As the writer was himself there he ventures to paint the impressions as he himself absorbed them. Sir William Lockhart, the commander of the Punjab Army, a veteran of the Indian Mutiny with the widest frontier experience, was to command two divisions. All the Army was duly elated at the prospects of seeing the Afridi Tirah, a spot exceeding Kashmir in beauty and climate . . . so '*bukhed*' the vain-glorious Afridi . . . which no European yet had visited.

It had been my good fortune to take some part in the operations for the Relief of the Samana posts as already described, in those hot days when the conflagration was still breaking out. I had been for years engaged in training the Imperial Service Mountain Artillery of the Kashmir Durbar for service on the edge of the Pamir, but had been sent up to the Samana trouble with Major Cookson, affectionately known throughout the whole army as 'Cookie,' with the Transport Train belonging to the State of Jeypur, at that time one of the few organized transport corps in India.

While the flames of insurrection roared and the

troops climbed on the Samana heights, we had brought up convoy after convoy of stores in our light carts from our railhead on the Indus, in intense heat. When the Government had decided to lift the Afridi Purdah, every mountain gun was wanted, and I was ordered back to Jammu to mobilize and bring up to Kohat one of the batteries I had been training (No. 1 Kashmir Mountain Battery) and in a couple of weeks returned to find a very large army forming under the high bastions of the old Sikh fortress in Kohat; and a very memorable sight it was. Two divisions were assembling and marching up to Shinawri, a plain lying below the Samana, forty-five miles from Kohat, under the great pass of the Chagru Kotal, above which the high cliffs of the Dargai ridge frowned down on the roadway.

As I marched with my guns into Kohat, long lines of troops and transport could be seen winding down from the pass which led from Peshawar, whence the troops who had been dealing with the Mohmands were now coming to join the rest of the Tirah force. As these filed over the passes, other brigades were passing from Kohat up to the place of assembly. The roads in every direction were full with gathering troops, Highland regiments, Gurkhas, Sikh corps eager to avenge Saragarhi, long lines of Indian cavalry, their lances standing high above the acrid dust that they stirred. By the side of the roads strings of laden camels padded on beside the troops, the jinkety-jink of the mountain guns, the skirling of the pipes, the haunting lilt of the *Zakhmi dil*, or 'Bleeding heart,' played on *dole* and *sarnai,* all contributed to the wild excitement and romance of the scene. General Yeatman Biggs, R.A., long known to his corps as Y. B., had the 2nd Division, of which a considerable portion was already on the Samana. Penn-Symonds, then of outstanding fame, had the 1st Division, which was assembling at Kohat. But while the divisions hastened to the gathering, another famous Indian soldier, Sir Power Palmer, or 'Long P.,' as we called him, was commanding the troops as they assembled and would control the communications. As we marched amid the echelons out of Kohat, he and his staff jostled past us on horseback, for the days of generals and staffs in motor cars had not yet come to jockey the marching troops. The weather had changed; the nights had grown cold, and the heat of the days had passed, for it was now mid-October, and the concentration at Shinawri was nearly complete. The 2nd Division was either there or on the Samana hill-top close by, and the 1st Division was already half assembled.

§ 5

THE CHAGRU KOTAL

Above the plain at Shinawri rose the great hills. Looking up at the *kotal* 4000 feet above us, we could see the mountain path, for it was little more, winding up a long spur. On the right of the pass, the Samana range itself came to an end in the mountain known as the Samana Sukh, which overhung the pass and the gorges on the far side. On the opposite side of the pass, and perhaps five hundred feet higher, the great cliffs of the Dargai ridge also overhung in sheer precipice the defiles down which the road wound to Karappa in the Khanki Valley, the home of the Orakzai tribes, who were now 'for it.'

From the top of the pass, the ridge of the Chagru Kotal was connected by a long steep spur with the Dargai Ridge, running into it by a narrow neck with precipitous sides, which joined the foot of the cliffs some four hundred feet from the summit, and from whence a goat track led slanting up the face of the cliffs. To the right of this neck the slopes fell away for many hundred feet in steep boulder and scrub-clad shale which led nowhere. To the right of the junction neck, the gorge dropped precipitous and dark, choked with scrub and fallen rocks, to the valley on the road to Karappa. Now it was fairly obvious and in accordance with all rules that it would be impossible to commit the long lines of troops and vast convoys to this deep gorge, or even to the top of the pass, without securing the Dargai Ridge, which was less than a mile from the bare top of the pass.

§ 6

THE TRANSPORT OF THE ARMY

Before we turn to the tactical action of the forcing and crossing of the pass, we had better look at the organization of the transport, for it is with this knowledge that we can learn some lessons which still hold good, and will hold good even when mechanical and electric mules scale mountain passes. The Army in India as a whole had very little organized transport, though the Frontier Force had excellent regimental animals. A very few mules and mule carts were maintained at the larger up-country stations. The work of the Army in its garrison was done by the carts and camels of the country-side, by contractors. All of which was very right and proper, for no country wants to feed standing transport in peace time. But on the other hand, unless it has some system of organizing the resources of civil life it cannot tackle sudden war. For generations this question of transport affairs painted a lurid streak in Indian campaigns and has torn the guts out of the Indian Exchequer. In the days of Lake and Wellesley, the country was entirely served by bullock and camel, and long years of war had produced an efficient system of using them, which was soon forgotten in peace. It will be remembered how the Commander-in-Chief in India and the European troops from the Simla hills trying to re-take Delhi after the outbreak in 1857 were delayed for weeks, while collecting 'carriage.' The story of the Afghan War of 1878-80 is largely the story of 'carriage.' The old art had been forgotten, and things were no better in 1897. The orders had gone forth to hire and to impress. But hiring is not always easy in times of danger, and to impress means animals without attendants. Tens of thousands of animals hastily impressed, dishonestly purchased, often without attendants and gear, were pushed up to the bases of the Army. Rubbishy gear

CONVOYS IN A FRONTIER CAMPAIGN

OLD STYLE

NEW STYLE

To face page 230

was hastily bought and manufactured, worthless attendants were crimped and clothed. Willing but inexperienced officers and N.C.O.'s from units not mobilized were brought up to endeavour to evolve order out of chaos. And a good transport officer, here as in South Africa, was worth his weight in gold. Soldiers who can fight are always available, men who can and will organize behind the line are harder to come by. When I went up to the Miranzai, with the Jeypur Transport, my father, an old-time officer, wrote, 'I don't much like this Carter Paterson business.' That was the old spirit that spoilt all efficiency of organization. The Knight and the Esquire would only handle sword and lance!

Now the above story is worth grasping, for it will point the moral and adorn the tale of the super-folly which ensued, and which was soon forgotten in the cheers.

§ 7

THE COMMANDER-IN-CHIEF'S PLANS

Sir William Lockhart's plans were perfectly straightforward. The force was to advance, the 2nd Division leading, into the Khanki Valley. Two more marches over the Sampagha Pass to the head of the Mastura Valley, then over once again brought you the headquarters of the Afridis at Bagh and Maidan, the 'Garden' and the 'plain,' the upland glory and boast of Afrididom. With the force was to go a long convoy of pack ponies with ten days' supplies for the two divisions. Ye gods and little fishes! The road was not fit yet for camels even. Pack ponies, the miserable little rats of the *Markomans* and other pack-carrying fraternities, thousands of little donkeys, all bought unwillingly, all equipped often with *chatts*[1] too big for them, all of which would have to wind over these difficult paths in single file behind two divisions! Each with thirteen battalions and three mountain batteries all marching in single file, miles and miles and miles of them! The head of the force must reach its destination long before the rear left camp, over pack paths that no one had ever seen. But so it was. Equipped with this information it is interesting too to see the mess that followed, nay, more than a mess – because we learn by such things – before we turn to gladden our hearts with the *élan* and gallantry of the soldiery.

On the morning of the 20th October 1897 the 2nd Division from Shinawri and the Samana were to carry the *kotal* and wend their way down to Karappa. And now a strange happening must be noticed. On the 18th that evil thing which crops up mishandled in every military age was to be carried out – a reconnaissance-in-force of the Kotal and the Dargai heights. A portion of the troops at Shinawri, under the command of Sir Power Palmer, were to carry this out on the 18th. The Dargai Ridge was actually carried on the morning of that day by the Gordon Highlanders, supported by a couple of mountain batteries, for thirteen casualties. The Orakzai tribesmen who held it were dislodged. For want of hard thinking and a

[1] The native saddle pad.

little *bandobast*, the troops returned to camp nearly 5000 feet below them at Shinawri, and lost fifty men in doing so. An Afridi lashkar camped in the Khanki Valley had swarmed up the heights and hung on to the British rearguard. By the evening the high cliffs against the distant sky were stiff with their standards. All the next day the sight remained to stir the gathering army.

An early start was made by the 2nd Division on the 20th, but a strange thing was ordered. The loading of pack convoys is a difficult and lengthy business, requiring much labour, which can only be done just as the animals start, unless they are to stand for hours under load, but this transport, including the ten days' rations, was to be loaded before dawn, for all troops. A wiser administration would have detailed a company[1] to remain behind with each corps to load when the time to join in the order of march approached. But no! Everything was loaded before starting, and the transport was not powerful government mules in disciplined corps, but the scourings of the country-side with the dregs of the bazaars in charge.

§ 8

THE STORMING OF DARGAI

Up went the head of the column before daylight, winding single file along the interminable road, Brigadier-General Kempster with the 3rd Brigade

[1] These were the days of eight companies to a battalion.

leading, followed by three mountain batteries. Even this force covered perhaps five miles of road. More troops cut in from the Samana, and a mountain battery and the divisional headquarters moved to the Samana Sukh. Kempster was to sweep along the spur leading from the *kotal* to the Dargai heights and to swarm up them as had been done on the 18th. Three mountain batteries on the *kotal* and one upon the Sukh were to support him. It was to be a bagatelle, and while Kempster held the ridge and the heights on the left side of the descent, the rest of the force, with its transport, would defile peacefully behind the leading brigade into the valley below. But the race is not always to the swift. Soon after daybreak the 1/2 Gurkhas under Lieutenant-Colonel Travers, followed by the Dorsets and supported by the Derbys (drawn from another brigade), started along the spur to the foot of the cliffs. The remaining two battalions of Kempster's Brigade, the Gordon Highlanders and the 15th Sikhs, waited on the top of the *kotal*. With them also were the 3rd Sikhs. The leading battalions passed the still smoking remains of Mahmud Khan, a fortified hamlet that had been destroyed the day of the reconnaissance, and formed up under cover in a small depression behind a ridge, whence the short neck already described connected the spur with the foot of the Dargai cliffs. The tribal standards waved on the troops and defiant cries were wafted down and re-echoed in the gorge. Soon after 8 a.m. the mountain batteries on the *kotal* and that high on the Sukh opened fire on the crest. Colonel Travers led his first few scouts across easily enough to some cover under overhanging rocks. Then the defenders awoke to what was in progress. The remainder of the Gurkhas, attempting to join their colonel in extended order along the narrow neck, encountered a tremendous fire, chiefly of Martini bullets aimed by the best marksmen on the frontier. Every expert in the clefts above had two or three loaders. Hardly a shot missed its billet. The men, dribbling over, were hit time and again, and rolled down the slopes on either side or lay on the fairway. Colonel Travers had hoped, as soon as a fair clump of men joined him, to begin pushing up the goat tracks where there appeared to be occasional cover from rocks. But his party did not increase. The accurately aimed fire swept off all who ventured to join him. Then, after some time had elapsed, General Kempster ordered the Dorsets to try, and a similar fate awaited them. It seemed impossible to get over that fire-swept neck. Then some of the Derbyshire Regiment were ordered to make the attempt – a futile proceeding. There were already crowds of men and stretchers behind the little ridge and in the depression. More men only added to the confusion. All the morning long, this *impasse* grew. The brigadier was impatient, but could not get the rush over the neck. He reported to General Yeatman Biggs, and asked if it was essential to carry the heights. General Biggs knew that the troops could not be committed to the gorges on the other side till the enemy, whose numbers seemed to be increasing, were driven from the cliffs. Another effort must be made. Then General Kempster sent for the Gordons and his Sikhs. By mistake the order got to a battalion not under his command, the 3rd Sikhs. The Gordons were moving off, and the 3rd Sikhs followed them. Colonel Mathias received his orders that the heights must be carried at all costs.

The afternoon was now advancing, and Mathias apparently realized that Gordon Highlanders were no more immune than anyone else, and that to dribble them over could only mean that the kilts would lie on the slope among Colonel Travers' Gurkhas and the Dorsets. Besides, it was obvious that a long climb up the face of the cliffs was to follow, and that only swarms of men following individual leaders would be likely to make the ascent. In fact, it seemed to all onlookers that even when the neck was passed in sufficient numbers, that a still more difficult task remained.

However, the first thing was to get enough men over the neck to be able to swarm up the cliffs. All the while there was a mass of tired, thirsty, and dispirited soldiers jammed up with ammunition mules and wounded in the small covered space behind the ridge. With difficulty Mathias got his men formed up in an irregular mass behind cover. He had realized that a mass alone would get over, that in the space of time they were on the ridge only a certain number of men could be hit.

Then occurred the inspiriting operation of which so much was written at the time. Colonel Mathias ordered officers and pipers to the front. The swagger with which the pipe-major threw his plaid and his drones well over his shoulder was magnificent. The Colonel strode out in front, and the pipes set up 'Cock of the

North.' And out on to that narrow ridge scrambled a mass of some six hundred cheering Highlanders. The artillery redoubled their supporting fire, and though many men fell, the mass, as the Colonel expected, got over, and in their train came Gurkhas, Sikhs and the men of Dorset and Derby. Piper Findlater, lying wounded in the neck, played his pipes as the men rushed on, a gallant incident that specially delighted the public.

The neck crossed, the companies set themselves in some confusion to scramble upwards along the slopes and goat paths and among rocks and crevices. It was a matter of at least three hundred difficult feet, and every one thought it would be the worst, but no! the heavy rifle fire soon died away, and the leading files gained the top at various parts almost unmolested. The tribesmen had seized their standards and had gone.

What had happened? Two things must have contributed to the result. First, of course, the impressive sight of the masses of Highlanders and other units swarming over the neck below, and secondly the artillery fire. The effect of the artillery was in this wise. The marksmen sweeping the neck were ensconced invulnerably among rocks and clefts when no shrapnel bullet could reach them. In absolute security they picked off the individual figures below them. But when it came to repelling the men swarming up the goat-tracks, it was another matter. The marksmen had to come out of their crevices, and the remainder of the line had to emerge also from behind the rocks and lean far over to fire on the climbers. But then the artillery came into play. From the spluttered marks of the shrapnel bullets it was evident that to do this now meant considerable exposure, while though the batteries below on the *kotal* could spatter the top of the rocks, the guns far up on the Sukh could bring a high angle of searching fire. This, together with the breaking of the original spell, destroyed the determination of the tribes.

That is the end of the story, but for learning and instruction let us see the aftermath of the loading order, and of failing to maintain an organization for the expansion of army transport. The ridge was not carried till late in the afternoon. It was quite impossible to think of continuing the march that night. The troops bivouacked as best they could. The convoys stood patiently all that night under load on the hill-side for the six or seven miles of road back to Shinari. On the *mazri*-clad plain below, thousands of animals which had not even started the ascent, stood in dark masses the night through. None were watered that night; only near a transport officer were any fed. It was quite impossible to take any loads off. Many a weakly animal collapsed under its load in the twenty-six hours they had waited. Then they began to file slowly down the *kotal* into the Khanki Valley. Thousands collapsed on the difficult ascent. Of those that got into camp at the far end, all had been unfed, unwatered and under load for the best part of forty hours. Thousands died or were destroyed, and the whole operation was delayed, while fresh convoys of food were organized and fresh beasts brought up from India, all from the folly of what in those days passed for staff officers. But it is a thing that might easily happen again, and it is worthy of remembrance as a warning. Plans may go agley, but even had the heights been carried without delay, those animals would have remained under load for over twenty-four hours without water. Had the course been taken of leaving a hundred men per battalion to load up transport when required, none of this would have happened.

It is not necessary to continue the story. The campaign continued with great endurance on the part of the troops, considerable audacity on the part of the tribes, and an exasperating want of good will in the higher machinery which was responsible for many of the regrettable incidents and disasters which took place. We learnt a good deal about frontier warfare in the face of the breech-loaders which was very different from facing the old sword and matchlock men. Some brigadiers learnt that it was their business to see that rearguards got home and were supported. General Kempster's brigade came in for several hard knocks after the storming of Dargai. To be 'Kempstered' became a ribald phrase which the Army used, and 'I'm kempstered if I do' a camp expression of dissent, which was perhaps hard on a fighting brigadier, but that is the way of armies.

That Piper Findlater should have turned an honest penny by appearing eventually on a music-hall stage was perhaps, by the standard of those days, regrettable. Perhaps to-day we should not be so nice.

Before winter came on in all its rigour, the main

force marched into the Peshawar Valley, having blown up and destroyed the fortified farms, of all those clans who would not 'come in,' and settle peace. Towards the end of the cold season, when success in the Tirah was assured, General Blood took a force into Buner, on the far side of the Peshawar Valley, to read their lesson to those thousands of black-shirted Bunerwals, who had quite unnecessarily flocked to the fun on the Malakand. The actual fighting involved in exacting retribution was not serious. Finally the Bazaar Valley, which runs into the open at Jamrud, was visited, then the Great Frontier War was over, and

> 'The King's Peace over all, dear boys,
> The King's Peace over all.'

CHAPTER TEN

THE NORTH-WEST FRONTIER IN THE TWENTIETH CENTURY

§ 1

AFTER 1897

THE eventful summer of 1897, followed by the campaign through the late autumn and winter months in the two Tirahs, settled the matter. Repentant tribes smoked the pipe of peace, and we have the extraordinary scene at a big peace durbar of Afridi chiefs in 1898, when the Afridis, notably the irreconcilable Zakkha Khel, took the horses from General Sir William Lockhart's carriage and drew him in triumph. But it left us with expensive military commitments, with large garrisons, which the Indian soldier hates, across the border, where the Malakand, the Khaiber, the Samana, the Kurram, the Tochi, Wana, and the Gumal area, were all held in force. The strain on the Indian finances after the war, with the wartime charges also to meet, was very serious.

The disturbance of the South African War hampered to some extent a military solution, and it was not till Lord Curzon began to make a competent survey that a decision was arrived at. When to him came also Lord Kitchener with a mandate to put the Indian Army on a more modern footing, then was the frontier policy, military and economic, set on to a scientific and comprehensive basis.

The strategical problem to meet outside aggressions was also overhauled and reconstructed, for the Russian railways had crept to the Oxus, and things were much changed since the days of 1885, when the Russians attacked the Afghans at Panjdeh, and half the Army in India moved to the Bolan.

§ 2

THE TRAGEDY OF GUMATTI TOWER

Before we tell of that reconstruction, there must come this story of a tragedy, staged early in the present century, typical of life on the frontier in its more desperate form, and a case to make angels weep. Close to the frontier cantonment of Bannu, an arm of tribal hills runs down, inhabited by a more than tiresome set of neighbours, the Kabul Khel Wazirs. There, just across the border through a pass of the same name, stood Gumatti tower and fort, a harbour for outlaws and bad-hats, for many a year. So long was the bill for outrage and damages, that an attempt was to be made by a small force to rout them out. News had arrived that one Sailgi, a famous leader of outlaws in every devilry that the world has ever dreamt of, was in harbour at Gumatti with half a dozen of his worst associates. Colonel Tonnochy, commanding the 53rd Sikhs (F.F.), a very famous frontier soldier, and 'Blanco'

White, his adjutant, with a few officers, were taking out a small military column to secure the gang, cutting them out if need be from the midst of the whole tribe.

At 2 a.m. the force started, and picketing the Gumatti Pass, which was unoccupied, succeeded in passing that grim defile unnoticed. By nine in the morning the column, which consisted of five hundred rifles of the 53rd and 54th Sikhs, eighty sabres of the 21st Punjab Cavalry, and a couple of mountain guns (10-prs.), had reached the open plain in the hills in the midst of which stood the outlaws' fort. The cavalry galloped out and surrounded it, and friendlies announced that Sailgi and half a dozen others were at home, but would never surrender. Donald, the political officer, with a confidence none too well placed, went up under a flag of truce, and opened negotiations. Sailgi announced that he would surrender if Donald would try him, if he and his companions were not handcuffed, and if his fort was not destroyed. As it was too dangerous to take such rogues unhandcuffed, and as Sailgi's fort was too ill-omened a place to be allowed to stand, his conditions were not accepted. After a while the mountain guns were brought up and tried to knock away a corner of the tower. Now and again the outlaws would appear and shout defiance. Guns drew closer in, and rifles covered every loophole. Sailgi was again offered surrender, but refused. Then he killed a gunner and wounded another, but the walls were crumbling. Tonnochy and Donald the 'Political' moved forward to see if a breach was practicable for a storming, and the former fell mortally wounded. The breach was not practicable, so weak were the little mountain guns, so strong the mud and stone of the tower. A withdrawal to Bannu meant the whole valley in arms. The place must be taken! Lieutenant Brown of the Engineers ran forward and affixed gun cotton to the bastion corner, unharmed. The fuse failed, and he ran across again still unharmed. The gun-cotton roared and the wall heaved, a huge breach was made. Blanco White led the storming party, and the Sikh native officer at his side was shot. The outlaws, driven from the tower, fought like rats, and poor White, swearing to avenge his colonel, was shot through the head as he peeped over a parapet. More breaches had now been made, troops poured in, and Sailgi and his brother outlaws, who might so well have been brave in a better cause, were shot or bayoneted. That was the end of it, a wretched purpose to put brave men to, even for the needs of the King's Peace, whether two thousand pounds of education of two most gallant English gentlemen, good yeomen like the loyal Sikhs, or brave, intractable ne'er-do-wells. Sailgi was found under the debris, his teeth clenched and his rifle gripped so tight that it took two men to loose it.

His wife and mother were in the tower, and Mr. O'Dwyer, the famous Sir Michael of the Punjab Rebellion, who was with the force as a *tamasha-bin*, a sight-seer, and who was nearly killed at Tonnochy's side for his pains, says the wife was the most beautiful woman he had ever seen. Happily the women were unharmed, and were taken away by relatives. It was said that when Donald turned to go after the parley, Sailgi raised his rifle, saying, 'I have got to die to-day. I may as well have another *faringhi*[1] to my credit,' but his mother struck up the barrel, saying, 'No, Sailgi, the *Sahib* has treated you fair and given you no cause.'

That night the force camped where they were, fired at pretty freely by the outlaws' friends, and O'Dwyer relates how, as he bicycled home next morning, when they had passed through the Gumatti Pass, he heard the explosions that meant the tower and fort had been blown sky high, indicating that, 'If the patience of Government was as protracted as a summer's day its arms were as long as a winter's night.' But somehow the price paid was a big one, even to vindicate the Sirkar, and to this day Tonnochy, the soldier, and Blanco White, his adjutant, are mourned wherever frontier officers congregate. Such things would not happen to-day, for many of the mountain batteries have howitzers and high explosive shell, that make frontier towers a jest.

§ 3

LORD KITCHENER AND LORD CURZON'S POLICY

The political, economic and military policies required the same measures. The political, in other words the governmental, policy wanted to see the tribes settled down, weaned to more peaceful pursuits, and refraining from molestation of the caravan routes. The commander-in-chief wanted his Indian troops and their British officers relieved of an undue propor-

[1] *Faranghi* : Frank, *i.e.* Christian.

tion of trans-frontier garrison duty, which curtailed the essential leave of the yeoman peasantry who composed the Army, and destroyed reasonable amenities to the officer. Further, on strategical grounds, it was important to get the regular Army back to stations where it could be trained, and available to take part in that *Grande Guerre* to which the world was obviously heading. In the immediate case it was the approach of the Russian railway system to the Afghan Frontier, from several directions, that demanded that the Indian Army should be free and not locked up by the garrisoning of unimportant valleys. The economic side demanded less military expenditure, in this case, largely due to the privileges and cost of maintenance of Indian troops beyond the border, and the general expense of carrying supplies to them. Then was developed the principle, not in itself new, either in theory or practice, of entrusting most of the border protection to units raised from the tribesmen themselves, as in the conception of the Black Watch on the Scottish Highlands, in the eighteenth century. Behind the tribal corps were certain bodies of regular troops organized in small brigades of all arms, located within the frontier. The new policy had among its advantages the finding of employment for the young men in the militias, as they were called, honourable employment with some prospects of career and pension. Further, roads and works that employed tribal labour were to be undertaken, and tribal labour, costly and inefficient though it often was, was to be employed, to the disgust of the engineers responsible. Nevertheless,

TRIBESMEN UNDER THE SHADOW OF A MILITIA POST

To face page 240

even this policy had common sense as its basis, for the frontiers must be brought forward in the general march of progress. Thus, with educational facilities for the sons of chiefs and elders, with dispensaries on the borders, and with also an increase in the number of trans-border men taken in the Army, the frontier progressed till the days of the World War. But the greatest factor of advancement was the practical fruition of an age-old design to have a 'Frontier' province. Hitherto the Punjab Government, controlling a growing and insistent province, was also concerned with the border. Somewhat cavalierly, if entirely wisely, the Punjab Government was shouldered out, and a Frontier Province was inaugurated. The logistics and conformation of the country-side did not permit, as Lord Lytton had envisaged years before, the inclusion of the Baluchistan portion of the border within this province. That tract had already been removed from the Sind Government's control, and placed under the Government of India, as a frontier province, and there was now created a second, so that there remain to this day, what are virtually a Northern and a Southern Frontier Province, known as the North-west Frontier Province, and British Baluchistan, of which the former contained the bulk of the tribes with whom we were so often at war.

But the former and to a lesser extent the latter province, do contain naturally within the border, settled areas that in some sense need a similar system to the rest of India. Yet half these tracts are so mixed up with the trans-frontier people, and suffer from the same violent conditions demanding special laws and regulations, that the demand by some of the intelligentsia for more political development had not been easy to accede to.

During this period, viz. from 1897 onward, the march of progress in all humane directions has been great. Canals, roads, agriculture, education, hospitals, all show remarkable advance from the rough-and-ready methods which were only possible for the first forty years. From the trans-border folk mission hospital dispensaries attract many patients, and spread the gospel of truth. Stones, goitres, wounds and the like are specially treated, vaccination is offered, and ladies who have lost their noses to jealous husbands come to have their features renewed.

§ 4

AFGHANISTAN

During these years of development our relations with Afghanistan steadily improved, visits of British missions to Kabul settled outstanding points of disagreement. Abdur Rahman himself sat on his throne chuckling with mordant laughter at our frontier imbroglios, which in his estimation we had asked for by handling these clans ourselves, and by our soft and kindly ways. He knew how to deal with such swine, not we! Having enjoyed his joke and incidentally knowing full well that when he liked he could always stir our tribes as a hint not to quarrel with him, he set himself down to develop his own country, and to plan with ourselves how to protect Afghanistan from Russian aspirations. Finally he died, ripe in years, having changed the face of his country and made it something of a nation.

It was Lyall who made him say when he first took the throne, looking out over the beautiful vista from the old Bala Hissar at Kabul, partly quoted already:

> 'Fair are the vales well watered,
> And the vines on the uplands well;
> You might think I am reigning in heaven,
> I know I am ruling in hell.'

Hell he had found it for the first fifteen years. Then, when he had finished the slaughter of all the tall poppies, confident that with an Afghan enemy the only safe motto was, 'Stone dead hath no fellow,' and helped by his British subsidy, by gifts of arms and the work of the sturdy Pyne and other Britons who went to serve him in Kabul, Afghanistan began to rise. By the Amir's fierce endeavours to be known as the '*Amir El Kebir*,' the 'Great Amir,' an Afghanistan had come into being to which his son Habibullah peacefully succeeded in 1904. That peaceful accession alone was a great tribute to his father's power and prestige.

The stories that are told of this rough period, this rough-hewing of a fiercely rebellious people, have been many, good and bad. Here is one, characteristic in its grimness, told me by Sir Salter Pyne one New Year's Eve, as we sat over a log fire in a lady's drawing-room in Peshawar, Pyne then having left the Amir's service, thankful to do so with his head on his shoulders.

Mr. Pyne, as he then was, had been summoned to see the Amir, whom he found sitting in a verandah overlooking the palace yard, 'A-heating hice cream,' as Mr. Pyne expressed it, for I have said that he was John Bull and more in his speech. He joined His Highness in an ice cream, and together they chatted of armaments and what-nots, when there was marched into the court below a gang of prisoners heavily escorted and chained, fifty in all. The Amir scowled at them. They were mutinous soldiery from Herat, some of the 'dog Heratis' of song. The Amir gazed for a moment under his beetling brow. . . .

'You *sag-parast*[1] swine,' said he. 'I'll teach you to mutiny. Poke their eyes out.' And it was done then and there, and as Mr. Pyne said, 'I couldn't finish my hice cream, but His 'ighness did,' and then Mr. Pyne told me a story of another court, and how he had amused the princess, and she had said to him, 'Lor', Mr. Pyne, you are a treat,' which no doubt he was. His description of his lunch party at Windsor was also effective. 'Nice little piece on my left, stiff old buster on my right.'

And he had a story of the Amir's fit of economy, when he ordered that the gun fired on the Behmaru Heights outside Kabul at the hour of high twelve should also carry out the day's execution, the blowing away of a criminal from a gun, an awe-inspiring finale enough, yet infinitely more humane than the slow process that passes for hanging in Kabul. There was a village below the heights, however, which lodged a

[1] *Sag-parast*: dog-worshipping.

petition. While recognizing the economic wisdom of His Highness' orders, still, high twelve was also the hour of their *alfresco* dinner meal in their courtyards, and the amenities thereof were, His Highness would appreciate, much disturbed by the falling of pieces of criminal among them, be he Afghan or be he Turk. And no doubt His Highness relented. On the other hand he may not have.

The Amir El Kebir published during his life his reminiscences, and in a somewhat remarkable volume edited for him by his chief Munshi, he discusses this matter of rebellion in this manner. 'Rebellion I have a horror of and the misery it entails. Afghans are a hard folk, and they must be ruled with an iron hand. But I seem to remember that the people of England (the gallery to which he was playing) hate rebellions too, and how not a century and a half ago (he wrote in the early 'nineties) England repressed her last rebellion with great cruelty. I read of English gentlemen hung in public, cut down while they were yet living, opened and their hearts cut out, and I do not pretend that Afghanistan is within a century of England in civilization.' And perhaps he was right.

§ 5

THE AMIR'S JESTS

It is told in Kabul of how the Amir El Kebir had a grim sense of humour, as indeed Kipling has sung in his ballad of the *King's Jest*, and once an elderly maiden relative reproached him with want of a sense of duty to her, in providing no husband. His Highness admitted the justice of the plaint, and gave her in marriage with sufficient dowry to make her acceptable, to an elderly nobleman of the country-side. The Amir disliked parting with his cash, and he felt that he had done well by her.

Imagine therefore his annoyance, when the lady appeared veiled at his durbar one day, and formally complained that her spouse had no teeth, and that as she had a headful, the bargain was not a fair one. His Highness drew a deep breath and swore by the beard of the Prophet.

'Woman!' he hissed. 'Teeth are given by God, but . . .' and here he paused and beckoned to some one behind him, 'man can remove them. You shall be equal. Remove her teeth.' And it was so.

There is a less grim and more human story of his humour, told of him when sitting as was his wont in open durbar, dispatching the business of the day. A female spy, with which his court was well supplied, slipped round and whispered that Nabbi Baksh, the Grand-Treasurer, who was kneeling on the foot of the dais counting tribute, was now and again slipping a gold piece inside his shoe. On the dais itself, in accordance with the sanitary custom of the East, shoes were discarded, but in the court and kneeling on the steps, shoes would be worn. The Amir looked up, but preferred a knight's move. He turned to Ghulam Hyder, his commander-in-chief, and made an unexpected attack.

'Ghulam Hyder! What beastly big feet you've got. Not fit to be seen on a royal dais.'

Ghulam Hyder was taken aback, gruff and stern of mien though he was, as befits an Afghan commander-in-chief. He shuffled, he stammered, he tried to hide his feet, which were certainly not small. 'Er, er! Your Highness, I am sorry . . . er . . . er . . . I don't think my feet are too large.'

'Don't argue with me, Ghulam Hyder, they are beastly feet. Now if you want to see well-shaped and small feet, you should see Nabbi Baksh's feet. They are a treat. Here, Nabbi Baksh, come here and let the world see your beautiful feet.'

The whole Court was now agog, but Nabbi Baksh, who had been busy with his coins, had not seen the first move. He was taken aback and began to stammer. 'He was ill, his mother was ill, he hadn't washed his feet for a month, they were unfit.'

Then the Amir bellowed at him, in the tone which had once made a vacancy in the Becket family:

'Come up on the dais at once, Nabbi Baksh, and take your shoes off.' Thus by a knight's move, to the delight of the court, was Nabbi Baksh on the stage, for as 'The Blackbuck is stalked by the bullock cart and man by jealousy,' so per the feet of Ghulam Hyder was Nabbi Baksh brought low as the coins rolled from his shoes. To save himself from jail and the bug-pit, he had to disgorge a lakh of rupees from his ill-gotten perquisites of two years in office.

§ 6

THE WORLD WAR

So Abdur-Rahman was gathered with his fathers in 1907, and 'Habibulla,' the 'Beloved of God,' reigned in his stead and did not even follow the Afghan custom of blinding his brother, so that it was evident that the strong hand of Abdur-Rahman, whose name means 'The Slave of Mercy,' had shown no mercy to some purpose. His new Highness came down to India in 1906 and was well pleased. And then it was that Sir Henry McMahon, aided and abetted by the Grand Master of all the Freemasons in the Punjab, no less a person than Lord Kitchener, by triple dispensation passed His Highness to the High and Sublime Degree of Master Mason in one night. Staunch masons looked askance one with another, but when a commander-in-chief is also Grand Master of Freemasons in the Frontier Province and the Foreign Secretary to the Government of India, who was also in the Masonic World Lord High Everything Else combined together, it does not much matter who does sniff at them. As it happened those two high masons builded better than they knew, better even than Solomon on Mount Tabor, seeing that they were Brito-Irish and that a war of survivals was on its way, as will be seen a little later.

The frontier decade of the new century then passed fairly equably. Sir Harold Deane, the first Warden of the Marches, held the frontier well, and gave the new province more than a good start. The Mahsud

Waziris of course gave trouble again, and, in 1907, were blockaded, cut off from the marts of the British border, and denied access to salt in the hope that it might bring them to their senses. This indeed, it did for a short while, stimulated, however, by what is known as an active period, when occurred a famous episode known as Tonnochy's raid on Makin. At Makin and Kaniguram there lived a very bitter hostile fanatic, the Mullah Powindah, which probably but means the 'tramping priest.' However that may be, he had ceased to tramp and had sat him down amid a lot of desperadoes and, like the 'good, kind Mr. Ghandi,' was determined to give the British no peace. And curiously enough he could not be bought, unless indeed the insult offered was too lowly.

So he and his haunts were raided by the daring Colonel Tonnochy and some picked frontier soldiers, with pretty useful results.

How little real effect, however, the blockade had on these miserable men of savage outlook, is told in the next chapter, under the title of a study in martyrdom. But all the while the militia system grew and, except in Mahsud-land, prospered. In 1907 the Zakka Khel, the section who alone in Tirah in 1897 went unchastised, grew above themselves, and were slated by Sir James Wilcocks in a week-end war, after trouble in the Khaiber which threatened at one time an Afghan War. Following this the Mohmands, bored with the years of quiet, broke out and had to be chastised also. And so in peaceful development as a rule, the frontier dreamed on, Sir Harold Deane passing away prematurely, and giving place to the equally strong hands of Sir George Roos Keppel. It is not too much to say that till the upheaval of the World War, the policies of the British were working well enough, and only the bogey of economic employment for the young mountaineers remained, mitigated *pro tem*, by military service and work on border roads, which could not, however, be found for ever.

Europe was now drifting hard to her fate, and when the World War came, every bitter mullah who could not let bygones be bygones, must needs seize his insistent drum. When the Sultan of Turkey joined the war, and proceeded to proclaim a *Jihad*, a world *Jihad*, and to cry from all the mosques and *minars* in Islam that the faith was in danger, then the frontier fat was in the fire. But Habibullah, the 'beloved of God,' master mason in the English Constitution, was mindful of his obligation 'Of the badge of friendship and the bond of peace,' and he sat very tight in Kabul. Rub-a-dub! Rub-a-dub! went the drums. '*Ya Allah! Ya Allah!*' yelled the priests. King Habibullah sent for the Moslem gentleman who was British representative in Kabul, and to King George sent greeting, 'Don't mind what I say, for I have kittle cattle to drive, but watch what I do.'

On the strength of that, as all the world knows, the Government of India and the Commander-in Chief, Sir Beauchamp Duff, took grave risks and threw the Army of India, British and Indian, to the Seven Seas in the cause of the Allies.

Only one hint sent the Amir: 'It will make it easier

for me to hold these wild devils if there are no frontier expeditions for the present.' So though the frontier boiled under the surface, there being no encouragement from the Amir, the untoward happenings were not too many. Generals V. B. Fane and Holland Prior gave some handsome ripostes in the Tochi and in the Yuzafzai Plain to some who tried it on, but there was nothing too serious. Habibullah handled Turkish and German missions with great art. To the Turks he promised a mighty army to aid them if and when they reached his border on their way India-wards, and the Germans he so played with that at last they went their way disgusted. As the war wore on, however, the Mahsuds were waxing more and more presumptuous. Getting more and more arms, their raids became military invasions, and at last the Government sent to the Amir and said, 'We are afraid we must put a stop to this,' and the Amir said, 'They are swine, aren't they! Don't I know it, and I agree that you must go for them. But for my sake I pray you don't send too cruel a general.'

And so an endeavour was made, but with very young soldiers, for all the best Indian staff officers and men lay dead in Flanders, or up to their eyes on the Tigris and in Sinai. The operations to prevent the impudent raids on the part of the Mahsud Waziris, which did not at times hesitate to cross the Indus, were carried out with a more or less success, but perhaps with less effect than had the usual seasoned troops been available.

In this matter of the frontier, it is perhaps well to

realize what a critical thing was the stirring of Moslem unrest by the entirely unjustifiable declaration of *Jihad* by the Sultan and his Sheikh – Ul-Islam – his 'Pontiff of the Submission.' Whether or no the Moslem world of the Persian Gulf, of the frontier, and of parts of India were to catch the infection and boil over, was decided really by two things. First, though not perhaps foremost, was the staunchness described of the Amir Habibullah to his friendship and obligations, but the second and finally the most important of all, was the victory of Sir John Nixon and his brigadiers, who bore the brunt of the battle at Shaiba, on the edge of the desert twelve miles from the Port of Basra. There a Turkish Army Corps, accompanied by hordes of Arab jackals and some Kurdish irregular cavalry, were trying to drive the British into the Persian Gulf, and nearly succeeded. In its effects on the British Empire it is hardly too much to say that it was the *decisive battle of the war*, this dog fight in the dust and heat haze of the '*gebel.*' All Islam was watching, and when it was over, the cry of the frontier mullahs and the sour-faced swine in the more fanatical of the Indian mosques lost its appeal, and died away.

The watch and ward on the Indus edge then went on, with only a remarkable attempt of one of the old Baluch tribes, who had not donem ore than knife a tax collector for half a century. They now caught some side pocket of the infective germs – the Maris and Bughtis, old forgotten troublers in that wild and little-visited massif which lies between the Indus, at Dera

Ghazi Khan and Sibi on the rail to Quetta. It so perturbed the authorities on their powder barrel in India, who had forgotten the Baluch, that they were for a moment frightened. The tribesmen, who had carried a Levy fort, were marched at with soldiery, and that was the end of it.

After that the World War rang to its close, the bitterness among the seditionists unfortunately bringing off their Indian Rebellion. It was not to be expected that Great Britain, triumphant after having supported the whole world, were likely to be injured, but a sad thing had happened in Afghanistan. Habibullah, the 'Beloved of God,' had paid the penalty of his staunchness. The sum of fanatical hostility had induced some party, whose name has only been hinted at, to murder him, in February 1819. Some there were who said that a skirt was a concomitant, for in Kabul Muhammadzai ladies are forthcoming . . . be that as it may, the sum of it saw our ally murdered to make an Afghan holiday, and Amanullah his son seized the throne from the heir, his effete uncle.

§ 7

THE THIRD AFGHAN WAR

Master Amanullah, whose presumption was greater than his 'guts,' now elected to throw in his lot with the Indian seditionists, and perhaps fearing that the army might vent its annoyance over the Amir's murder on him, launched an invasion of India, the first since the days of Zaman Shah, over a century earlier. His privileged agent, the Afghan postmaster in Peshawar, really a spy and propagandist, issued an absurd proclamation calling on all and sundry to rise against the British. Despite the fact that the hot season had commenced, despite the fact that the Army in India was demobilizing, his rather worthless Afghan soldiery were driven back and never reached the Indus. Beaten after some sharp fighting in the Khaiber, an armistice was asked for after the British were marching in Jalalabad, and about to bomb Kabul. In the Kurram, General Nadir Khan advanced to the leaguer of Thal, but was defeated by General Dyer. On the Quetta side, the British crossed the frontier for the first time since 1881, and captured the Afghan fort of Spin Baldak. Then was an armistice patched up, to the huge relief of Amanullah, who hid his chagrin under a proclamation of exaltation.

The British, too war-weary to go to Kabul, eventually made a peace that did not redound to their prestige, but at any rate struck the note always in their minds, that of the attainment of a strong and prosperous Afghan neighbour. They succeeded, too, in getting out of the old payment of a defence subsidy to the Amir, the loss of which must have been a severe handicap to Amanullah when his trouble arose. But the Afghan invasion, vain and ineffective though it was, had one terrible result. It tore up all the civilizing work of twenty years. It stirred all the old wild feelings of the clansmen to overrun Hindustan. The Waziris, almost *en bloc*, joined the Afghans, and poured over the border, destroying the smaller garrisons, murdering British officers and burning Government property. In the Khaiber most of the Khaiber Rifles deserted or were discharged as unsatisfactory and unsafe. They have not been re-raised.

On all sides the general prestige of the Frontier Province Government was lowered, and it was necessary to set about at once settling the tribes of Waziristan, who incidentally had practically destroyed all of the Southern Waziristan Militia who would not desert their officers. In Zhob, the tribes had risen after years of quiet, and our half-baked troops and inexperienced officers had been severely handled.

To Major-general Andrew Skeen was now entrusted the carrying out of a punitive campaign against the Waziris. He fought several thousand tribesmen, exceedingly well armed with all the derelict rifles of Europe, stolen from the Turks, lost by the British, or sold by the Russians, and ammunition was also for the first time like sand on the seashore. The troops to be employed were largely children, men enlisted of unwarlike races in the attempt to enlarge the Indian Army beyond the capacity of the very few races in India with the heart to bear arms. And the story of his defeat of the tribesmen is one that reflects the greatest credit on his leadership and wisdom. The Mahsuds were reduced to order, but it took close on two years. The Afridis had already been dealt with.

§ 8

THE FALL OF AMANULLAH

Some allusion is necessary to the fall of Amanullah, the young man who thought he could compel the world by biting the British hand that had fed him and his dynasty. He came back from Europe primed with the theories of Angora and Moscow, and without the character to ride a storm, tried to compel his people to ways that were not their ways. He fell before the arms of a tribal Rob Roy. Habibullah, the water carrier's son, succeeded in leading against him and the civilization that was growing in the country-side the same wild rush of Kohistanis as had surrounded Lord Roberts in Sherpur. Amanullah fled, and at once his armouries and treasuries were pillaged. Now none so poor as do him reverence. The work of years was overthrown. Those Europeans who made so much of their share in Amanullah's glorious development, notably the French scientists, watched with chagrin their card-house crumble. Happily for Afghanistan, there were enough patriots to rally to his uncle, Nadir Shah, who returned from Europe to be offered the throne. The wild caterans were expelled, and the water carrier's son, who had the impertinence to call himself Habib ullah '*Ghazi*,' or the 'Defender of the Faith,' was, with his leading officers, hung in due and ancient form as the illustration shows, in the market place at Kabul. Now Nadir Shah is endeavouring painfully to rebuild his kingdom to some prosperity.

THE WAGES OF REBELLION. HABIBULLA GHAZI, THE USURPING KING OF KABUL, AND HIS MINISTERS REAP THEIR REWARD FROM NADIR SHAH, IN KABUL

GHILZAIS MARCHING DOWN TO INDIA TO SPEND THEIR WINTER WITH KING GEORGE

To face page 262

The trouble in Kabul was a factor that naturally greatly upset the calm of the border, added to the anxieties of the chief commissioner, and the Government of India, and no doubt contributed greatly to the troubles of 1930 in the Peshawar Valley.

§ 9

THE FRONTIER TO-DAY AND ECONOMIC PROBLEMS

The North-west Frontier to-day is the direct result of this wicked Afghan invasion, an attempt to rebuild and develop the confidence in the Curzon policy. The last few years, as evidenced in the summer of 1930, it has pleased the lads of the country-side to ally themselves – for a price – with the sour sedition-mongers of India, who do not hesitate to foul their own nest in their spite, to annoy the frontier authorities. It still stands in its alignment and principles as when we first succeeded to it, tempered, as explained by the policy of controlling as far as the Afghan border, the important trade routes. Sheer and black with their crown of snow in the winter, raw red and lost in haze in the summer, still stand the border hills. It has been said and repeated by a certain school of thought that to have had this problem with us for seventy years and more, to have spent huge sums on frontier expeditions, and still to have the problem before us, is a great slur on our acumen and capacity. In a certain sense that may be so, but we have to remember that an attempt to take over hills across the administered border, disarm the tribes and occupy the area would have meant prolonged bloodshed and ill-will. It would have been done at the cost of many British, Indian and tribal lives and at the cost of the Indian taxpayer, for by no stretch of imagination could it ever have been possible to make the administration of these tracts pay for themselves. It is easy to be pound wise when seventy years have passed. Further, another difficulty often forgotten, was that until the middle of the 'nineties the frontier with Afghanistan had never been agreed on, and in many places was in constant dispute, notably in the case of the Wana Plain, and to this day the delimitation is not complete, nor indeed till Abdurrahman with British help made that very new thing, a stable and definite Afghanistan, was it possible to do so.

Again, even had we been in direct administration of the frontier hills, we should not have been in a much better condition to tackle the real trouble, the want of land that can be tilled, the want of occupation for the increasing population. Moreover, had there been the King's Peace over all, the increase in population would probably have been very much greater.

The unrest in Mahsud-land after 1918, however, has led the Government of India to embark on an experiment which has produced interesting results. Tired of marching troops over the hot stretches of the Indus whenever a Mahsud clan stretched itself, it decided to make a large upland cantonment at Razmak, dominating the tribal storm centres, and containing a big gun or two, that could counter attacks in the camp by dropping monitory high explosive shells on the tower of any malik, or the mosque of any priest, who was responsible for keeping the clansmen in order or in ferment. Further, Government ran a motor road of some twenty or thirty miles through the country, and lo! the tribes have been so taken with motors that all the old junk in India has got up there to play, tied up with string and wire but still working. A Ford car manages to carry a dozen tribesmen to market, within the border, but – you cannot do this with rifles, bandoliers and knives stuck over you. So these items of toilet are for the first time being left behind, and without them perhaps civilization may peep in. A similar policy in the Afridi country is obviously required, and the new road in the Aka Khel Plain south of Peshawar is the first step in this direction by a timorous and withal hard-up administration.

Times are changing in many ways, and apart from the political follies in progress, such follies as red shirt organizations, first allowed by a timorous Government before the last Afghan War – follies that would make any of the older men who could rule, turn in their graves – there are many new factors at work, some good as some bad.

The old Afridi chiefs, who in Roos Keppel's days kept their clans in order, now live in wealth in Peshawar. They keep as much of the Government allowances to themselves as possible, and their clansmen are restless and discontented. With the Army and Militia largely closed to them by their own folly, they are hard put to it to live. They want more land, and they want work, not indeed hard work, but fairly easy work, with good pay . . . in this they have long subscribed to the modern principles that govern labour politics. How to give it them is a problem. But it is now not too much to say that, give them work and opportunity, press on them such civilizing things as dispensaries, travelling dispensaries if necessary, let the medical missionary work to his full capacity, take the young men as much as possible into the forces, hit them as hard as you can when they transgress, a great future of ameliorization may be opening up, the fruit of earlier endeavours. But without opportunity the tribes are more dangerous as neighbours than ever, and ripe to join any glorious movement that promises subversion of authority. If the King's Peace and control in northern India is to be weakened, then God help the humbler folk within the more civilized border. Once again let us quote from the great Sir John at Gadshill. 'Young men must live, and gorbellied knaves with fat purses are fair games.' The Hindu merchant fills the bill as a gorbellied knave most adequately.

It is not without its humorous side that in this valley of Peshawar, where Avitabile in his embroidered jacket held his tasselled gibbets, and where Sidney Cotton did not hesitate to blow mutineers from the guns, and disarm his Purbiah regiments, rebellious and revolutionary bodies should have been allowed to work close to a powder mine, in the presence too of the best-equipped body of troops in India. Perhaps the effort of holding Europe in the World War has left us so helpless that all strength of character is in suspense.

Perhaps we are very wise, and are handling foolish people with such consummate wisdom that our and their good may blossom tenfold. But the picture of a thousand Afridis hired from Calcutta to shoot up the British, penetrating to the edge of cantonments for the glory of God and His Prophet, at the instance of Siva and Vishnu, is one that hardly bears looking on, save by those to whom the world is but a comic stage.

§ 10

THE COUNTRY-SIDE

Among the many changes which the frontier has seen, especially since the development of the frontier province, has been the method of dealing with the tribes. In early days negotiations were largely conducted by means of '*Arbabs*,' men of some standing or relationship, trade connection and what not, with the various clans or sections. These middlemen were indispensable in our first years, as knowing something of the ways and wants of an unknown people. As time passed, however, our own officers became highly versed in the habits, divisions and customs of the trans-border folk and could deal directly with them, and encouraged them to come into meetings. The middleman – a system always with inherent objections – is especially difficult to control in the dishonest intriguing East, and a good deal of our troubles came from crooked *Arbabs*. The *Arbab* system died sooner on some parts of the frontier than others. When the tribesmen were out for a straight deal they would wish to deal direct with the *sahib*, and when they had some deep seated intrigue on, an *Arbab* might help them, especially for a consideration, to dust the eye of authority. The locating of officers on the border for the most of their career, did produce a very efficient, strong and sympathetic race of officers, fit successors to some of the old names, Edwardes, Mackeson and Nicholson that had been so famous in early days, of whom Deane, Roos Keppel, Barton, Donald, O'Dwyer, Keen and many another stand out. Some modern softness in high places, quite unsuited to the frontier, has induced a deterioration, it is said, that has largely helped in some of the recent contretemps. However understanding and sympathetic a frontier officer may be, an exact knowledge of when to change from soft speech to hard, stern orders is essential, and the frontier is no place for kindly souls with academic theories to air. Indeed, it is a place of antitheses, as some of the stories related show. The writer well remembers waiting outside a changing place for the ponies that drove the mail cart. The panting ponies were being taken from the cart after their stage, and a fiercely intractable pair were arguing the point as to whether they should or should not be put in the shafts in their place. With him was a stout companion, another Englishman, and two Afghan lads were lolling hard by. Said one lad in Pashto, 'I've a mighty good mind to jab my knife into yon fat swine's belly.' 'Better not,' said his companion, 'The deceitful brute has probably got a pistol in his pocket.' From which I deduced that when travelling on the border, it is fairer to show your arms, and thus put temptation out of the way of high-spirited lads of the village.

Often as I have wanted in the course of this story to get away from bloodshed and warfare, from the flying bullet, the vendetta and all 'that man unto man has done,' I find it hard. The allusion to Sailgi's beautiful wife within the bleached tower, of Muhammadzai ladies on the Kabul roofs, and of Captain Warburton marrying a Durani Princess is all that I have been able to introduce in the skirt line, for, as I have said, skirts do not much enter into border drama, for reasons good and for some impossibly bad. Away in the villages a lot of hard-faced women lead a hard life, but as girls must possess the same features that make the lad so comely. Among the humbler ones the work of the fields is largely theirs, and inside the fortified towers they lead a secluded life, with few amusements and interests outside their domestic problems. There was an Afridi officer I once knew who had come to great fame in his regiment, and who had been given the rank of 'captain,' which is very highly prized. Once at the end of his service he persuaded his wife to come down to a regimental gathering in India so that she might see the consideration in which he was held. 'Ah,' she said, 'now I know, truly you are a man of importance, but I never knew before what all you told me meant.'

In some of the frontier hills the women drive donkeys five miles a day and more for water, twice a day if the store gets upset. The feasts of marriage are of course their occasion and in Afghanistan itself, where the Amir's writ runs as in British India, the daily life is full of the little things that count. Among the grim hills of the independent tracts, where a blood feud often prevents a man leaving his tower by day, there is not too much of the *joie de vivre* for the women. 'Bangles ring softly and sadly.' It is indeed from the state dispensaries along the border and the mission hospitals alone that some conception of the softer side of life alone comes.

Schools there are practically none, save those of the Mullahs, where small boys may learn a few Arabic texts by heart and are taught to call all who have a different faith by the opprobrious term of Kafir. Amid scenes of rough life, likely lads with the faces of angels are taught the hard creed of revenge, and at times are made themselves to finish off some victim of vendetta, to blood their hesitating hand. Into these ruthless hills alone, do the world's missionaries fail to go, so hopeless is the prospect and so sure the death. Dr. Pennel, and Dr. Pennel alone, has been allowed to go, led by some chief or outlaw who needed his aid perhaps for his family.

§ 11

THE DRAMA OF MOLLIE ELLIS

There is a frontier story of very recent days which must be told here, and which does illustrate very emphatically the type of scoundrel with whom our frontier officers often have to deal. The scene is laid in the old-world frontier station of Kohat across the Indus on the road to Miranzai and Kurram, a station in which the *point d'appui* is still the old Sikh fortress which looms over the station. The house of the general commanding the station lies in the centre, and not far from it and its armed guard was the house of Colonel Ellis, the senior staff officer of the district, who at the time of the tragedy was absent in the district. With Mrs. Ellis dwelt their daughter Mollie, a lass approaching maturity. One night an alarm was given, there had been some sound, and the servants entered the house to find Mrs. Ellis in bed with her throat cut, a handful of a black beard in her hand, and Mollie, with several rugs, gone.

What had happened no one knew, but evidently Mollie had been abducted by the same hands as murdered her mother. The station was aroused, and a hue and cry sent forth. Mounted troops, with many extra officers on horseback and in cars, started to scour the mountains and country round and the way to every pass. Police and infantry searched the nearer country, and aeroplanes began to soar over a wide area with no success.

At last information was obtained that Mollie was alive and being carried and led far away into the mountain side by a notorious outlaw and his following. A Pathan political officer offered to go across the border to see how the land lay, and treat for release, stirring the frontier chiefs and *maliks* to exert themselves to remove such a slur from their good name. When news came through as to her whereabouts and that certain of the *maliks* would see to it, then a wonderful lady of the frontier, widow of a mission doctor in Peshawar, who had been murdered by a patient, offered to go out and comfort the child and stay with her till she was brought back.

After considerable adventures, Mrs. Starr,[1] with Kubla Khan, the political officer referred to, succeeded in reaching Mollie in a fortified tower far across the border, and eventually bringing her away from her abductors, none the worse and fairly recovered from the first horror of her position. The abductor apparently had carried out his ruffianly act in revenge for some raid on a *cache* of stolen rifles said to be in his house. Mrs. Ellis was probably murdered because she had tried to raise an alarm, and had then fought for her life. The abductors had hoped to get away undetected with the girl rolled up in rugs. She was, however, unexpectedly sleeping beside her mother, owing to Colonel Ellis' absence. Never before had such an outrage occurred, and up till now, or at any rate till bombing had upset the frontier conventions regarding women, molestation of any English lady had been almost unknown. The whole matter caused the greatest sensation, and aroused great indignation. Loud was the praise of Mrs. Starr for her devotion, and of Mollie for her steadfast bearing in her astounding trial. Happily, ere long, the abductor, whose dossier was a long one, paid the penalty on a frontier gallows.

[1] Now Mrs. . . . Dr. Starr was murdered by a tribesman.

§ 12

THE MILITARY PROBLEM

This book is not the place to discuss the military problem at length. But it may be well to observe that on this frontier that problem has two entirely different aspects. There is a major and a minor problem. One is the age-old one of the protection of India, which really includes Afghanistan, from outside, from the rollers of the north, in modern times Russia, the intermediate and accessory problem of a hostile Afghanistan either alone or leagued with Russia; the other the entirely separate one of the tribes themselves. One is a matter of forethought and big arrangements first, but on a modern footing since the Russian War scare of 1885 already referred to, and brought to more modern form by Lord Kitchener, now the matter for daily anxious study by the General Staff of the Army in India.

The other, the daily one, the insistent lesser problem of the tribes, has been considerably illumined in these pages. One of the disappointments of modern times is the uselessness of the Air Force in handling the problem. It was hoped that solution might have been found. But it was soon realized that bombing has no material effect against tribal skirmishers and sharp-shooters. Even machine-gunning hits no one amid rock and crag. The Air Force pilots on the North-west Frontier have been the admiration of the world in their rescue of the Europeans in Kabul during the late usurpation. They fly most daringly into the mountains. They do, it is true, bring notice of tribal gatherings, they can poke their noses up tribal valleys and they can overlook, to the huge annoyance of the clans, but that unfortunately is almost all. In the late Peshawar troubles the results of their activities, in themselves beyond praise, was in the nature of things trivial. Even punitive bombing has now been realized as of little avail. To bomb unwarned means destruction of families. To bomb after warning is absurd. Dispersal is the matter of moments, and half the year the tribes live in caves. How difficult is punitive bombing is well illustrated by the following story from the Euphrates. A friendly sheikh rode in to see the political officer. After salutations said he, 'They were bombing down my way yesterday. I think it is rather rough after all I have done for Government.'

'Oh,' said the political officer, 'I am sorry. There must have been some mistake. I hope no damage was done.'

'Oh no,' replied the sheikh. 'Nothing to mention. Praise be to God! Only a cow and a wife I hated.'

The bomb, once released, is no chooser of persons. When tribes have to be tackled, the infantry soldier and the mountain gun is still the only remedy, with a handful of lancers if the valleys be open enough and the *mazri* scrub rideable. But if the King's Peace could only be obtained by economic means then wars and rumours of wars might cease.

AT KANIGURAM IN WAZIRISTAN

THE BRITISH COMMANDER DICTATING TERMS TO THE MAHSUD WAZIRIS

To face page 274

CHAPTER ELEVEN

IOD-I-GUL

THE GARLAND OF STORIES

For many chapters now the reader has been wearied by sheer history, even if history packed with drama, and it is now time that he be cheered with some lighter food. The story of Chikai, the famous freebooter, is typical of many who have hacked their way to power by way of battle, murder and sudden death, but it is a jaunty story withal, and to follow it is a 'Study in Martyrdom,' which will show the British frontier officer in some of his day's work. A little bundle of lesser stories will tell of Subahdar Dilawur Khan of the Guides, the man of whom it might be said by his father, 'Belike they will make thee *Resaldar*[1] when I am hanged in Peshawar,' and maybe it was the story of Dilawur Khan that prompted Kipling in his *Ballad of East and West.*

§ I

THE STORY OF CHIKAI, THE FREEBOOTER

In the tumbled lawless mountains, whence the young men harried the gorbellied knaves of trades,

[1] *Resaldar:* a captain of cavalry.

there are men who have hacked their way to power from humblest origins, and none more strangely in modern times than one Chikai, the Zaimukht free-booter, whose story is told at some length by the famous Dr. Pennel of Bannu aforesaid. We may take him as a sample of many such, and in following his life story we but follow that of a type.

In one of the villages that lie in the upland valleys, close to the Afridi Tirah, was born of humble but dishonest parents one Muhammad Sarwar, who grew up to boyhood amid the walnut trees and the poplar or two which fringed the village stream. His people were too poor to have much concern with the feuds that took place with the clansmen across the valley, which now and again sent the village headman climbing up into his tower pulling his ladder behind him. Nevertheless, young Muhammad loved to hear the rifle bullet whiz through the keen air and see it smash and flatten against a stone, and dreamed of the day when he too should own a rifle and have a bell-mouthed pistol inlaid with silver and a couple of knives in his waistbelt. Since his father had neither flocks to attend nor land to till, Muhammad at length took service with a miller. The stream had been taken off into a mill-race that drove half a dozen stone *chakkies*, great rough wheels that ground the corn and left the nourishing glutens with the flour. Because of the mulberry tree that overhung the mill, and the pleasant shade on the turf above the mill-race, many an idle man came there to lounge and gossip. The gossip of raid and feud and murder, of rupees and stolen rifles, was at times exciting enough, and the lad would listen agape. A lad of his acquaintance but a little older, and an equally penniless loon, by name Abdul Asghar, was making money, owned some land and half a dozen sheep. That seemed better than minding the mill stones. How was it done? Then he heard that Asghar was wanted by the border police, in the *thana*[1] in Miranzai for highway robbery. How Muhammad's ears pricked up! A highwayman! That was what his fancy had always painted for him. He had once heard a man tell with gusto how his knife had slipped into the belly of a fat merchant as into butter! Aha! that was the goods for him! So one day he asked Asghar to take him, and was then and there added to a cattle-lifting gang. He soon became an expert assistant, and then one day Asghar was shot, and Muhammad, now a nice-looking lad with a profile like a Greek statue, started on his own. Now it was that the nickname of 'Chikai,' the 'lifter,' was given him, exactly as if his name might have been Armstrong or Napier. Then he had a chance to widen his rôle to that of hired assassin, which can be blended so easily with the lifter's art. Mullah Darwaza, of the village of Saman in those parts, had an enmity with a *malik*, or notable of the village, who had enticed away one of his *talibs* or boy disciples, a beautiful lad of thirteen years of age, for his own disreputable purposes. Now instead of the lad reading the Qoran and learning from the illuminated book of the poet Shaikh Sadi, the brat was swaggering around the village with his eyes blackened with antimony, and

[1] *Thana:* police stations.

a gold-braided puggaree on his head, the most impudent catamite for a dozen miles round. The saintly Mullah would gladly have stabbed the seducer himself. But that would have meant loss of sanctity, added to the discomfort of having to avoid revenge. The Mullah, reading prayers one day, saw Chikai among his congregation, and whispered to him to come see him that night. Chikai met the man of God, and came away with a bag of rupees, and two days later the *malik*, washing himself before prayers on the bank of the stream, fell forward shot by an unknown hand – shot through the heart, and no one the wiser. This whetted our lad's appetite, and 'removals' soon became more lucrative than 'lifting.'

Ere long Chikai became known as an expert 'remover' that would hardly give Chicago best, and as his fame increased many secret commissions came his way. With success came danger. Chikai, with money to burn, did not, like Dick Turpin, frequent good houses of call and cheer, but built himself a strong tower with a solid base that none could undermine, and equipped it with a rope ladder to the loopholed storey, which he could draw up when he had said his prayers and would go to bed.

Now and again fortune kisses a man on both cheeks. Chikai, having grasped the lesser opportunities that had come his way with the hand of courage, now was to come to his 'big business.' Among the tribes of the Tirah and Miranzai there is that strange division of which the origin is obscure. In one valley, clans of the same tribe will be 'Gar,' in the other 'Samil,' meaning, as already explained, little more than 'Oxford or Cambridge,' or 'French and English' would mean in a school, save that the point is often argued with rifle and tiger's-claw. Through many tribes the factional difference runs, and it is one of the queer things of the world. One day, the Chikai story runs, a prominent 'Gar' *malik* was shot in a 'Samil' village and then the fat was in the fire with plenty of blood to flow. After a good deal of promiscuous shootings and night murders in prosecution of the feud, the Samil faction realized that they had no leader worth writing home about. Then someone bethought himself of Chikai, and the idea caught on. The freebooter was approached, and was as willing as Barkis – on terms. If he was successful – if the Samil section of the Zaimukhts overcame the Gar – then he was to be acknowledged to be the head of the Zaimukht tribe. This was accepted by the Samil folk, who had much fear of being 'downed' by the other faction. Chikai therefore brought to the clan a posse of outlaws who lived in his hall, and these reckless yet wily men led the rest of the clan. In engagement after engagement the Gar party were defeated. Their name was as mud, and all were weary. Further, a very important fact, the crops were ripe and needed reaping, at which time as all the world knows, only fools fight. Both sides summoned their *jirghas*, their meeting of elders. The two *jirghas* amalgamated. Twenty fat sheep were slain, a gargantuan feast was consumed, ending with a dance round a blazing fire in which the deadly enemies of yesterday danced one with another, and Chikai emerged as the leader of 8000 well-armed men. He built himself a fine fort at Chinarak in the Zaimukht Mountains, and lived as 'The Zaimukht' should, and as The MacNab had lived before him. Chinarak was garrisoned with his own special bodyguard of outlaws, some of whom were refugees from British justice, and some from the noose and the execution gun of Kabul. But he had developed some sense of politics and some worldly wisdom. He realized that in his somewhat accessible valleys under the great Safaid Koh, they had plenty of good fish to fry, without running a tilt at the British Government. So he kept his folk clear of any risings and prospered accordingly. Whiles, he played at being the simple mountaineer, and showed up by his simplicity beside the more gaudy entourage of the political officers, on whom from time to time he came to call. But, plain though his clothing was, and black with a plain fringe his puggaree, it would be observed that his rifle was the finest there, and his revolver of the best pattern, so that the young men round gaped with admiration. His demeanour was cheery and boisterous, but at times his humour was grimly sardonic.

Pennel relates one of the well-known stories of his ruth. One day his favourite barber was pleased to tell him that an enemy had offered him a large sum to cut the freebooter's throat. When the shave was finished, Chikai drew his revolver and shot him, lest he should yield to temptation another time. Dr. Pennel also relates how he visited the stronghold of Chinarak in response to an invitation to doctor some sick, the missionary being in camp within reach. He went, and after he had seen the sick, Chikai said that he had heard that the doctor was an *anjil*, a preacher of the Gospel, and he would hear him preach so that he might compare the teachings of Christianity with all Islam. He summoned the Mullah to sit on his other side to preach in his turn. And so amid a circle of the most proper looking cut-throats as ever scared a simple man, the doctor gave the 'message,' pressing a Pashto Testament into the strong man's hands, and ever maintained that Chikai's ways softened somewhat therefrom. In any case his abstention from joining the 1897 rising very materially helped matters in the Kurram, where the situation was difficult enough in any case.

Alas! 'Be the day short or be the day long, at length it ringeth to evensong,' and Nemesis was to overtake the devil-may-care free-lance of the border. Growing careless perhaps, he with a party of his bodyguard were waylaid by a section of the Khabul Khel Wazirs, with whom was an ancient quarrel, and they all fell riddled with bullets. Chikai's heart was cut out, and carried off in triumph by his enemies, who boasted that it weighed twenty pounds. Such indeed is the end of most of these master-spirits of the border side.

When the British Army gets them, it makes fine soldiers of them and takes them round the world behind the Union Jack.

> 'Last night ye had shot at a border thief,
> To-night 'tis a man of the Guides.'

§ 2

A STUDY IN MARTYRDOM

The Keep of Doom.

'Glory for all and heaven for those who bleed.'

Five o'clock on a frontier afternoon, and the walls and loopholes of the militia fort at Sarwekai in the mountains of Southern Waziristan stood out sharp against the hill-sides and in the lengthening shadows above the main walls rose the inner keep on which all eyes in the garrison were directed. And an observer would have noticed that while there was no enemy to be seen, yet the garrison were under arms and gazing seemingly up at the keep. Half hidden by a mud-plastered buttress on the rampart, a British officer and two Indian officers also gaze upwards, also with rifles in their hands and with them an Indian corporal.

Then a khaki-clad figure climbed to the top of the keep parapet, rifle in hand, stretched himself erect and flung his rifle down among the soldiery gazing at him and cried, '*Allah ho akbar!*'[1] The corporal raised his rifle, aimed at the erect figure on the keep and fired. The figure remained for a moment poised still erect, span round and then fell with a crash into the terre-plein of the fort below. A prolonged Aah-a-h-h of relief went up. An assistant surgeon knelt over the body for a while and then waved his hand, on which

[1] 'God is great!'

four men brought up a stretcher covered with a white cloth, raised the body and bore it away.

It was not the only corpse within the walls of the fort on which the British Jack flew. Up in the officers' quarters awaiting portage to consecrated ground, lay the body of Major B – of the Political Service, murdered in his bed the preceding night, by the sentry on duty outside the officers' quarters, merely to make a Mahsud holiday. The strange scene just witnessed was no less than the execution of the murderer in due if peculiar form.

En avant, les enfants perdus.

> *Plantez un croix sur son tombeau,*
> *Gravez son nom, son numereau.*

It has been explained how, in accordance with Lord Curzon's policy, militias were organized to take the place of the Regular Army in guarding the trades routes in the tribal territory. Further, the militia corps were to provide that very necessary employment for the lads of the trans-border villages. Money to burn would quicken the interest in things British, and civilization and influences would slowly percolate.

It has been said how the tribesmen to many of the best young Britons, offered a delightful material on which to work. Virile, active, jaunty, warlike, many loved them and asked nothing better than to train and lead them. So the Viceroy's policy was admirably backed by the eagerness of high-grade young officers to serve in the Militias. On the other hand, some

Englishmen there were, indeed, to whom the Pathan character, with its infinite capacity for treachery – cruel and black-hearted treachery – was repugnant, and who could not weigh the good and the evil in the balance, and they had some reason for their dislike.

In Waziristan there were to be two Militia Corps. One, the Northern Corps, was to protect the Tochi and neighbourhood, the Southern, with its headquarters on the Plain of Wana, was to protect the Gomal and its passing caravans. Into this corps the Mahsud Waziris, long the leaders of the wolf's-head and stormy petrel business, were to predominate, steadied partly by some companies of clansmen from within the British border.

In addition to the Militias, there were Border Military Police and tribal levies of the type known throughout the frontier as 'Catchies,' which is short for 'Catch-'em-alive-oh,' a term referring more to the needs of their toilet, than their methods with prisoners. The organized Militia, with all the dress and gadgets of a regular corps, were far superior to such gentry, and sniffed accordingly. The Waziri Militias, especially the Southern Corps, were admittedly 'hard cases.'

But the more difficult and adventurous the job, the more the better type of Briton comes forward, and the Waziri Militia were soon officered with enterprising efficient officers, to whom service with Pathans was a joy.

But arrogant childish vanity, vanity of peculiar inhuman kind, is included in the Pathan make-up, and more especially in that of the Mahsuds, and most especially in that of the Shabi Khel section of the clan. It had entered into the head of a militia-man of the Shabi Khel, that however contented with their lot and attached to their officers they might be, it would redound to the credit of his clan if he murdered a British officer, the more important the better. Further, the political officer of the area was now sleeping under his protection as sentry on duty ten yards off. Whereon he up and shot him in his sleep. Having done so, he retired with his rifle and ammunition to the tower of the keep, which was unoccupied, and from there began to fire on anyone who approached. The officer commanding, who had hurried to the scene with the men of the post, ordered all under cover till daylight. The Indian or rather Pathan officers and the British officers were in parley, and the question of how to secure the murderer without loss at his hands, was discussed. Communications, at first confined to abuse, with the desperado, were entered into. Men of other tribes, furious at the deed, now covered every loop-hole of the murderer's sconce with their rifles, and now and again a marksman's bullet spat into the loop-holes behind which he was lurking. At last it was agreed that if he was shot by any ordinary man a blood feud would ensue. That this penalty should not be thrust unmerited on any individual, the men of the tribe in the corps, and the Pathan officers generally, had come to the conclusion that the proper thing now was for the murderer to be shot by a relative, and thus come into the category of accidental death.

The murderer's exaltation had now effervesced, and

before him loomed a dog's death on the ramparts after a snarling fight to a finish, or hanging in pigskins in front of a British prison, with all the world a-watching, to witness his discomfort in this world and the next. So that when the proposal came to him that he should stand forth and be shot cleanly through the heart by a blood-brother and a marksman, he gladly accepted, stipulating only that his corpse be restored to his relatives. To this request those in authority themselves agreed thoughtlessly, lest worse befall.

And it was the closing scene in this strange chapter from the white man's burden that is described at the opening of this story. Before passing on to the sequel, there is an interlude. The friends and relatives of the Shabi Khel bore their scion away, and buried him in ancient form with the recess for the questioning angel to sit by the body in the grave. But they also built a shrine above it, which was lit up with flickering chirags o' Fridays. All the country-side came to pay homage, and say their prayers at the grave of one who had so upheld the clan's reputation for irresponsible evil and ruthless treachery, and all the young sprigs of the country-side thought to do likewise. And thus were two young men martyred by the evil of one.

The Glamour of the Shrine.

> *'Shoot straight who may, ride hard who can,*
> *The odds are on the cheaper man.'*

It was not long before the first fruits of the lighted shrine were gathered, the result of the promise that the officer in Sarwekai had so thoughtlessly, though to Christian minds so reasonably, given. A few months later a new regiment came marching up into the frontier station and cantonment of Bannu on the banks of the Kurram River. It was that most beautiful of all seasons on the Indian Frontier, early spring. The air was yet clear of haze and the ring of snowy mountains of Pir Gul and Shuidhar and their spurs glistened in the morning sun above the cobalt hills that formed the Waziri habitat.

The brigadier-general commanding and his brigade-major had ridden down the road that wound from Kohat below the Kafir Kot, the hill of the unbelievers, where ruins of Macedon survive to this day. A dozen officers of the garrison and their wives were with the party to welcome the new arrivals and with them the band of the outgoing corps.

Up the road came the new battalion, playing on *dole* and *sarnai*[1], that lawless haunting Kabul love song, *Zakhmi dil*, the 'Bleeding heart,' so lilting and yet so lawless that no man dare put it into English, and the tired legs of the marchers responded. Half a mile from the station the brigadier met the newcomers, and set himself at the head, with the new band and all the welcomers, and in front of all the brigade-major. Then to 'My love is like the red, red rose,' to which in India men sing, 'The boar, the boar, the mighty boar,' the battalion swung along, past the clump of bamboos that waved a welcome, past the shrine and the old faqir who muttered under his breath as in duty bound, 'God

[1] Afghan drum and pipe.

smite their souls to the nethermost hell!' past the cemetery, where murdered officers and dead English babies lie in witness to the wandering race, over the bridge on to the *place d'armes* in front of the fort. Then just as the band broke to 'Garryowen,' a shot from under the culvert – it was hardly a bridge – and the brigade-major at the head of the procession fell from his horse. . . The men of the leading company flung themselves into the spruit and dragged out a tribesman, bayoneted, hammered with rifle butts, half scragged, and wholly man-handled, before the officers could intervene.

'Let them finish the brute off!' but the brigadier called out, 'Take him alive! We must find who sent him,' and so sufficient pieces to hang at leisure were collected, and all the while an English gentleman lay by the roadside dying, his wife and two surgeons by his side, and a ring of furious soldiery around, most of them frontiersmen at that.

A litter soon arrived, the battalion re-formed, and, dragging the murderer in their midst, filed to their lines, but with all the excitement and *éclat* of their arrival faded.

The Frontier Crimes Act loses no time in the administration of justice. The wretch before the court admitted that he belonged to the Shabi Khel, that he had come to murder a *sahib* to show what dare-devil lads his clan produced, and because the Mullah Powindah had promised a straight pass to paradise to all who slew an unbeliever. La la! The ignorance that would class a Christian one of the *Ahl-i-Kitab*, one of the 'People of the Book,' as 'unbeliever'! So the garrison cursed their old enemy the Mullah, and the clansman went to his doom as they shoot a mad dog, his doom of the gallows in a pigskin, to disabuse his mind and any of his friends of mistaken ideas of paradise for such as he. Before he died the prisoner was consumed with grief to learn that he had missed the general, who he thought must be riding first, and his dying moments were further saddened to hear, as he was falsely told, that his victim would live.

And this was all of a spring morning well into the twentieth century, when two more souls left the world before their time.

The Harvest Moon.

'Rien n'est sacré pour un sapeur.'

But tragedies such as I have related are but the cracking of the kitchen pipkins of Imperial policy, and the months rolled on and the militias grew in strength and discipline in the hills beyond the border. After the Saxon manner the officers of each battalion declared that theirs and theirs alone justified the Curzon experiment. In the Southern Waziristan Militia all was especially well, for they had the very best of all the frontier officers as colonel, one who understood the Pathan inside out, loved them all and was loved by them, yet the book of their uncurbed vanity and folly and all their ways, both good and bad, lay open before him. Discipline, activity, reliability, was the reputation they were acquiring and on the mountain tops in the

Himalaya the good Lord Curzon and his advisers rubbed together the hands of wisdom and prescience. But they had reckoned without their Shabi Khel. There had been no outrage on the border for some time, an attempt to murder an officer on the golf links at Bannu having failed. It had not been possible for the tribesmen to obtain the body of him that hung in the pigskin, and the shrine of the hero of Sarwekai alone bore the burden of remembrance. But on that the Mullahs set great store, and once a month held feast thereat, lest the youth of the glen should forget. Every Friday the little lamps flickered and leapt, and the pious dropped a stone on the growing cairn hard by.

In the fort on the upland hill-girt Plain of Wana, which was the headquarters of the Southern Waziristan Militia and guarded the great trade route of the Gomal to Ghazni, the colonel of the battalion sat at dinner with his officers, to the number of four, which included the political agent of the district and a subaltern of engineers who attended to the roads and the posts. Suddenly the mess havildar rushed in and shouted, '*Sipahi agya.*' 'A soldier has come.'

Behind him a young militiaman in uniform raised his rifle, the good Martin Henry of Government make, and shot the colonel across the mess-table through the heart. All was uproar, a dozen sepoys sprang from nowhere, an officer felled the assailant with a chair, the guard rushed and secured the prisoner but the colonel lay a-dying – dying to make a Mahsud holiday once again, for the murderer the third time was a Mahsud Waziri of the Shabi Khel.

But that was not all the story. Men of the garrison knew that something was a-foot, and several men of the Mahsud company had been seen to run from the vicinity of the officers' quarters. The Mahsud company happened for that month to be in charge of the inner keep and to be quartered therein. Within the keep was all the ammunition, the rations and the water reserve. How far was the company cognizant of the outrage? What were their intentions?

The officers of the corps held hasty conference with the native officers of the non-Mahsud companies. It was agreed that the first thing was to get that company out of the keep, and put a company beyond suspicion in. It was a most delicate and difficult matter, and to this day no one quite knows how the subahdar-major and two others persuaded that arrogant, unreasonable and excited crowd to come out. At last, however, after some hours of anxiety, the move was achieved. The Mahsuds filed out, laid down their arms and proceeded to tents outside the fort. The British officers now breathed more freely, for the nearest troops were close on a hundred marching miles away on the Indus banks, save for some small outposts. Four Europeans alone stood to hold some three hundred odd excited border militiamen, of whom a large proportion came from outside the actual border, over whom through their families authority had no control – excited militiamen with arms, precious Martin Henries in their hands! Happily a bold front was shown, and happily the Mahsud is hated as the princes of faithlessness along the whole border. The other clans stood staunch, and seeing it was so, the old British instinct to rule and lead shone forth. After an anxious night the murderer was put on his trial, while the Militia and no doubt the tribes around, wondered. There could but be one sentence, and that the magistrate under the Crimes Act promptly awarded. To hang by the neck till he was dead.

But it is one thing to condemn a Moslem to death under such circumstances, and quite another to carry out the sentence. Who was to do it? Not the Darwesh Khel Waziris! Not the Afridi of Orakzai! Not the Khattak or Bangash! That were trying loyal men and fellow Moslems too high. Not the scavengers of the fort establishment. Nay! That would be a deadly affront to all believers.

His Majesty's Royal Engineers are the handmaids of the Army, as well as its guide, philosopher and friend. The subaltern of engineers should make a gallows and a noose, and with the officers as sheriffs and warders, would be hangman. Vengeance, the vengeance of law, must be carried out at all costs, or the whole country-side might see the *sahibs* had fear.

So that subaltern of engineers set about his business, which the formation of the keep made easy enough for a man of resource. The keep was open; that is to say its four walls contained barracks and store rooms with rampart above, with a crenellated parapet on the outside, and a plain one on the side that surrounded and looked down into the inner court. A stout beam thrown across a corner of the inner court would serve as a gallows tree, with a rope and noose of sufficient length. Two Afridi officers brought up the murderer, who was duly trussed by British officers.

The sun had set, and the long shadows had fallen on the valleys, as the harvest moon came over the eastern hills, the well of the keep stood deep in gloom, and the crenellated parapet caught the last ray of after glow. An Afridi held a torch, as the engineer adjusted the noose, and at a sign from the magistrate, the officers heaved and the murderer hung into the gloom below, his limbs a-quivering. . . It was not in derision that the bugler sounded and all the officers stood to attention, but in tribute to the Empire whose writ ran once more, even as Admiral Parker raised his hat and thanked the mutineer at the Nore as the body was hauled to the yardarm.

*

One more task remained in the fort. There must be no more of the shrine and illumination business to inflame young men's minds. The body was taken by officers and scavengers out in the still moonlight through the postern at dead of night, and buried beneath the scattered heaps of burning litter from the mule lines, so that in the morning no man could tell the spot. A hundred miles away they buried the colonel in consecrated ground, with muffled drums a-moaning, and then as the troops marched home to jaunty airs the frontier set itself to the old task, policing, doctoring, teaching, relieving, in the hope that some day good might come of it.

*

And that is the story of three British officers martyred to make a Mahsud holiday, and how three highland vanity merchants whom God had made for a better end, left the world by way of bullet and glamoured grave, the pigskin noose, and the dung-yard, with six mothers a-grieving. 'But the leaves of the trees were for the healing of the nations.'

§ 3

SUBAHDAR DILAWAR KHAN OF THE GUIDES

One of the interesting and pathetic stories of the frontier, told at length by Sir Francis Younghusband, in his *History of the Corps of Guides*, is that of Dilawar Khan, the 'Lord of Courage,' an outlaw of the Khattak clan of Pathans and a native of the now well-known village of Jehangira near the Kabul River, between Attock and Nowshera. Before the Mutiny, when Major Lumsden commanded the Guides and was responsible for the rough-and-ready methods of quietening the frontier in Yuzufzai, Dilawar Khan was a well-known and enterprising wolf's head, whose ultimate end was obviously the gallows. But Lumsden always felt that hanging was a poor use to which to put brave men if you could avoid it, and sent for him, offering a safe conduct. Dilawar Khan knew every corner of the country-side, and it had occurred to Lumsden that he would be a very useful soldier of the Guides. Dilawar Khan came in on parole, a thing he

WITH THE EXPEDITION TO TIBET IN 1904
8TH GURKHAS AT PHARI JONG

'CHOICE YOUNG MEN AND GOODLY'
RAJPUT MOSLEM GUNNERS OF A MOUNTAIN HOWITZER

To face page 294

would never have done to any Sikh or Afghan official, and the two strong men held converse one with another. Lumsden explained that dodge him never so cleverly the Khattak must one day be hanged, there was no escape. 'Come to me and live a life of credit and honour.' But Dilawar Khan laughed and went away. He had been brought up for the priesthood before he took to outlawry, and had a penchant for religious dispute, generally been flung out for asking too persistent and searching questions on points of Moslem doctrine, far beyond the ken of ignorant frontier Mullahs. Then one fine day he came back, and asked to be enlisted, only bargaining that he should be excused the goose-step, for he had seen the contortions which that brought to splay-footed Pathans. 'No,' said Lumsden, 'enlist you may, but the goose-step you will learn like any other soldier,' and it was so. Dilawar Khan became a true and faithful soldier, helping in tracking many a robber and outlaw, and rising to be a native officer in the Guides, than which there is no higher thing. During his life he had many affrays by disputing with the Mullahs and then, lo! he embraced the Christian faith, and a devout and sincere Christian he became. Sent on secret service in his old age to Chitral he was imprisoned by the Mehtar, but released, and unfortunately died in the snow on his way back, a monument of faithfulness, and also to the influence that men like Lumsden had over such wild spirits.

§ 4

THE STORIES THAT COME THROUGH THE PASSES

The Cannon Balls

The stories that have come to India through the frontier hills are queer enough, and bear re-telling; some you will hear round the frontier mess tables, some I have heard from the lips of Sir Salter Pyne, the bull-dog Englishman who was so long head of the Amir Abdur Rahman's munitions factory, others from trans-border officers of frontier clans in the frontier regiments. Here is the yarn of the two rival chieftains in the Bazaar Valley, who long were at feud with each other.

They both lived in stone castles built, as in Genesis, with 'slime for mortar.' High loop-holed towers stood at their corners, with solid plinths that could not be mined, and solid embattled walls surrounded the dwelling, and the courtyards where the women pounded the corn. One, who we will call Alif Khan, was the proud possessor of an old iron cannon, filched in days gone by from some Afghan or Mogul passers-by. But while a cannon adds to prestige it needs cannon balls, and cannon balls were hard to come by. Alif Khan, in fact, had but six. Over the river which ran through the valley stood the equally solid castle of Beta Ali Shah, the head of another sub-division of the tribe, placed dourly enough on a bluff of conglomerate that overhung the camel track and the water mills by the river bank. Alif Khan and Beta Shah had been at some enmity all their lives touching a claim to water, and a few murders between the sections in years gone by. Both were old men now, and neither had killed his neighbour, and they were now inclined to let things be. But old feelings die hard, and whenever Beta Ali Shah came out to see his flocks or what not, Alif Khan would fire a round or two from his six-pounder gun, and if his eye was in would probably get a goat or two, and had once knocked his neighbour's headgear off. When, however, he had fired away all his rounds, there was nothing for it but to stand by. But Beta Ali Shah had all the Afghan desire for trade and profit. He would have the round shot collected, and sold to the Sikh *buniah*[1] who lived by the shrine and the pomegranate orchard. The Sikh, knowing the game, would sell them back to Alif Khan, so that the game might go on. And when you come to think of it, it was not a bad way for two old men to keep their hand in, the one for war and the other for trade, and quite as good as bowls on Cumberland turf.

Bangles ring softly and sadly.

Now let us turn from the ruth and think of fairer things. It is not unamusing to remember the somewhat unabashed courting that went on in Kabul during the first war. Our young officers with their pleasant manners soon attracted the attention of the, at best of times rather larky, Muhammadzai, and other ladies of birth. Many of our unattached officers had lodgings

[1] *Buniah*: trader.

in the city, and there was a good deal of flitting about the house tops. Afghan lords and masters were often dour and unapproachable. Afghan ladies, fair of hue and of peach blossom skin, were attractive enough to those who had been across the Indus a twelvemonth and more. The *burqa*, the great overall hood, with slits to the eyes, is useful for many purposes, and was born of intrigue as well as seclusion. So the sound of the British bugles that re-echoed against the Sher Darwaza heights, and the echo of the drums and fifes, had more than one message for the Afghan folk! Indeed, it was said that the uprising of the sudden wave of bitterness was not lessened by the knowledge that Afghan ladies themselves looked favourably on the newcomers.

True romance also flourished with all probity. Captain Warburton of the Shah's Artillery married in 1840 the widow of an Afghan chief, who was herself a niece of the Amir. Sir Richard Warburton of the Khaiber was born on 24th September 1842 in an Afghan fort between Gandamack and Jellalabad during the retreat of Elphinstone's brigade, offspring of the union. Mrs. Warburton had a small son by her Afghan lord, who was brought up by his stepfather as an English lad, and was well known for years as Mr. Warburton of the Punjab Police, well known also to be pure Afghan in blood.

The border march referred to so often played on pipe and tabor by the frontier corps, known as *Zakhmi dil*, the 'Bleeding heart,' was set to English metre by a band-sergeant in Kabul, where he had heard it in this first campaign. It is a lilting, jaunting air, with words, as I have said, that make your hair curl, in the Persian as well as the English, though no doubt there is a milder version. But to meet a frontier corps a-playing it on *dole* and *surnai*, the native drum and chanter, is to hear all the charm and romance of the wild border life, and even to see the Rohillas flocking to the loot of India.

The hard life of the frontier clans, however, makes no great shape of love and love-making, and the frontier lasses soon wear hard with all there is to endure. 'Romance' with a big 'R' is hard to find and little to last, for there is no man who makes of his wife a more drear chattel. Jealousy is fierce enough, and a nose may be sliced off for an escapade which the husband's conduct but richly justifies. Indeed, on the frontier side, if you would see what sort of comeliness lies behind a veil, the remark that the 'poor lass has surely lost her nose' will probably be rewarded with a glimpse that will reassure your doubt. Whether it is worth having when all is said and done is another matter.

Tender ruth on the border.

Still must this story of the frontier be a hard one. Of scarred ravines and rush of swordsmen, of all that is fierce and cruel and ruthless, and there has been little of touch of women and love of charm and rest by the fountain side. But then the frontiersmen are grim and bony, little given to life's easements and caring little therefor. For their cruelties enter into daily life, as this story once told me of his childhood by my orderly, Hamid Gul, a Ranizai from Swat. He and a band of children of his village were playing near a stream which divided them from another village, with which they were at enmity. Often had their mothers urged them to keep away and on no account to cross the burn, lest they be murdered or sold as slaves by their rivals across the valley. That day, as they were playing knuckle bones, none being perhaps over ten years of age, they noticed a child from the opposite side, a lad, perhaps of six years of age, had paddled over the burn chasing butterflies on this side. Immediately the children rushed down and seized him, and without ado stretched his poor little weasand and slit it with some boy's pocket knife. That in a nutshell is the trans-border life, to which, however slowly, British neighbourliness has brought some softening.

Sikh and Afghan.

Between Sikh and Afghan there was no love lost, nor is to this day. When Afridi and Orakzai attacked the posts on the Samana Range in 1897, they captured the signal tower of Saragarhi, as already related, which connected Forts Lockhart and Gulistan. They put the survivors, all of whom were wounded, to a short death, but the two Sikh cooks they roasted alive. If a Sikh or Gurkha find a wounded Afghan on the hill-side, as likely as not, if no *Sahib* be about, 'twill be, '*Ahre Bhai! Matches hai?*' 'Have you matches, comrade?' They would set the man alight for the fun of seeing his powder pouch or bandolier explode. I have seen a wounded tribesman strapped down to a native bed by four followers, non-combatants of our own, and a fire of dried thorn prepared below. Our arrival alone saved the wretch. But followers, on the other hand, receive scant mercy from a Pathan, and I've seen one murdered with his heart cut out, so cruel and fierce is the border law of enmity and hatred, and 'All that man unto man has done.'

There is a story well known on the frontier years ago now belike forgotten. It was just after the battlefield of Shabkadr in 1897 when the Mohmands had invaded British territory and had been attacked by a column out hot-haste from Peshawar. The 13th Bengal Cavalry, which had made their famous charge under Joey Sahib, was just over. The weary Somerset Light Infantry, hot and thirsty, were resting while the general and staff were surveying the field. Here and there spattering shrapnel pursued groups of Mohmands making for their own hills. A little way off lay a wounded clansman, whom none had helped away. A Sikh trooper of the 13th rode up, dismounted and propped the wounded man against a stone. Five hundred yards away the general was looking through his glasses. 'Look!' he cried, 'look! People tell me of the bitter hatred between Sikh and Pathan, but that trooper has got off his horse to tend and relieve that wounded Mohmand.' The staff got out their glasses and looked. The Sikh had got to his horse, mounted, and shook out his lance. Then he cantered away. A hundred yards on he turned about, held his lance aloft, clapped spurs to his horse, which started with a bound in the air. On the breezes came the exultant cry as he galloped at the wretch he had propped up, as men gallop at a tent peg. '*Ah-h-h Khalsa ka Fatteh Sirkar ka Fatteh.* I'm Jowand Singh. *A-h-h-h Hamara dushman hai.*' 'Victory to Sikhdom and the English. He is my enemy.'

And the luckless man was struck fair in the breast, and the trooper looked back along his lance as it cleared from the corpse.

CHAPTER TWELVE

THE NORTH-EASTERN AND EASTERN FRONTIERS

§ I

THE NORTH-EASTERN FRONTIER

IT is now time to turn from the maze of events connected with the age-old making of India staged on the North-west Frontier and look again on those other thousands of miles of frontier outlined in Chapter One. From the very nature of things, they do not scintillate with battle, murder and sudden death, as do the hills of Roh, and their story, while worthy of many books on many subjects, must stand outside to a great extent, a work dealing with The Romance of the Frontiers, when the word 'Romance' is made to stand for war and armies and migrations.

But to minister to that side of the many-headed word which deals with pike and gun, let it be said that four war medals of the British Army deal with this frontier also. First and foremost in interest is the India Medal to 'The Army of India,' which ran from 1799 to 1826, and covered the wars of Lord Lake and Arthur Wellesley; the first Burma War, and the capture of Bhurtpore, has two clasps for active service on the Eastern and North-eastern Frontier, viz.

'*Nepal*' and '*Ava*,' for 1814-16 and 1825 respectively. The 'India Medal of 1854' has for the North-eastern Frontier clasps '*Bhootan*' (1864), '*Sikkim* 1888,' '*Looshai*' (1871-2), '*Manipur*' (1891), '*Naga Hills*,' '*N.E. Frontier* 1891,' while on the Eastern Frontier we have '*Pegu*' for the Burmese War of 1853-4, we have '*Burma* 1885-7,' '*Burma* 1887-9,' '*Burma* 1889-92,' '*Kachin Hills* 1892-93,' and '*Chin Hills* 1892-3.'

For the Tibet War of 1904 there is a special medal with clasp '*Gyangtse*,' and among the clasps on the 'Third India Medal' is a clasp '*Abor*.' So much for the sheer swashbuckling, apart from gentler matters.

It has been explained how the Buddhism that was born in India is seemingly more suited to the people of the Mongold Fold than to Aryan and Semite. We have seen India fall away from Buddhism eventually, while centuries before, this philosophy had spread into the mountains and across to China and Tibet. We have seen the British fighting in the 'nineties among the beautiful ruins of a time when Buddhism joined forces with the art of the Greeks in Bactria, and filled a great kingdom with its carvings and art. As India fell away China long remembered whence its enlightenment came, and for many years, right up in fact till fierce Islam chased away the Buddhist calm, the pilgrims came to India to visit the monasteries in Swat and to see the shrine in which lay the ashes of the Buddha. And those ashes lay in that same city of Peshawar, the city of violence and the come and go of armies, so sung of in the previous chapters and so unlike anything to which Buddhist pilgrims would wish to visit.

This northern pilgrims' road is very fascinating to us, and it is largely to the adventurous travels of Sir Aurel Stein of the Archaeological Department that it is so. We can see amid the dead poplar forest the high valleys where the ancient races lived and where the Chinese armies fought and whence they even entered India, remembering that the great Chinab, one of the five rivers of the Punjab, but means 'River of China.' Some day, as already suggested, when we can really explore Swat, we shall find much more about those long dead civilizations that crowd on our frontiers. When a frontier faces north-west and also north-east, there must be an apex where the two meet, and that apex is near where the northern pilgrim route came out of Yarkand and over the Mustagh or Karakorum Range, and down the Indus Valley to Skardu. The little Dardic states which fringe the apex have been already described under the north-west face of India, and we need not trouble them again, but look over the corner to the north-east and see Chinese Turkestan with Yarkand and Kashgar, the dead forests aforesaid, and the Lobnor and other spots of dread high interest. Here we see Buddhism and Islam, inter-mingling and struggling, and we shall meet the Tartar with the Moslem name and similar folk who profess the Buddhism that so much better suits their mentality, when they have a mentality worthy of any name at all.

The Indus Valley, we shall see from the map, curls away south on and on for many a hundred miles, till it becomes the Gartang River by far Gantok, in Tibet, and nearly meets the Brahmaputra which curls north for many a hundred miles, reaching almost to the holy lake of Manasarowa, which actually gives source apparently to the Sutlej, a tributary of mother Indus, the two great rivers thus curling round behind the Himalaya till they almost meet in their sources, a very remarkable geographical phenomenon.

If you march up the gorges of the Indus, up and down, up and down, over the giant spurs, you will come to the Tibetan province of Kashmir that men call Ladakh, and there at the town of Leh you will find the famous Himis Lamasery, the best known to all travellers of the Buddhist monasteries of Tibet. Here, years ago, was written by a young Cossack officer who had broken his leg in the mountains and was recovering and being cared for in the Lamasery, a work that caused some excitement. There he had access, or was said to have had access, to many old and strange documents in the possession of the monks, which were known to exist. When he returned he amazed the world by publishing a Life of Christ, which he had, he said, discovered in the Himis Lamasery. And for a short while he 'got away with it.' There was some slight colour to such an idea in the fact that the Moslems in Kashmir reverence and show a so-called 'Tomb of Christ,' based on one of the many Jewish stories of survival from the Cross and subsequent world wanderings. Master Nicholas Notovich, an attractive-looking young gentleman in his Cossack uniform, had successfully pulled the legs of the Pundits, by his amazing cheek, which, apart from the unsuitability of

THE EASTERN FRONTIER
THE GEKTEEK VIADUCT, SHAN STATES

THE POTALA AT LHASA, THE VATICAN OF CENTRAL ASIA, WHERE DWELLS THE DULAI LHAMA

To face page [illegible]

his subject, is in itself an achievement, even if on the wrong side of the blanket.

§ 2

TIBET

Tibet itself is a mighty land and a mighty subject, from its barrier of the Kunlung Range, which separates it from Chinese Turkestan in the north, to its merging in the south with the undefined and unbounded northern marches of British Burma. Like so much of the eastern world, it has had some relationship and some subservience to China in the past, and it has always, as said, been the wish of Great Britain that Tibet should stand by itself free of Chinese and Russian domination, and remain aloof as the spiritual home of a branch of Buddhism.

From early years the British in India have entered into friendly relations whenever possible with her, and as a 'nation of shopkeepers,' trade, its assistance and stimulation, has always been in the forefront of our policy. Tibet, like China, however, has been subject to fits of sulkiness and aloofness, added to a great impertinence in the neighbourly conduct of essential business. When these fits have been on, often due to some Chinese or Russian influence, friendly relations have been impossible. So far back as 1887, a British trade mission was proposed with the general consent of China, but was refused admission by Tibet. The Tibetans then took upon themselves to invade Sikkim, a little state under British protection. They erected fortifications, blocking the trade route in Sikkim and endeavoured to include that state within their dominion. A British expedition came to the support of Sikkim in 1888, and duly expelled by force the invading Tibetans. The British troops crossed the Jalep Pass, and pursued them as far as Chumbi, which they had richly deserved. China then agreed with India on a frontier boundary on behalf of Tibet, and proposed certain trade conventions. For a good many years no very satisfactory relations supervened, and by 1902 the situation had become acute, and a Russian Buriat, by name of Dorjieff, was exercising considerable influence over the Dulai Lama, the spiritual as well as temporal ruler of the state. Buriats are a Mongol Buddhist race, long subjects of Russia, and in the whole of Russian Mongolia there are hundreds of thousands of Buddhists who look to Tibet as a spiritual home. Through them Russia has always an opportunity to intrigue in the country.

Tibet still refused trade and friendly relations, and even hinted at Russian support. A British Mission, with escort under Colonel Younghusband, proceeded to the frontier to endeavour to get some discussion and settlement, but the Tibetans refused to negotiate, and endeavoured to delay the Mission so that it should be involved in the hideous cold of the Tibetan winter. Additional troops were sent to the base of the Mission, and eventually it was decided that Tibet must be taught to be a reasonable neighbour, and that the Mission should advance, till the Tibetan Government should send someone to meet it and discuss affairs. Brigadier-General J. R. MacDonald was given command of the escort, which was now a compact force specially selected for the extremely arduous work to be done. The most complete winter outfit, resembling that of an Arctic expedition, was issued to the troops, and the supply question which was obviously going to be the crux of the campaign, secured by organizing a magnificent corps of the best pack mules in India, and hiring large numbers of Yaks, the pack bullocks of Tibet, alone suited for work in the high altitudes.

By December 1903 this all-weather force started on its mission, the like of which had never been seen. It was to penetrate into almost unknown regions full of witches, devils, strangeness and romance all invoked to withstand us, while far away over lofty passes and rivers lay the holy unseen Lhasa, of which not even a photograph had reached the outer world.

Climbing and nursing their transport, and halting long at Phari to collect supplies, the force marched through Sikkim and eventually reached Guru, a hundred odd miles on the road to Lhasa. There were 3000 Tibetan troops, with civil officials, and the Mission was requested to return. This was not acceded to, and hundreds of excited Tibetans were seen swarming in their defences close by, but the British troops were forbidden to fire. They, however, concerned themselves with bundling the Tibetans out of various stone works that threatened the force. Eventually the latter were all collected round their generals, and surrounded by the British, who had a force of four guns, two hundred mounted infantry, and nine companies of infantry. The Tibetans were then told they must retire or lay down their arms, Tibetan and British officials mingling together while the discussion was in progress. Suddenly a shot was fired. It is said that the Tibetan general drew his revolver and blew off a Sikh soldier's jaw. In the mêlée which ensued, several officers were cut down. The fat was now in the fire; our troops replied, and the Tibetans, suffering very heavily, fled. It was all over in a few moments, some ammunition and a few Russian small bore rifles being abandoned by the Tibetans. The remainder of the enemy, to the number of several thousand, then withdrew towards Gyantse. More supplies arriving, the British pushed on their thrice adventurous march by the shores of the frozen Lake Bhamtso.

The Tibetans were now reported in force at Zamdung or 'Red Idol' Gorge, eighteen miles from Gyantse. To capture the Zamdung position, a climb of 3000 feet by a party of Gurkhas was necessary, while British and Tibetan guns exchanged shot for shot. At last, high up above the force, came the sound of the Gurkhas' rifles. The force then advanced, and the position was carried. The Tibetans, hopelessly inept and foolishly stubborn, lost heavily and fled to Gyantse, which our troops reached on the 11th April. Next day fort and town surrendered, and was found to have plenty of grain, which was a very great asset. This town, like most Tibet towns, is picturesquely perched on steep and rugged rocks, stands some 13,000 feet above the sea, and is the third biggest town in Tibet. So here we see a small British force hundreds of miles from home campaigning about the level of Mount Blanc.

§ 3

TO HOLY LHASA

The British were not prepared to take over the jong, and they moved their camp to Chunglu, some three-quarters of a mile from the town. It was now pretty evident that the Mission would have to go on to the holy city, a matter of two hundred miles and more. This would mean more troops to hold the long line of communications, and far more complex arrangements for maintenance. General MacDonald therefore returned to Chumbi to discuss the matter with Government and make preparation, leaving Colonel Brander at Chunglu. All was quiet at Gyantse, but no signs of Tibetan envoys or the expected Chinese Amban. But while MacDonald was marching back amid terrible blizzards, Brander learnt that the Tibetans were establishing themselves in force at the Karo Pass, some fifty miles ahead on the road to Lhasa. The road from Gyantse makes a curious twist to the south-east for some miles, and at the Karo Pass the Tibetans could threaten the road from India by another route. Brander, a man of action, decided to attack and disperse them forthwith, and moved forth with a small column. Three thousand Tibetans were entrenched at a height of 16,400 feet, and to circumvent them our turning parties climbed to the astounding heights of

19,000 feet above the sea. The Tibetans, when turned thus, fled after suffering considerably. Captain Bethune, a daring officer of the 32nd Pioneers, was killed, and eighteen men killed or wounded. While this was in progress, two thousand Tibetans attacked Major Murray of the 8th Gurkhas, holding with eighty rifles the post of Chunglu. Major Murray had no difficulty, however, in repulsing the Tibetans, who lost heavily. Reinforcements, however, had began to arrive, and an adequate supply depot established, thanks to the supreme energy and endurance on behalf of man and beast of the transport service.

It was now ascertained that the Tibetan forces, to the number of some 16,000 men, were collected at various places on the route to Lhasa, but that supply difficulties prevented them concentrating.

In June, as preparations for the move on Lhasa were nearly ready, the chief of Bhutan, the Tongsa Penlop, arrived in camp and was intensely impressed with what he saw of the force. He eventually accompanied Younghusband and MacDonald to Lhasa, and was helpful as an intermediary. General MacDonald, with further reinforcements necessary for a move to Lhasa, left Chumbi on 12th and 13th June, and by 22nd June the leading column was at Kangma, forty miles from Gyantse.

During his longish wait Brander, outside Gyantse, was more or less invested, and the Tibetans were now in force in several places round about, and were holding the Gyantse jong itself in great strength. As soon as MacDonald had succeeded in effecting a junction with

Brander and defeating various parties of the enemy, he attacked Gyantse jong, and breached the walls. The breach was then stormed by a party of the 8th Gurkhas, supported by the Royal Fusiliers, a pretty desperate service in which Lieutenant Grant of the 8th earned a Victoria Cross; indeed, the whole tenor of the fighting was severe, the Tibetans displaying great courage.

From Gyantse the road to Lhasa ran south-east for a while before bending round to the River Tsangpo, which, also known as the Lu, is but the Brahmaputra of Bengal. By 16th July, a force destined for Lhasa was on the summit of the Karoo by a glacier 16,000 feet above the sea, with vast snow peaks on either side. Again were our troops in their turning movements up to an altitude of close on 20,000, a feat to make Alpinis themselves marvel. It was not till 24th July that the force was able to complete the descent into the valley of the Brahmaputra. The crossing, which had to be made by ferry boats, was an arduous business, taking seven days, and during it one of the most indispensable men, Major Bretherton, the chief supply and transport officer, was accidentally drowned. By now Tibetan officials were continually arriving offering any terms to prevent us approaching the Holy City. The time for negotiation, however, was past, and it was realized that now only, by occupying Lhasa, could a real lesson be given, and the hide of the wilful misunderstanding and insolence of the Tibet state-craft be pierced.

By the 2nd August, the force, in great expectation,

halted at Trilung Bridge, whence the shining roofs of the Potala were visible six miles away. The Tibetans now expressed a desire for peace, and only craved that their holy places should be spared. That of course, went without saying, and the troops had been scrupulous enough in this matter already, during their advance.

A full description of Lhasa would be a wonderful thing, but while the city was foul and dirty in many ways, the great hill of the Potala on which was built the palace and monastery of the Dulai Llama, the 'Vatican of Central Asia,' came up to all expectations, standing up pile on pile, scarp on scarp. Half the population was monk or nun in the portion devoted to monastery and nunnery, and in the remaining half women predominated.

The Tibetans were now ready enough to negotiate a reasonable and friendly arrangement, such as any responsible state would have been glad to accept from the first, and when this was concluded, on 23rd September the forces started back.

As the force was leaving there was a pleasing enough scene. The Ti Rimpoche, or Regent, caught up the column on the march and asked for an interview with General MacDonald. When this was granted the old man called down blessings of Buddha on his head, presenting him with a small golden image of 'The Master,' thanking him for his humanity and praising the discipline and conduct of the troops.

By the 19th October, the force, after considerable vicissitudes from blizzards, had safely descended from the great uplands and was at Chumbi, where it broke up, amid the congratulations of His Majesty and all in authority. The altitude map attached gives some idea of the feat accomplished, which probably no other army but our own could have carried through. It may be noted that the distance from Silluri to Lhasa is some 400 miles, the distance from London to Aberdeen, and to this must be added the height above the sea, and the well-known difficulty of continuous marching and climbing at the average altitude of 14,000 feet, with excursions to 20,000.

And thus it was that one of the world's most romantic veils was lifted, and the world was not disappointed in the scene behind it.

Since this somewhat brusque inception of friendship, the seed laid has flowered greatly. In 1921 Sir Charles Bell, the political agent on the Tibet border, spent eleven friendly months there, and while the attitude of a new China is an anxiety, the checking the design of Soviet Russia – Imperial Russia had definitely disavowed any interests in Tibet – will always call for watchfulness, and the careful maintenance of friendly relations with Lhasa. Happily those do continue, for a new phenomenon has recently occurred, for in 1930 the British Agent at Gyantse, Lieutenant-Colonel J. L. R. Weir, and his wife, actually reached Lhasa on the invitation of the Dulai Lama, Mrs. Weir being practically the first European woman to reach the holy city.[1] She has actually – a woman, an English woman – sat chatting and laughing with His Supreme Holiness himself, to whom all women are anathema, and apparently,

[1] Other than a French lady smuggled in some years earlier.

thereby, still further stimulating the Lama's friendly feeling to everything British, and especially to his most charming visitor. In fact, never have there been such goings on before in Buddhist circles.[1]

§ 4

NEPAL

In Chapter One some outline has been given of the friendly and independent neighbour whose territory marches with British India for five hundred miles. The early campaign has been alluded to which the British fought for over a year about the time of Waterloo, too remote a period for the details of the war to be given here at length. It was a war that clinched a friendship, and in which the prisoners were promptly enlisted into the British Army, as the Sirmur, Malaon, Kumaon, and Nasseree Battalions.

Forty years later, in 1857, Jung Bahadur brought a large force of his troops down to assist us in the capture of Lucknow, giving also six battalions to complete General Franks' division fighting rebels on the Gogra River, before the assembly for that clinching operation. In 1917-18 again did the Nepal Government bring troops to assist in the protection of India, and actually now lets the Government of India recruit twenty battalions for the Indian Army from among the Mongoloid subjects of that Rajput throne of Nepal.

[1] We may expect, in due course, to hear more of it from the adventurous lady herself.

Perhaps one of the graver anxieties from which the Indian Government suffers is that Nepal shall quarrel with Tibet, a habit of long standing. The aloofness of Tibet and her dislike of strangers may indeed be attributed to some of the deeds of Nepal. When Rajah Pritwi Narain of Gurkha,[1] commenced his career of aggrandisement in the middle of the eighteenth century, he soon came to loggerheads with Tibet, commencing his incursions in 1768. As a result, by 1792 all trade with India was stopped, and the period of aloofness commenced. As has already been said, the possible world complications inherent in the India border, are always a matter for care and for central direction, and must always remain in the hands of the Governor-General.

The actual border between India and Nepal is largely made up of a swamped and overgrown forest land, known as the Terai, chiefly famous for its big game harbours. The routes into the interior, along which trade and population go to Katmandu and other populous centres, are few. The Terai and lower reaches of Nepal are more than malarious at certain seasons, and a contrast to the fine uplands of the interior. Britons who are accustomed to the short thick-set little Gurkha soldiers who serve His Majesty, do not realize that what in effect is the ruling race, are tall Aryan Rajputs. The Nepal army itself enlists many of these races, who in the Indian Army serve in the 9th Gurkhas alone. It is to be remembered that Nepal is a semi-Tibetan country, conquered by Rajputs and

[1] Gurkha is a town in Nepal.

colonized by that race in parts, where the Mongoloid tribes adopted in some rather indefinite way such attributes and practices of the Hindu religion as were permitted to them. It is their unconcern in the more ritualistic rules of Hindu life that makes them such good soldiers in the field. The high caste Indian soldier's food restrictions are inimical to his health under active service conditions, and it is with difficulty, despite priestly dispensation, that he will do without them. For this reason the Brahmin regiments failed absolutely in the World War, refusing to feed in messes and touch food in the trenches. Not so Magar and Gurung, the favourite tribes from which our Gurkha soldiers enlist. Among the quaint little romances of Army life in India, none is more noticeable than the *camaraderie* between the Gurkhas and the British soldier, especially developed when the corps be Rifles or Highlanders, the former a memory of the Siege of Delhi, and the blood alliance between the Sirmur Battalion and the 60th Rifles. The Indian soldier and his British comrade are usually more aloof. All the regiments that enlist, hillmen and Punjabis, encourage the Scottish pipes, which indeed in some form or other is the instrument of all mountaineers. In the Gurkha corps it is a serious cult, and the pipers wear the plaids of various Scottish setts. On a guest night in a Gurkha regiment, after the pipers have played round the mess-table, the Gurkha pipe-major will take his tot of whisky and call *Slanthe!* with any pipe-major in Christendom. There is a story of the Afghan Amir, Shere Ali, who not only put a regiment into Highland dress, but made his men wear pink fleshings on the knees. The Gurkha soldier of the British enlistment is, as has been said, thick-set and short. During the World War in France and elsewhere, he found himself hard put to it when taking over the trenches of Europeans or ordinary Indians.

The little Gurkha women who accompany their men to the British lines are a pleasing roundabout little folk, who make merry on every occasion. It is said that the wife proper stays at home to look after the family corn patch, and that some merry stepney takes her place in the regimental quarters, and no doubt it may be so, for the ways of the East are simpler than the ways of the West.

§ 5

SIKKIM AND BHUTAN

East of Nepal lies the small state of Sikkim, close to our Himalayan hill station of Darjeeling, where the great panorama of Everest (which is in Nepal) strikes the eye. Sikkim is a country of scarcely 3000 square miles and under 60,000 Mongoloid Tibetan people. In 1888, as related, it was necessary to send an expedition against the Sikkimese, for which a medal was granted.

After some period of misunderstanding, Sikkim now remains content and prosperous in her trade with British India. The military expedition to expel the Tibetan invaders, already described, is commemorated by the clasp '*Sikkim* 1888,' in the 'India Medal of 1854.' East of Sikkim lies the much larger state of Bhutan, also Buddhist and consisting of a Mongoloid people akin to the Tibetans. Campaigns in the past have also been necessary against Bhutan, but of no very desperate nature and but a preliminary to better understanding. In the days of Warren Hastings, excellent relations had been set up with the Bhutanese, and their slave raids into Kuch Behar brought to an end. During the first half of the nineteenth century the country was in the hands of powerful chiefs, who defied their spiritual head, the Shapdung Rimpoche, incorrectly known in India as the Dharma Rajah, and the temporal authority through whom he worked, the Druk Gyalpo, called in India the Deb Rajah, and relations with India were unsatisfactory. After the Indian Mutiny in 1863-64, a military expedition entered the country to enforce better relations and put an end to slave raiding, since when excellent relations have prevailed.

Sir Ugyen Wangchuk, formerly a local chief, the Tronsa Penlop, was elected in 1907 by the other chiefs as Maharajah of the whole of Bhutan. The year before he had come into India to meet King George, then the Prince of Wales. Since his election he has held his barons happily together and kept his state in admirable relationship with the paramount power. In this picturesque country the population almost all dwell in fortified single farms in Saxon fashion, there being no villages, and only the governors own jongs or hill-top castles. It consists of three zones, the lower lying below 4000 feet, feverish and uninhabited, the second 4000 to 10,000 feet, the inhabited part, and in the third or northern and more lofty zone, live in the grazing months the cattle graziers and the like. Bhutan, however, holds itself aloof from India, and save on occasion Europeans other than Government representatives are not encouraged. When princes have toothache the dentist is welcomed, and in times of cholera missionary ladies have also been allowed to come to the aid of the stricken districts.

§ 6

THE ASSAM BORDER

A glance at the map will show that the long arm of Assam has frontiers, as explained in Chapter One, on both its sides inhabited by Mongoloid tribes of varying proclivities. North are the indefinite hill tracts which merge into the Tibetan Himalaya, in which are a series of small tribes, the principal being, beginning in the west, the Akkas, Daphlas, and Miris, and then on both sides of the Brahmaputra after the turn to the north has been made, that very tiresome folk the Abors. When the great river turns north there flows into it from the north-east the Dibang. On both sides of that river are the Mishmi tribes, and from here the hills curl round to meet those from Burma, and we come to the Singphos who are but Chingpaws or Kachins in other guise. The hills continue now to the south to make the southern frontiers of Assam, and contain the wild head-hunting Nagas, the Lushai Hills, the States of Khasia and Jaintia, containing Garois, Jaintias, Khasas and Cacharis, referred to in Chapter One.

There have been innumerable small expeditions against most of these tribes in the last eighty years, carried out as a rule by the three Gurkha regiments formerly stationed in Assam, which had six mountain guns. The Abors for many years were most troublesome, but in 1911-12 were very thoroughly handled, and since then have settled down. The Lushais have given great trouble in the past, including a very serious rising in the 'seventies, when Kohima was besieged. The 'India Medal of 1854' has clasps for '*Looshai*' (1871-2), '*Lushai* 1889-92,' '*N.E. Frontier* 1891' and '*Naga Hills* 1879-80,' while the strange rebellion on the State of Manipur which lies south of the Lushai Hills, described in Chapter One, earned the clasp for '*Manipur* 1891.' Reference has been also made in Chapter One to this story. The withdrawal of the Gurkha escort, taking with them Mrs. Grimwood, the widow of the murdered commissioner, will long be remembered. The whole rather miserable episode was enlivened and redeemed by the famous advance to Thobal of Lieutenant Grant with a small party from the Burmese side, who made naught of the Manipuris. Lieutenant Grant very properly was awarded the Victoria Cross.

The Abor Expedition of 1911-12 earned the clasp '*Abor*' to the new frontier medal.

Assam and its borders have now, however, passed happily into the piping times of peace. Civilization and progress have won the day, and regular troops are practically no longer needed. An admirable force of military police enlisted from Jerwas and other local tribes managed on Gurkha lines is sufficient to put a stop to any recrudescence of the old ways. The military police, however, have a soldiering record of which any frontier troops might be proud.

§ 7

THE EASTERN FRONTIER

The Eastern Frontier of India is, as has been outlined in Chapter One, the frontier of the Province of Burma. The Province of Burma, which may ere long become a separate country, as distinct from India, has a long mountain border, which divides British territory from China, French Indo-China, and Siam. Burma, as will be seen from the study of a detailed map,[1] contains certain areas of 'Native States,' *i.e.* states that are managed generally by their own chiefs and Tsabwas, and certain tracts which are directly under the Governor and not under the parliamentary Government of the province. They are in all cases the hills of backward and aboriginal tribes, or tribes whom the King of Burma could not control, but who have been brought into order since the days of the annexation.

The Province of Burma has been falling into our hands since 1826, always as the result of the greatest

[1] That published with the First Part of the Simon Report, is as good as any that can be obtained.

disregard by the Burman throne of all the fair interests of British and Indian trade, the ill-treatment of our nationals, and the most studied Chinese-like insolence in answering all representations. The British first were compelled to go to war with Burma, *i.e.* the throne of Ava, in 1824, in the campaign known as the First Burmese War, again in 1853-54 and thirdly in 1885. After each campaign, certain tracts of country were taken in lieu of indemnity, and after the third war, when any other settlement seemed hopeless, the whole country was annexed.

A clasp for '*Ava*' on the 'India Medal' was awarded for the first war, that for '*Pegu*' on the 'India Medal of 1854,' for the second war, and that for '*Burma* 1885-7' for the annexation. The subsequent pacification was a lengthy business of very hard marching and fighting by small bodies of men led by junior officers, occasioned largely by the army of Thebaw being allowed, after the capture of Mandalay, to disband with their arms in their hands. It earned a clasp, '*Burma* 1887-9.'

Two of Rudyard Kipling's ballads tell the story of the jungles on the Burman frontiers with lilt and feeling, the Ballad of 'Bo Da Thone,' and 'The Grave of the Hundred Head.' The former aptly describes the scrambled hasty fighting of the frontier troops.

'The word of a scout . . . a march by night . . .
A rush through the mist . . . a scattered fight,
A volley from cover . . . a corpse in the clearing . . .
A glimpse of a loin cloth and heavy jade earring.'

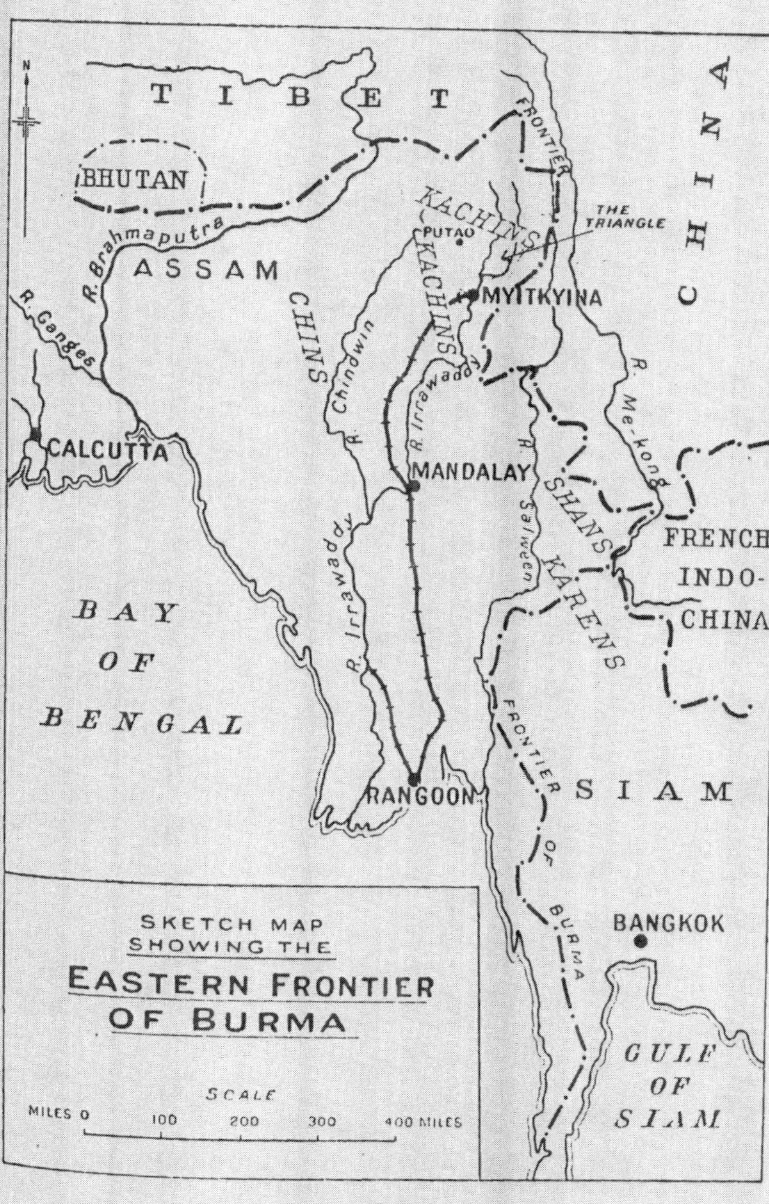

SKETCH MAP
SHOWING THE
EASTERN FRONTIER
OF BURMA
SCALE
MILES 0 100 200 300 400 MILES
N
TIBET
CHINA
BHUTAN
ASSAM
CHINS
KACHINS
KACHINS
KACHINS
PUTAO
THE TRIANGLE
FRONTIER
MYITKYINA
R. Brahmaputra
R. Ganges
CALCUTTA
R. Chindwin
R. Irrawaddy
R. Irrawaddy
R. Irrawaddy
MANDALAY
R. Salween
SHANS
KARENS
R. Me-kong
FRENCH
INDO-
CHINA
BAY
OF
BENGAL
RANGOON
FRONTIER
OF
BURMA
SIAM
BANGKOK
GULF
OF
SIAM

And then the press through the long grass by the river-side and the rice patch:

> 'The wind of the dawn went merrily past,
> The high grass bowed her plumes to the blast,
> And out of the grass on a sudden, broke
> A spirtle of fire, a whorl of smoke.'

After the pacification of Burma proper, and the extermination of the innumerable bands of soldier-bandits with which the country-side was terrorized, the attention of the Government was directed to the hill tribes on the borders, whose behaviour on the trade routes was anything but desirable.

The province of Burma had two frontiers, that which divided it but distantly from India, by a large area of jungle mountains inhabited by a slave-owning head-hunting folk known generally as Chins and nearer Assam as Nagas. With these for six or seven years after the annexation, small military and police columns wrestled mightily, and wearily, till at last the folk settled to realize that they must not raid and must not head-hunt. For these very continuous raids there are clasps on the 'India Medal of 1854,' '*Chin Lushai* 1889-90,' '*Burma* 1889-92,' '*Chin Hills* 1893' and '*Kachin Hills* 1893.'

But the romantic part of the tribal tracts as outlined in Chapter One are the Kachin Hills. These hills run far north on both sides of the two branches of the Irrawaddi, the 'Nmaikha and the 'Nmalikha, amid bamboo jungles and mighty teak forests. In the far north they are still unexplored and the actual British limit so far as China or Tibet is concerned still unfixed and likely for long to remain so.

§ 8

KACHIN LAND

The Kachins are a race or a *mélange* of races which for many generations and indeed many centuries have been pressing down from some undefined matrix in the north. Mongoloid like the Chins, and, but more attractively so, more Tartar and less aboriginal, they have many attractive qualities, and of recent years have taken to military and police service. In the far flinging of the British legions during the World War, a battalion with several hundred Kachins in its ranks went to Mesopotamia and took a leading part in operations against those very Kurds whom Xenophon called 'the shrill-voiced Carduchi' from their habit of calling across deep valleys one to another. The author saw active service against these very Kachins in 1892-93 and took part in the opening up of the trade routes with China on which, like the mountaineers of the North-west Frontier, they grew fat on despoiling or at least extracting heavy blackmail from 'gorbellied knaves.' Twenty-seven years later it fell to his lot to serve with them instead of against them, and to be the commander-in-chief, under whom the Burma Rifles, full of Kachins aforesaid, served against the Kurds. It was his privilege then to decorate a Kachin corporal for gallantry at the storming of the Bazian Pass at the entrance to the Kurdish Hills of Sulimanieh, when the last time of meeting had been on the top of a captured Kachin stockade emptying his revolver on to the tribesmen inside. And very fine little soldiers they make, somewhat like Gurkhas in appearance.

The sketch map in the text will show the general habitat of the Kachin tribes who have been pressing steadily south for so long, but who now, at any rate while the *Pax Britannica* lasts, have become stabilized except so far as any organized colonization may allow otherwise. To get the locations clear let us for a moment glance at the mighty Irrawaddi. The Irrawaddi *is* the province or Kingdom of Burma, the great spine which for the greater part of the land runs down its centre. Far up its waters above the Third Defile, viz. the third range through which it has carved its passage on its imperious way to the sea, lies the town of Myitkyina. From Rangoon close down to its mouth, to Myitkyina, the 'town of big fish,' and almost the limit of its navigable waters, is 1100 water miles, although the rail which also terminates here is but 724. Myitkyina is the most northerly administrative centre, now a growing flourishing town, with a garrison of two Gurkha battalions of military police. When the author knew it, it was nothing but a few booths and the stockade in which were three hundred Rifles of the Mogaung Battalion. That, too, was before the Kachins caught *Boh* Burton, the *Kanu Burha*,[1] asleep and burnt the stockade over his head.

[1] The one-eyed old man. He wore an eyeglass.

Twenty miles above Myitkyina is that mysterious or formerly mysterious spot, the 'Confluence.' Here the Irrawaddi ceases to be the Irrawaddi, and breaks into two rivers, the 'Nmalikha the western branch, and the 'Nmaikha the eastern branch. The 'Nmalikha is a douce and peaceful stream, coming down through the Shan state of Hkampti-Long from the far distant Putao, where Fort Hertz has been established of late years; *Ultima Thule* if ever there was one. The eastern branch, the 'Nmaikha, is a very different stream, running fiercely in a V-shaped gorge, amid rapids and huge boulders, while from its left bank the hills rise steeply to the divide that separates it from the Salween, running parallel and close to in surface measurement, but infinitely far in terms of scaled mountain paths. The 'Nmaikha again has a confluence of its own far up, where the Taron is the larger stream, and may be said to be the ultimate Irrawaddi. For many years the course of the unknown reaches of the Irrawaddi was a matter for speculation, and many thought it might even be the Lu River of Tibet. Modern adventures have, however, proved the Lu River to be the Brahmaputra, and that the Irrawaddi flows from the north and probably no great distance from where it becomes the Taron.

The Kachin tribes and their location can now be expressed in terms that have a meaning. It may be said that this race occupies a tract the shape of a horse-shoe, the curve lying across the country between the two branches above the 'Confluence,' an area now known as the 'Triangle.' The sides of the shoe reach down, on the right bank of the Irrawaddi, to below Bhamo, and on the left bank in the hills bordering the Hukong Valley and down towards Mogaung and Mainkwang till they touch the Naga Hills and the Singphos of Assam nomenclature. In the valleys are the settlements of the Shan, who at one time must have dominated the Kachins or at any rate awed them by their civilization, so much so that they – the fire that keeps the Kachin warm – to quote from Mr. Barnard, are still held in some semi-contemptuous reverence. They were always, however, mercilessly raided by the Kachins and until the coming of the British in very recent years to Hkampti-Long, 'The place of gold,' they have had a pretty thin time.

For many years the 'Triangle' has been left severely alone, though it was visited by Major Yule's column in 1892, Sadonkong itself being reached via the 'Nsentaru ferry. In modern times it was not till the British Government decided to stop the slave-holding and slave-raiding by the Kachins of these distant fastnesses, that the 'Triangle' has been entered. One of the closing works of Sir Harcourt Butler's long service to the people of India and Burma was the eradication of this evil . . . long ended in the Kachin lands that were in touch with us, and only existing in these remote Kachin Valleys and among the more distant tribes of the Chins, to whom also like the Nagas human heads were an *objet d'art*. Sir Harcourt, after arduous journeys, himself conducted the final negotiations for liberation including the arrangements for the economic life of the liberated slaves.

The Kachins in touch, as so many of the tribes have been for a generation and more, with British influence, have shown themselves a race capable of great advancement. Missionaries and civil officers have reduced their unwritten language to character and grammar. They are giving admirable service in police and in the Army, and are undoubtedly, together with the Karens, the future race, from which any indigenous soldiers required by the Government of Burma will be drawn.

Their hard-working women, while not so attractive as the gaily-clad Burmans, are comely and taking, sturdy and enduring as mountain folk's women must be. The admixture of Shan blood from female slave-holding has improved the looks. Many Kachins have Shan Talok wives, and the Shan Talok lady is wholly attractive and graceful. The author has a lively recollection of a brother officer courting the Shan Talok wife of a Kachin Tsawbwa, with four Gurkha sentries mounting guard outside.

§ 9

FORTS HARRISON AND MORTON (AND THE DEFENCE OF SADON)

There are two forts in the Kachin Hills east of Myitkyina, bearing names that recall the wars of the earlier pacification. In 1892, the British Government had made up its mind to pacify the trade routes with

China as far up as the latitude of that town. Sadon, a large village close to the Chinese border, was the centre of much blackmailing and looting of caravans, and two military columns were to operate in the hills between the Irrawaddi and China. The column, under Major Yule of the Devons, moved to Sadon and proceeded to establish there a stockaded fort. Leaving some details and convalescents under Lieutenant Harrison of the Royal Engineers to complete the post, Yule crossed into the 'Triangle.' In his absence Kachins and Chinese black-flags, or robbers, from all sides swarmed on Sadon and attacked the post, the whole country-side being up. It was fourteen days before Captain Davies from the south brought a column to the relief, but on the second day the author, who was marching quietly up in charge of an important convoy with twelve mounted infantry, cut his way in. Eighteen miles from Sadon, having no news of the rising, his advance guard was ambushed crossing the Namli River, and he decided to try and fight his way through. For the eighteen miles he sustained a running fight, arriving after dark at Sadon Fort to lose his convoy at the last moment, in a fierce attack of Kachins in Sadon village, when most of his ammunition was spent, and himself and several of his men wounded. He was then able to share with Harrison the remaining twelve days of the defence, which at times was desperate and included constant sorties for water.

The fort was named after the officer in command, Fort Harrison.

In 1930 occurred one of those coincidences which

add to the charm of British Army service. During the trouble in Peshawar, my son was in charge of the signal centre in one of the bastions of Peshawar fort, during the re-occupation of the city. With him on the bastion was a subaltern in charge of a party of infantry, whom he did not know. Passing the time of day with each other, they found that they were Harrison and MacMunn, sons of the Sadon defenders. Whereon they grumbled, saying, 'Don't suppose anyone will give *us* D.S.O.'s.'[1]

The year after Sadon, it was decided to open another post some thirty miles or so to the south at Sima, another commanding and pacifying centre. A very similar incident occurred. The force, military police this time, had established a post and left a garrison under Captain Morton. Again huge masses of tribes attacked it, and police and military columns were hurried to the scene. Morton was killed in a sortie, and also Lieutenant Masters, and Surgeon-Major Lloyd gained the Victoria Cross. That campaign, however, was not finally over till Major Davies led a column from Bhamo to support the police. Since then these hills have settled down, and the King's Peace has meant much advance and prosperity.

As the years rolled on several officers have lost their lives in the gradual carrying of reconnaissance and peace farther north and their names may well endure in those places where names of the brave live for ever.

'The Grave of the Hundred Head' touches the very

[1] Which had been awarded to their fathers for the Defence of Sadon in 1892.

lacrymae rerum of the task of spreading peace, and extirpating the bandit who

> 'Shot at the strong and
> slashed at the weak,
> From the Chindwin scrub to
> the Salween teak.'

For thus the first verse runs of the son of the widow in Chester:

> 'A snider squibbed in the jungle,
> Somebody laughed and fled,
> And the men of the First Shikaris
> Picked up their subaltern dead,
> With a big blue mark in his forehead,
> And the back blown out of his head.'

§ 10

THE SHAN FRONTIER AND KARENNI

As we come down the Eastern Frontier we come into a most interesting and indeed fascinating area of an ancient conquering and ruling race, the Shans, who inhabit a large portion of British Burma which at one time they must have dominated. They belong to a Mongoloid race known generally as Tai, who form compact groups in Siam and in the Lao States, between the Salween and the Mekong. They are a semi-civilized race of Buddhists, and have obtained considerable culture in many directions. After the first general occupation of Upper Burma and the assertion of British rule they have lived happily and contentedly. The bulk of the Shans are found in the two groups of the northern and southern Shan States, the former consisting of a few large states, the latter a multitude of small statelets. The two groups federated as one whole in 1922, which assisted in the consideration of Shan interests. It is in the Shan States for the most part that the British frontier in this part of the world marches with Siam and French Indo-China. But the Shans will be found also scattered along the Irrawaddi in the Hukong Valley, in the valleys among the Kachins as Shan Talok or Chinese Shans, and far up above the confluence is the isolated Shan state of Hkampti-Long, already referred to among the Kachins, showing how far this race had at one time made its way.

These frontier Shans have many of the ways of the Burmans, but being hill men have the energy of a more vigorous climate. The charm of their bright silks, their pretty chattering women, their tinkly temple bells, their rich jungles and beautiful hill-sides, have all the romance of Burma itself added to the hill-sides and the scenery. For many years now has a railway run through to Lashio, deep into the Shan Hills, from Mandalay, and the trade and prosperity in and through the states is considerable. Plans for railway extension eastwards have long been discussed.

The states generally form something of a plateau, but two large pums or mountains dominate the horizon, the peak of Loi Ling being 9000 feet above the sea, and Loi Maw 8000. The total number of

Shans in the states and scattered in up the Irrawaddi is over a million.

A word must be said of the most southerly of the tribes and tribal tracts on the Burma Frontiers. South of the Shan States come a group of tribes known as Karen Mongoloids also, from some part of China in the centuries that are gone, quite unlike the Shan, however. The Karens are divided into several big groups such as the Red Karens and the like. In the midst of the Karen Hills is the State of Karenni, something like the Shan States in its status, though not so large or important. The Karens, of whom many have embraced Christianity for several generations, serve in the military police and, dressed in Kilmarnock caps like Gurkhas, resemble them greatly, and are undoubtedly among the military races of Burma, will take a greater share in the necessary forces. Their normal religion is of the usual *animist* or spirit and ancestor-worshipping cults which seem to prevail among all the primitive tribes of these parts.

FINALE

Atque Vale

To traverse four thousand miles in the space of one short volume can be no satisfying experience. A thousand questions should rise to the reader's lips, if the author has been able to communicate any of the romance with which he has thrilled himself. The smell of the camels, the drawl of frontier speech, the cool breeze down the pass, the Ghilzai lass laughing at you from the top of a camel, the frowning black Unbelievers' Castle, far older even than Rome, the Buddhist shrines and Graecian friezes, the throb and lure of little drum and jaunting pipe of the frontier troops, the jinkety - jink of the gun mules, even the smell of the acrid dust, they bite deep into one's blood and bones. The surge and thunder of the north-west gives place happily enough to the peace of the Himalaya, the 'Abode of Snow,' and the infinite calm of the snow peaks, the tumuli of cloud on Gamnotri and Jamnotri, the breasts of the mother of Time, the curved eaves to the woodland temples that hint of Pekin, the convoys of shaggy yaks making for Holy Lhasa, the Buddhist pilgrim out of *Kim,* that tramps down the road, flip-flop in his iron-shod sabots, who of those who love the road can ever forget it, and to hike in the Himalaya passes the hike on the South Down.

But though the Mountains of Solomon and the Abode of Snow are all very well, and have such a glamour as makes one's heart ache to think of, there is just one better land to remember farther south. There one can sit with one's eyes shut, and remember, nay actually *feel* the sun on the *taungyas*, *Feel* the green of the bamboo clumps, while the partridge pipes hard by, and the girls laugh on the river banks, where the tinkly temple bells ring again and again, and the gong beats men to prayer, and one yearns with Kipling's soldier on the road to Mandalay. 'By the old Moulmein pagoda looking eastward to the sea,' and then one thinks perhaps of the brother subaltern, dead, with a big blue mark in his forehead, because

> 'A snider squibbed in the jungle,
> Somebody laughed and fled.'

It is a memory of men who marched and fought for the world's peace and plenty, and the safety of this great continent of India, with which the paper men now ply scissors and make their dollies, while all the time there is always a man's work to be done without them, in peace and in war. As Lyall has it:

> 'O men of the wandering sea-borne race
> Your venture was high, but your wars are done.
> Ye have rent my tent, ye behold my face.
> What is the land that your arms have won?'

INDEX

INDEX

INDEX

INDEX

INDEX

INDEX

INDEX

INDEX